D1500134

PRINCIPLES OF BANK OPERATIONS

PRINCIPLES OF BANK OPERATIONS

American Institute of Banking

SECTION THE AMERICAN BANKERS ASSOCIATION

NEW YORK, NEW YORK 10016

Preface

BANKING is a business of many facets. The well rounded banker must comprehend the dynamic function of banking in our economy. In Principles of Bank Operations, therefore, the activities of the commercial bank are presented from the functional standpoint. Thus, the text is concerned with the principles behind bank operations rather than with actual operating procedures. The banker student enters the bank with the customer learning *what* the bank does for the customer, and then in each case, the student is led to observe the banking side of the operations learning *why* the bank conducts the transaction in a specific manner.

The major banking functions are presented in sequence, the receiving, the paying, the bookkeeping, and the loaning functions, and the function of collection. Specific chapters are devoted to such banking services as trust, safe deposit, and foreign financial transactions. Attention is given to general bank accounting and to service charges. The roles of the Federal Reserve System and the Federal Deposit Insurance Corporation in banking are explained.

This course is the first of a series of three courses dealing directly with the banking system. The three courses, Principles of Bank Operations, Money and Banking, and Bank Administration analyze and describe the way the banking system actually functions.

George D. Bushnell, vice president, American National Bank and Trust Company of Chicago, served as chairman of the critic committee that rebuilt this text. He is the author of two prior Institute texts in this field, Bank Organization and Operation (1937) and Fundamentals of Banking (1946) and, for many years, has taught this subject in Chicago Chapter.

A critic committee of outstanding bankers gave generously of their time in outlining the text and in reading the manuscript. These men were: Frank M. Dana, vice president and supervisor of operations, Bank of America National Trust and Savings Association, San Francisco, California; James J. Durkin, cashier, Colorado National Bank, Denver, Colorado; Melville M. Parker, executive vice president, The First National Bank of Lebanon, Lebanon, Pennsylvania; Harold W. Wallgren, vice president, The Philadelphia National Bank, Philadelphia, Pennsylvania; J. C. Welman, president, Bank of Kennett, Kennett,

Missouri; George R. Amy, deputy manager, American Bankers Association. The Institute most gratefully acknowledges its debt to these men for their efforts in behalf of banking and for their devotion to the education of young bankers.

Chapter material was furnished by bankers and educators, each of whom is recognized as an expert in his field. The contributors were: George R. Amy; Karl R. Bopp, vice president, Federal Reserve Bank of Philadelphia, Philadelphia, Pennsylvania; George D. Bushnell; James J. Durkin; A. Anton Friedrich, professor of economics, Washington Square College, New York University, New York, New York; John A. Guilbert, Bank of America National Trust and Savings Association, San Francisco, California; Neil G. Greensides, supervising examiner, Federal Deposit Insurance Corporation, New York, New York; Clarence H. Lichtfeldt, comptroller and vice president, First Wisconsin National Bank, Milwaukee, Wisconsin; James A. McBain, assistant vice president, The Chase Manhattan Bank, New York, New York; Gordon W. McGinley, assistant cashier, The Farmers and Merchants National Bank of Los Angeles, Los Angeles, California; Harry E. Mertz, assistant vice president, La Salle National Bank, Chicago, Illinois; Richard P. Brown, vice president and trust officer, International Trust Company, Denver, Colorado; J. E. Renstrom, comptroller, The First National Bank of Denver, Denver, Colorado; Philip M. Stone, Federal Reserve Bank of San Francisco, San Francisco, California; T. Graydon Upton, vice president, The Philadelphia National Bank, Philadelphia, Pennsylvania; Harold W. Wallgren; Harold T. Zuecca, vice president, Broad Street Trust Company, Philadelphia, Pennsylvania. To these men the Institute extends its appreciation for their expert services.

The Institute wishes to express its appreciation to Philip M. Stone for his timely services in preparing the manual for instructors and the practical exercises for correspondence students.

This volume is designed to acquaint young bankers with the many phases of banking. It is hoped that, through a study of the text, they will develop a broad-gauged view of banking. Thus they may be inspired to provide the leadership necessary to maintain banking in the vanguard of our economy.

LEROY LEWIS
National Educational Director

Contents

Charts, Forms, and Tables

CHARTS

FORMS

TABLES

PRINCIPLES OF BANK OPERATIONS

PRINCIPLES OF BANK OPERATIONS

CHAPTER I

THE ECONOMIC ROLE OF BANKS

The Purposes of This Chapter:

1. To show the economic importance of banking.
2. To discuss the deposit function of modern banks.
3. To present the loan function of banks of today.
4. To mention the money function and related bank services.

PRINCIPLES of Bank Operations is concerned with what bankers do and why they do it. The primary purpose of this text is to provide an understanding of the basic functions and the operations of a banking enterprise. The emphasis, therefore, is on the underlying objectives, the end results, of bank operations rather than on the specific details of methods by which bankers achieve these objectives.

This book is not a handbook; it does not state how operations should be performed. Such a book would have a limited value and for an obvious reason. The specific techniques used by bankers may be varied or changed from time to time. A specific technique which may be successfully used when employed by a large bank may be very costly and uneconomical when applied in a small bank. New office machines may cause changes in the ways in which certain operations are performed. Although the ways of conducting bank operations may be changed the underlying principles remain the same.

What operating objectives do bankers wish to achieve? What problems do they confront in the operation of a bank? How do they go about solving their problems? These questions guide our discussion throughout Principles of Bank Operations.

1

The Economic Contributions of Banking

Consider the role that banking plays in the overall operations of our economic life. The economic role of banking is a very important one; in fact, it is difficult to imagine how our economy could operate without the services which banks provide. All of us (workers, farmers, businessmen, and the government) depend directly and indirectly in many ways upon the activities of the banks.

What are the contributions which banking makes to our economic life? This presentation is necessarily brief and in summary form, for a full discussion of the economic functions of banking would take not one chapter but several books. The student may find a fuller treatment of this subject in the Money and Banking text published by the American Institute of Banking.

Banking in Ancient Times

In studying the economic importance of banking we notice the fact that banking is one of the oldest economic institutions. We do not know when banking first began or just when the first bank was organized. These facts of history are lost in antiquity. There were, however, banking enterprises in the earliest commercial civilizations. Apparently the need for banks developed along with the use of money in organizing agriculture, industry, and trade.

From the sands of Arabia archeologists have uncovered clay tablets which date as far back as 2000 B.C. These tablets indicate that, in ancient Babylonia, a money and credit economy had developed to an extent which required the services of banks. For instance, one ancient clay tablet has an inscription that is obviously a promissory note given by a farmer to a bank in exchange for a loan to purchase seeds. It reads:

Warad-Ilish, the son of Taribaum, has received from the sun-priestess, the daughter of Ibbatum, one shekel of silver by the Sun-gods balance. This sum is to be used to buy sesame. At the time of the sesame harvest he will repay in sesame, at the current price, to the bearer of this document.

This ancient inscription is self-explanatory. Warad-Ilish, as do farmers today, relied on a bank loan to finance his purchase of seed. The bank loan was in the form of a promissory note which was payable to bearer and thus negotiable. Apparently Warad-

Ilish was in good credit standing at the bank, for the sun-priestess asked only for his signature to the note.

This type of lending activity is common practice in modern banking, suggesting that in this respect banking in ancient Babylonia was much like banking today. There was one point of difference, however; in ancient Babylonia banking was an activity of the temple rather than of secular organizations.

Banking was an enterprise of the wealthy religious cults of Babylonia, in the beginning, and remained a monopoly of the temples for many centuries. There were valid reasons for this religious monopoly. The religious organizations owned extensive lands, and their revenues from the farms and from other sources were very large. Thus the money to lend was chiefly concentrated in the hands of the religious cults.

Another equally important reason for this religious monopoly was that temples were considered sacred and were held in confidence and trust by the people of Babylonia. It was only natural, therefore, that the Babylonians regarded the temples as safe places to leave their gold, silver, and money—safe not only in the sense of protecting their valuables against theft but also in the confidence that the temples would render an honest accounting of their deposits. Thus the temples became the first banks of deposit.

The history of banking in ancient Greece, Egypt, and Rome followed a pattern similar to that in Babylonia. The first banks were the temple banks; but the temples did not retain a monopoly of banking indefinitely. Private banks developed, during a later period, and private initiative took the lead in banking.

These early banks provided many of the financial services which are characteristic of banks today. They provided places for safekeeping, they took deposits on which they paid interest, and their deposit credit was used as a means of payment, that is, as money. Temple banks acted as agents for their customers and sold letters of credit to merchants engaged in foreign trade. They were executors of wills and they managed estates for the benefit of the heirs. They financed commerce, agriculture, and government.

The Economic Functions of Present-Day Banking

Of the many financial services (Chart I) which banks render to the American people, there are three services that, from the economic point of view, stand out above all others. The three basic contributions of banking to the economic system are:

1. Receiving deposits. Banks collect and assemble the greater part of the surplus funds of the people.

2. Making loans and investments. Banks make funds available to producers, consumers, and governments.

3. Creating money by extension of credit. Except for the relatively small amount of coin and currency issued by the government, banks create all the money we use in carrying on our economic activities.

For the purposes of this discussion, these three basic economic contributions of banks are designated as: (1) the deposit function, (2) the loan function, and (3) the money function.

THE DEPOSIT FUNCTION

When an individual deposits money in a bank, he receives in exchange the bank's promise to pay money of equal amount when called upon to do so by the depositor. If the individual does not expect to use his money for current payments, he opens a time deposit account and allows the balance to accumulate. If he intends to use the money for current expenses, for instance for the payment of monthly bills, he opens a demand deposit account from which money is payable on demand or is transferable to others through a written order on the bank called a check.

The Viewpoint of the Individual Depositor

Why do individuals deposit money in a bank? Among the reasons given are: (1) A demand or checking account provides the depositor with a convenient means of payment, (2) the bank statement produces a record of the money he has received and paid out, and (3) the bank is the safest place in which he can keep his surplus money.

Currency and coins are frequently lost. Deposit credits cannot be lost; they cannot be filched by pickpockets, extorted by robbers, or stolen by burglars. If a clever penman successfully forges a depositor's signature, it is the bank, not the depositor, who takes the loss. Thus a bank, in receiving deposits, provides a place of safekeeping for money.

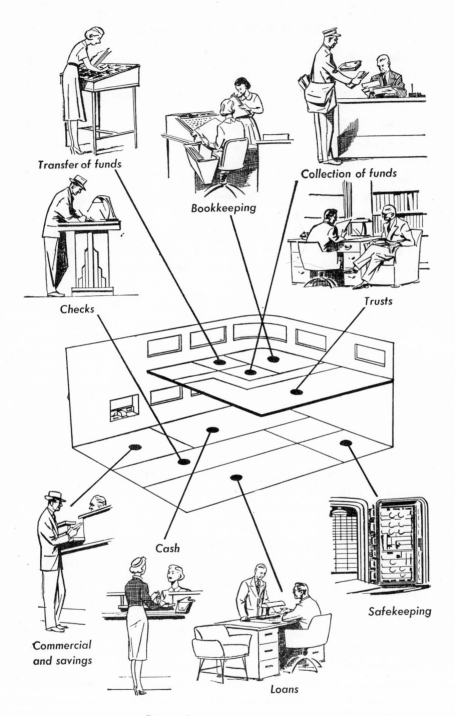

Transfer of funds

Bookkeeping

Collection of funds

Checks

Trusts

Cash

Commercial
and savings

Loans

Safekeeping

CHART 1. PEOPLE NEED BANKS

5

Historically, the safekeeping of money was one of the earliest services offered by banks. Today, it remains a service of great value to individuals, families, and business organizations.

Economic Significance of the Deposit Function

From the viewpoint of the economist, matters of greater economic significance are involved in the function of receiving deposits.

Deposits are surplus funds, that is, money which the owners, at the moment of deposit, do not intend to use for immediate payments. In some instances, the money deposited is a surplus fund only for a very short period of time, as in the case of an individual who deposits his monthly check on the first day of the month and has disbursed a large part of the deposit by the tenth day of the same month. An individual may, however, allow his deposit balance in a saving or time deposit to accumulate for years before he draws against it, perhaps withdrawing in order to make a downpayment on the purchase of a home or to make major home improvements.

When an individual deposits funds for which he has no immediate use, his surplus funds are joined with the surplus funds of other depositors, including not only other individuals but also business organizations and governments. Thus the surplus funds of the entire economy are accumulated in banks.

This vast pool of surplus funds does not remain an idle hoard of money. Through the lending operations of banks, the funds are kept continuously active in order to finance the activities of industry, agriculture, and government.

It is interesting to note that one of the earliest formal definitions of banking emphasizes the deposit function of banks. The following definition of banking is attributed to Gerard de Malynes, who wrote in 1623:

A bank is properly a Collection of all the ready money of some Kingdom, Commonwealth, or Province, as also of a particular City or Town, into the hands of some persons licensed and established thereunto by public authority of some King, Prince, or Commonwealth.

Except for the minor details of the style of writing, this definition would serve very well as a partial definition of a present-day bank.

THE LOAN FUNCTION

The "collection of all the ready money" of the economy is only part of the business of banks. Just as there are individuals and organizations who have more money than they need at any given moment (that is, they have money to hold), so there are others who need more money than they possess. Another important function of banks is to provide a place in which the ready money of the community can be collected and from which it can be made available to those who need it.

The loan function is the counterpart of the deposit receiving function of banks. Depositors store money in banks; banks, in turn, lend to consumers, farmers, businessmen, and government. In so doing, banks maintain an active circulation of money ready to finance the production of goods and services, the moving of finished goods through the channels of distribution, and the final sale of those goods to consumers.

There are, generally speaking, three major classes of borrowers: businessmen, government, and consumers.

Loans to Businessmen

Banks lend money to businessmen for many purposes and for varying periods of time. If the nature of the business is seasonal, a businessman may need additional money to finance a seasonal expansion of his payroll and inventories. A merchant, for example, builds up his inventory of toys in the late summer and early fall in anticipation of Christmas sales. A toy manufacturer, on the other hand, has his busy season in the first part of the year, and he then needs additional money for the purchase of raw materials and the hiring of additional workmen. A farmer may borrow for the purchase of seed and fertilizer with the expectation of repaying his loan at harvest time. In these cases the time interval between the making of the loan and its repayment is a matter of months. Such loans are referred to as short term credit.

The credit needs of a business, however, may extend over a longer period of time. A farmer buying a new tractor may not be able to repay the loan out of his current income. He may, therefore, ask that repayment be spread over a period of several years. A manufacturer may also require longer term credit when he is adding one or a few machines to his equipment. A storekeeper who is remodeling his store, perhaps in order to display his merchandise more attractively or to increase his stock of goods, may find that insufficient net income makes it difficult or impossible for him to repay his loan within a period of a few months. Banks make loans in such cases to suit the financial circumstances of the borrowers. A loan with repayment extending over a period of several years is called intermediate term credit.

For some purposes, businessmen need relatively large sums of money, far more than can be repaid from one or several years' income. A farmer may need to add acreage to his farm or to build a new barn or silo. A manufacturer may need to build an extension to his factory. A storekeeper may wish to replace his old building with a new modern one. In these cases the borrowers will want a long term loan, such as a mortgage loan which can be repaid over a span of many years.

The needs and purposes of business borrowing are more numerous and the financial circumstances are more varied and complex than those indicated in the few illustrations mentioned. These instances, however, indicate the ramifications of bank credit and the extent to which bank credit enters into every phase and operation of the business system.

Over the years banks have developed new credit facilities to keep pace with the growth, the expansion, and the variety of enterprises in our economy. To help keep the economy strong, to facilitate a high level of current operations, and to provide for its growth and development—these are the obligations of bankers as well as their opportunities for profitable operations.

Loans to Government

Banks also lend large sums to government. By means of short term loans in anticipation of tax revenues, banks finance the current operations of government and of its many subdivisions. Through their purchase of government bonds, banks accommodate the long term credit needs of government.

The Federal Government in time of war finds it necessary to resort to borrowing from banks in order to meet the costs of war. Some idea of the extent of government borrowing for the purposes of war can be gained from examining the net debt for 1916, one year before our entrance into World War I. During that year the net debt of the Federal Government was slightly more than $1 billion. At the present time, after the financing of three wars, it is close to $275 billion.

Not all the huge increase of federal debt, however, is the result of war expenditures. The Federal Government, in recent years, has greatly expanded its peacetime activities. As a consequence, there have been only a few years in which federal revenues have exceeded federal expenditures. These annual deficits have added their totals to the debt.

Financial institutions other than banks, as well as individuals, buy government bonds and thus help in the financing of the federal deficit. A large and important part of the federal debt, however, represents borrowing from commercial banks.

Local governments also borrow from banks. State and local governments, school and irrigation districts, and highway and other authorities make use of credit to finance a large proportion of the public improvements, such as public buildings, schools, roads and turnpikes, irrigation and water development projects, and many other public works. Again banks are called upon to provide an important part of the credit used for these purposes.

Loans to Consumers

The total of bank loans to consumers runs into many billions of dollars. Consumers borrow for personal reasons—to pay for doctor, dental, and hospital bills and to make any other unusual and generally nonrecurring expenditures. A large part of consumer borrowing is in the form of instalment loans to buy automobiles, refrigerators, ranges, and other household equipment and to modernize their homes. Only a very small number of the homes purchased are paid for outright. The purchase of a home depends primarily upon the availability of mortgage credit which is supplied largely by commercial banks.

"The spice of variety flavors all of banking today," was said by Fred F. Florence, a past president of the American Bankers Association. "Banks are lending money for dental bridges and drawbridges, for carports and airports, for kitchen ranges and cattle ranges."

Bank lending reaches into all phases of public and private life; it touches some phase of each life, that is, as a consumer, as a home-owner, as a worker, as a businessman, as an investor, as a farmer, as a merchant, or simply as a citizen in a community.

THE MONEY FUNCTION OF BANKS

The money function, though last, is not the least important in our discussion of the three primary economic functions of banks. All but a very small part of the money we use as a means of payment is supplied by banks.

Kinds of Money

The following is a list of the kinds of money in common use and the amounts outstanding December 31, 1955[1]

Treasury currency—total	$ 5,009,000,000
Federal Reserve notes	27,519,000,000
Demand deposits exclusive of interbank and Government deposits	109,700,000,000

From this list we note that the money issued by banks makes up approximately 96% of the total supply of money used as a means of payment. Of the total supply of bank-issued money, four of every five dollars consists of demand deposits subject to check. This money is variously referred to as bank balances, checkbook money, or deposit currency.

When an individual deposits coins, currency, or checks drawn on other banks, the sum is entered in his account as a deposit credit. This transaction is commonly called a primary deposit. When a businessman or a consumer borrows from the bank, the proceeds of his loan are usually entered in his account as a deposit credit. It is commonly referred to as a derived deposit, that is, a deposit which originated in a loan granted by the bank. Whether the deposit is a primary or a derived deposit, it can be checked against by the depositor and used as a means of payment.

Although checks are not legal tender, they are widely used for the payment of bills and taxes, for the purchase of goods, and for the payment of wages and salaries.

Demand deposits are debts of the bank. They are the promises of banks to pay at any time upon demand. One may ask why the debt obligations of banks are so widely accepted by individuals, by

---

[1] Data taken from Federal Reserve Bulletin, March 1956. pp. 243, 244.

businesses, and by government as money. The answer is that people generally have confidence that banks make good on their promises to pay. The general usage of checks is evidence of an almost universal confidence in the promises of banks and in the accuracy and honesty of their record keeping.

Uses of Checks

The convenience of using checks has made them a popular form of money. Checks can be drawn for the precise amount required. They can be sent through the mail at very low cost, regardless of the amount involved. Consider, in contrast, the difficulties involved in sending any sizeable amount of money in the form of currency, bullion, or coins over any appreciable distance, such as from New York to Seattle. When checks are used, the transfer of funds is handled through the clearing of checks by the banks without either the payer or the payee giving the matter a moment's thought. Canceled checks provide the additional advantage of serving as receipts for payments made.

It is not surprising, therefore, that bank deposit money dwarfs all other forms of money in the extent of its use. The familiar statement that more than 90% of the total dollar volume of all payments are made by check may well be true.

The money function of banks is so briefly treated in this chapter that many questions are left unanswered. For a fuller treatment of this function, including the source of bank credit money, the amount of money banks can issue, the backing behind the money, and the relation of bank deposit currency to bank loans and investments, the student is referred to the Institute text Money and Banking, particularly Chapters V and VI.

OTHER SERVICES OF BANKS

In addition to the three primary economic functions, banks provide a large number of more or less related services. In the following sections we discuss some of these services.

Keeping Records for Customers

It is clear that a bank must keep a full and accurate record of all money received for deposit and of all withdrawals from each account. At regular intervals, often monthly, the bank renders a statement of the account to the depositor, returning to him his canceled checks. This record keeping is a necessity to the bank; it is also an important and useful service to the depositor. Not only does the statement keep him informed of how his account stands with the bank; it also provides him with a running record of his financial activities. If a person deposits with a bank all the money he receives over the year and if he makes all his payments by check, he will have an accurate record of his income and his expenditures for the year.

Acting as Collection Agents

In servicing demand deposits, commercial banks act as collection agents for checks deposited with them and drawn on other banks, which may be located in the same community or elsewhere in the United States. Banks also collect many other items for their customers, such as promissory notes, drafts, bills of exchange, interest coupons on bonds, and other credit instruments. To effect collection, the customer merely turns the item to be collected into the bank; from then on the bank handles the matter. When the money is received, the bank credits it to the account of the customer.

Providing Places for Safekeeping

In ancient times, when temples were sanctuaries, people deposited gold, silver, precious stones, and other objects of great value with the temple banks for safekeeping. Today people leave valuables with banks for safekeeping. Instead of gold and silver plate, the safe deposit boxes of today usually contain important documents, wills, deeds, stocks, bonds, promissory notes, mortgages, and any other items of personal interest, about the safety of which the individual is particularly concerned. The protection banks now provide is not the religious sanction of a temple; the protection now is the vaults with thick steel walls, which are proof against fire, burglary, and most other contingencies.

Holding and Administering Property for the Benefits of Others

Holding, administering, and managing the property of others are called fiduciary services. The word fiduciary is derived from the Latin root *fiducia,* meaning trust or confidence. As we have previously noted, the rendering of trust services was an activity of some ancient banks. Today it is an expanding activity of some modern banks.

There are numerous reasons which may motivate an individual to have his property administered for his own benefit or for the benefit of others. On retiring from active business life a business-man may wish to be free of all responsibility for managing his property. He may set up a trust at a bank with himself as bene-ficiary. He may establish a trust for the benefit of others who in his judgment may not be capable of managing the property them-selves, as would be the case when minors are the beneficiaries; or he may specify in his will that his property shall be managed by the bank in trust for the benefit of his heirs. Thus, in the course of their trust services, banks act as guardians for minors, as con-servators of property for incompetents, as trustees, as executors, or as administrators for the estates of deceased persons.

Promoting Thrift

Another activity of banks is to promote and encourage the development of habits of saving. Banks provide special accounts (time deposits) for receiving and recording the savings deposited with them. They promote the formation of savings clubs in schools. Thus, as part of the school curriculum, children are taught to save. Through the establishment of Christmas and vacation clubs, banks encourage individuals and families to plan the orderly management of their personal finances and thus to anticipate a future need for funds.

Banks also contribute to the savings program of the Federal Government. They are the sole distributors of the E bonds (sav-ings bonds) issued by the Federal Government. They also redeem the bonds upon demand. Banks render these services without cost to the individual.

Rendering Incidental Services

There are a number of incidental services which banks con-tribute to the convenience and profit of individuals.

Assume that you intend to go abroad. In order to pay your expenses, you will need francs in France, lire in Italy, marks in

Germany, and pounds, shillings, and pence in Britain. You could take the necessary money in a lump sum in United States currency and exchange it abroad for local money. But this would be an awkward and probably a costly way to do it, and your currency would be subject to the risk of loss or theft. There are easier and safer ways to get the foreign money you will need.

If you are going to stay only a short time, your bank will issue to you a letter of credit or traveler's checks, according to your preference. If you intend to be abroad for an extended stay—as a student at a foreign university, for example—ask your bank to open for you, in a foreign bank, a deposit account on which you may draw at your pleasure and according to your needs. Your bank will transfer your American deposit balance either to its foreign branch, if it has one, or to foreign banks with which it has correspondent relationships. If your bank has no foreign connections, it will arrange the matter through an American bank which does have the necessary foreign connections.

Giving Credit Information

Banks are often called upon for credit information. Not only are they informed on the credit standing of individuals and businesses in their own communities, but through interbank connections they can assemble credit information from most distant communities. Just as banks have developed channels of check collection, so they have developed channels of credit information both on a national basis and on an international basis. It is not surprising, therefore, that many bank customers depend upon banks (as a matter of routine) for basic credit information.

Banks also are a rich source of information on local business conditions and opportunities as well as on national economic trends and general business conditions. Because of the contacts, knowledge, and facts that banks have, they are often called upon to give financial guidance and assistance.

SUMMARY

Principles of Bank Operations presents the *what* and *why* of banking operations. This chapter is concerned primarily with the economic functions of banks and the services they render to individuals, families, businessmen, farmers, and government. Banks assemble the surplus funds of the community and the nation. They make these funds available to industry, trade, agriculture, government, and consumers. Banks are major sources of the money we use to conduct our transactions, and they render many other services which are important to the operations of a well ordered economy and to the convenience and profit of individuals.

The following chapter analyzes and describes one of the principal functions through which banks provide their many services efficiently, economically, and profitably, in other words, the receiving function.

Questions Based on Chapter I

1. Discuss the role banking plays in the overall operations of our economic life.
2. What institution fulfilled the role of banks in ancient Babylonia?
3. What does the individual depositor receive when he deposits money in a bank?
4. Name the three major classes of borrowers.
5. What types of credit are available?
6. How is the deficit of the Federal Government financed?
7. Are demand deposits subject to check important in the money function of today's banks?
8. What is a primary deposit?
9. Name some of the services banks perform.

Question for Investigation

How many services does your bank render? Name them.

A MODERN BANK LOBBY

CHAPTER II

THE RECEIVING FUNCTION

The Purposes of This Chapter:
1. To list the channels through which deposits enter a bank.
2. To discuss the duties of the receiving teller.
3. To outline the principal receiving teller systems.
4. To describe the process of proving deposits and the method of distributing items received.
5. To discuss the organization of the mail and messenger department.

THIS CHAPTER and the next several chapters are devoted to a consideration of what banks do in order to provide the varied services they offer. Emphasis is placed on *what* processes are used generally and *why* they are used, with only such reference to *how* they are accomplished as will aid clarification. Though the details are different in different banks, the steps that must be performed to complete each function are essentially the same. The sources of deposits and what processes are used to handle deposits properly are discussed in this chapter.

As in other well run businesses, coordination is the keynote of bank operations. Each item must be processed systematically, beginning with the department which receives it and proceeding through those which record and route it to its final destination. This processing is the result of many years of thought, planning, and experiment. To the outsider, the processes involved in the receiving function appear very complex; actually, the mechanics of the process are simple and logical.

Items are received by a bank in a variety of ways, each of which is the starting point for systematic processing. The principal channels through which deposits enter a bank are considered first.

The Receipt of Deposits

There are many channels through which deposits are received by banks. The processing of deposit items must begin at the point at which the items enter the bank. Items are received in the following ways.

1. The receiving teller. The receiving teller is the principal point of contact with the depositor. Some idea of the teller's importance may be gained when consideration is given to the volume of deposits received through the teller's window.

2. Other bank departments. Other bank departments, though not directly concerned with taking deposits, may engage in transactions that result in the creation of deposits. For example, the loan department may grant a loan, and the borrower may wish to have the funds deposited to his account.

3. Mail and by special messenger. Banking by mail is a growing phase of bank operations. Many banks now offer this service.

4. Wire transfer. No matter where a customer may be, it is nearly always possible for him to place a deposit to an account in his own bank. The deposit may be made by telegraph, usually through the intermediary of the bank most convenient to him at the time. The banking business makes extensive use of wire facilities. Wire transfers of funds are discussed in Chapter IV.

5. Night depository service. Many businesses that remain open on certain nights during the week wish to avoid the danger of holding cash and checks until the following morning. For this reason, some banks provide a night depository service. This service is extended by means of a specially constructed chute, which has an opening on the outside of the bank building that leads to a safe within the bank. The depositor is provided with a key for opening the chute. When inserted in the lock, this key operates a rotating cylinder until an opening appears to admit the deposit pouch.

The customer using the night depository fills out an agreement stating that he will abide by the bank's rules regarding the use of this service. He is charged with the key and with a deposit pouch that is numbered and recorded in his name. The procedure to be followed is simple. The customer fills out an ordinary deposit ticket and places it, together with his deposit, in the pouch. Then he seals or locks the pouch and drops it in the chute.

There are two methods of handling bank deposits received in this manner. In one method, double or triple custody of the safe is required, that is, two or more employees are necessary to work the combination. The pouches are taken, still under the custody of two persons, to a special receiving teller window. There, in the presence of witnesses, the teller verifies the deposit and sends a receipt to the customer.

The second method of handling these deposits requires the presence of the customer or his representative, and double or triple custody of the safe is maintained. The sealed or locked pouch is turned over to the customer or his representative, who receipts for it, opens it, and makes his deposit.

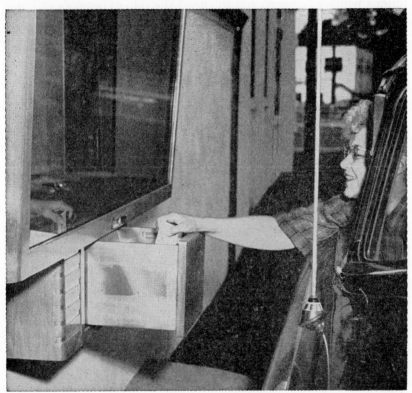

The Franklin National Bank of Franklin Square, New York

DRIVE-IN TELLER'S WINDOW

6. Lobby depository and other services. Some banks provide a special chute in their lobbies, to be used by customers during rush hours. The customer obtains a special envelope from a counter in the lobby, seals his deposit in it, and drops it in the chute. The chute leads to a vault. The envelopes are opened later, and the tellers put the deposits through in the usual manner. In order to

avoid disputes, the customer is required to write on the outside of the envelope the amount of cash enclosed. All deposits containing cash are opened and proved by two tellers. Some banks have these lobby depositories placed so that they may be used even when the bank is not open.

With the movement of urban populations to suburban areas, many banks have established a service that tends to eliminate the parking problem for customers. This service consists of a drive-in teller's window, constructed to afford the teller complete physical protection in the event of an attempted robbery. The customer drives up and passes his deposit through a specially designed window. His receipt is given to him, and he drives away.

The Receiving Teller

The receiving teller meets practically all types of people in the course of his daily work. To each of them, from housewife to businessman, he represents his bank. His cheerful willingness to help them transact their banking business promptly and properly is of first importance to the future of his organization, since it has been truly said that a bank can grow only by the consent of its customers. Thus the teller must know how to get along with people and how to earn their respect and good will. He must also know money and the instruments which represent money, in order to discharge the responsibilities of his position.

Time Deposits and Demand Deposits

Since people deposit money for a variety of reasons, there are several different kinds of accounts. Each account is designed to fulfill a specialized need of the customer. All accounts, however, belong to one of two classifications; they are either time deposits or demand deposits. These accounts, together with saving accounts and commercial accounts, are discussed in Chapter VII.

Cash Items and Collection Items

The customer brings to his bank a variety of items for which he wishes to receive either cash or a credit to his account. These items fall into two broad general categories, and the first step in handling them is for the teller to decide in which category each item belongs. These two groups are called *cash items* and *collection items*.

Cash items, which include coin and currency, are items accepted by the bank for immediate credit to the customer's account. The great majority of items brought to the bank are cash items. Although there are minor variations, the fundamental characteristics of cash items are easily recognized.

1. They are payable on demand and not at some specified future date.

2. There are no documents, securities, or other accompanying papers attached to them.

3. The necessary instructions for presenting these items to the persons on whom they are drawn and for obtaining the funds they represent are simple and uniform.

Cash items taken on deposit increase the balance of the customer's account immediately.

Collection items are items which are credited to the customer's account only after the bank has presented them to the persons on whom they are drawn and has actually collected the funds they represent. The details of the procedure involved in processing collection items are discussed in Chapter XIII.

It is possible that, from time to time, the bank may receive items which resemble collection items (in that they are accompanied by documents and require special handling). Such items may be payable on demand. The bank, as a matter of judgment, may be willing to give immediate credit for them. These items are called *cash collections*. The customer may cash them or deposit their value to his account. The bank is required to give special handling to each individual item.

The Deposit Ticket

The deposit ticket (deposit slip or deposit tag) is a record of the cash and cash items presented for deposit. A copy (termed a duplicate deposit ticket) may serve as customer's receipt when appropriately stamped or noted by the teller.

The Process of Receiving a Deposit

There are six steps to be taken in receiving a deposit. In many banks the receiving teller handles all six steps; in other institutions certain operations may be taken care of in the proof department in order to expedite customer service. These six steps should always be taken. One of the cardinal rules for the receiving teller is that he should *always follow the same order of procedure*. The steps can never become mechanical, in the sense that they are performed automatically. In each instance the teller must concentrate upon what he is doing, and if he makes a practice of following the same order of procedure each time, he may be certain that no step has been omitted. These six steps are followed in receiving a deposit.

1. Verify the amount of the cash.
2. See that all currency and coin are genuine.
3. See that all items taken for deposit are cash items.
4. Check all items for proper indorsement.
5. Verify the total of the deposit.
6. Issue a receipt for the deposit.

The receiving teller first verifies the amount of the cash by actual count.

He sees that all currency and coin are genuine. This operation is performed while the teller counts the cash.

He sees that all items taken for deposit are cash items. In this operation the teller's knowledge of the basic differences between cash items and collection items is important. He must be able to tell at a glance whether the items can properly be taken on deposit.

His fourth duty is to check all items for proper indorsement. Each cash item must bear the customer's indorsement on the reverse side. This indorsement identifies the customer, who assumes responsibility for the item. In the event of nonpayment of the item when presented by the bank, the customer (indorser) must reimburse the bank.

Either the teller or a proof clerk verifies the total amount of the deposit. The amounts shown on each individual deposit ticket must be totaled accurately, for the obvious reason that the customer's account has to be credited with the right amount.

The teller issues a receipt for the deposit, usually by making an entry in the customer's passbook, by issuing a machine-produced receipt, or by issuing a duplicate deposit ticket.

Classification of Items Customarily Received on Deposit

The items which the teller receives on deposit may be grouped in the following manner.

1. Coins and currency.

2. Checks on us. Checks drawn on the teller's own bank are referred to as checks on us or "us" checks.

3. Clearings items. Checks drawn on other local banks are known as clearings items.

4. Transit items. Checks drawn on out-of-town banks are known as transit items.

5. Miscellaneous items. Such items as bond coupons are classified as miscellaneous items.

Each of these items has a separate destination, and the proper distribution of cash and cash items is an important part of the daily work. It is a characteristic of the receiving function that each working day is complete in itself; that is, no items are carried over from the previous day.

Each of the cash items received on deposit has a specific destination. Coin and currency are delivered to the cash vault. Checks on us are routed to the bookkeepers. Clearings items are sent to the out-clearings clerks. Transit items are routed to the transit clerk. Miscellaneous items may require special handling and are accordingly forwarded to the employees designated to take care of them.

Receiving Teller Systems

The principal systems used in receiving teller work are (1) the alphabetical system, (2) the numerical system, (3) the general window system, and (4) the unit teller system.

1. In the alphabetical system, each receiving teller's window is assigned specific letters. The customers make their deposits at the appropriate window, that is, based on the initial letter of the last name of an individual customer or on the initial letter of the first name of a corporation or a partnership. Thus, one receiving window might handle all customers whose names begin with the letter "A," starting with Albert Adams and ending with Azure Paint Co.

2. In the numerical system, each account is numbered and the receiving windows are assigned blocks of numbers. One window may take all accounts numbered 1 through 1,500, the next 1,501 through 3,000, and so forth. This is common practice in handling time or savings accounts.

3. In the general window system, a customer may use any receiving teller window regardless of the name or number of his account.

4. In the unit teller system, each teller is both a receiving and a paying teller. In many banks, he handles time, as well as demand account transactions, and in some cases, he also serves in other capacities such as note teller or collection teller.

The primary purpose underlying all receiving teller systems is that of rendering the best possible service to customers. Therefore, a number of variations in the systems listed have been made. For example, some banks in industrial districts are faced with extremely heavy work loads on pay days and therefore designate certain tellers' windows only for the cashing of pay checks. Other banks specify that business deposits are to be made at certain receiving windows; therefore, the individual customer will not have to wait while the teller counts large amounts of cash and examines many checks for proper indorsement.

Proving Deposits

As mentioned earlier in this chapter, one of the six basic steps in receiving deposits is that of verifying the deposit totals. This step is usually taken in conjunction with that of routing the cash items to their proper destinations. There are two ways of verifying the deposit total: (1) by the individual deposit proof method or (2) by the group deposit proof or batch system.

1. Individual deposit proof. The proving of deposits by tellers is satisfactory in some banks. The teller checks the addition of the deposit tickets by whichever method is most convenient, sorts the cash items into checks on us, clearings items, transit items, and miscellaneous items. Then he assembles the totals of each group on a receiving teller's proof sheet. Each time the teller makes a proof sheet, the items themselves are sent to the respective departments for handling. The teller adds the totals of all groups on his proof sheet at the end of the day. This figure plus the cash received must equal the total of all deposit tickets received during the day, and thus the teller's operation is verified, or *balanced*. A typical receiving teller's proof sheet is illustrated in Form 1.

2. Group deposit proof or batch system. In the group deposit proof or batch system both the deposit totals and the total of each group of items are proved in one operation. This method is based on the premise that if every deposit in the batch is totaled correctly, the sum of the deposit totals equals the grand total of the

various items. Batches may be run on the adding machine by individual tellers or by interior proof clerks. In either case the procedure is the same.

A group of deposits is taken. All the cash items listed on these deposits are sorted according to their classifications. The totals of the deposit are listed on the left-hand side of a large batch sheet; on the right-hand side each group of cash items is listed, together with the cash received. The total of the groups of cash items plus the cash received must equal the total of the deposit tickets. If it does not, and there are no errors in listing by the customer or by the proof clerk, then one or more of the deposit tickets has been added incorrectly by the customer. Form 2 illustrates a simplified batch sheet.

FORM 1. RECEIVING TELLER'S PROOF

The cash received on deposit is, of course, retained by the teller. Various methods are used to give the total of cash received to the

Commercial Deposits	Savings Deposits	General Credits		Checks on us	Clearings Items	Cash Rec'd.
$1,496.14			$	110.40	$ 900.00	$ 320.00
629.05				96.31	51.50	11.19
36.14				11.19	75.00	500.00
554.26				5.00	10.00	36.40
81.40				25.00	30.00	25.00
1,327.02				14.48	150.65	900.55
					72.70	
4,124.01T				262.38T	91.60	1,793.14T
					205.75	
					1,587.20T	

Loan Payments		Transit Items	General Debits	Loan Debits
	$	51.09		
		30.20		
		125.00		
		275.00		
		481.29		

	TOTALS	FOR PROOF
	4,124.01	4,124.01

Date_____

Listed by_____

Batch No._____

Teller_____

FORM 2. TELLER'S BATCH SHEET

26

employee who runs the batch. In some banks, the proof clerk simply picks up on his adding machine the cash totals listed on each deposit ticket. In other banks, the teller substitutes for the cash a memorandum called a *cash ticket*; the person proving the batch uses the cash ticket for listing the cash on the batch sheet.

Organization of the Central Proof Department

Many banks, in which the volume of incoming deposits necessitates the proving of deposits by someone other than the teller, find it helpful to organize a proof department. The size of this department naturally varies with the size of the bank. In small banks only part of the time of an employee is needed to process the work. In large banks the department itself may become so large that it is necessary to subdivide it into sections, each of which handles the work of a group of tellers. This department also customarily handles the work of the paying tellers.

Speed of operation is an important factor in the organization of the central proof department. Clearings items, for example, must be processed each day in time to make the deadline hour at the clearing house. In banks which handle a large volume of mail deposits, a night force is often used to operate a distribution division. This force prepares the mail items for distribution to other departments at the opening of business the next day. It may also handle transit items and send them out the night they are processed, thus saving a day or more in the time required for collection.

It should be borne in mind that clearings and transit items are instruments against which the bank has either advanced cash or for which the customer's account has been credited. Therefore, speeding these items to their destinations expedites the bank's recapture of the funds it has advanced. The dollar amount of items in the process of clearing and in transit collection is called *float*, and an unnecessary amount of float is a needless expense to the bank.

Central Proof Systems and Routing Methods

The method used in proving deposits and routing cash items is geared to the volume of deposits handled by the individual bank. Several methods, illustrated in Chart 2, are in general use.

In the first of these methods, the receiving teller proves the de-

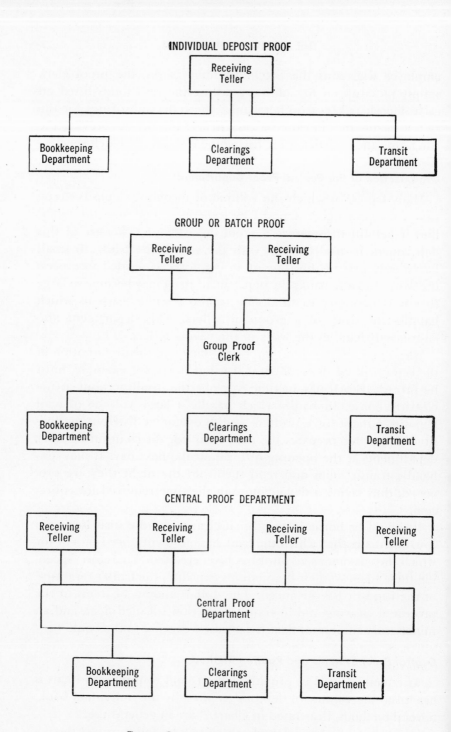

INDIVIDUAL DEPOSIT PROOF

Receiving Teller

Bookkeeping Department

Clearings Department

Transit Department

GROUP OR BATCH PROOF

Receiving Teller

Receiving Teller

Group Proof Clerk

Bookkeeping Department

Clearings Department

Transit Department

CENTRAL PROOF DEPARTMENT

Receiving Teller

Receiving Teller

Receiving Teller

Receiving Teller

Central Proof Department

Bookkeeping Department

Clearings Department

Transit Department

CHART 2. METHODS OF ROUTING ITEMS

posits by the use of his individual deposit proof sheet and distributes the items.

In the second method, a group proof clerk proves the deposits of several tellers by means of the batch system. Where the volume warrants, a central proof department is established to handle the work of all the tellers.

Equipment Used in Proving Operations

The equipment used in the proving operations varies from the ordinary adding machine to the complex sorting and calculating equipment. The volume of activity, type of deposits, and the number of destinations of the items deposited are the principal factors determining which equipment is most appropriate. The simple adding machine can be used to verify the total of each deposit ticket and to obtain a total for each classification into which the items are sorted—for example, clearing, transit, and checks on us. More elaborate equipment provides sorting pockets to receive the checks and a separate total accumulator for each pocket. In one operation, these machines verify deposit ticket totals, sort the checks to a large number of classifications, give individual totals for each classification, and provide two grand totals (1) of all classifications and (2) of all deposit tickets.

Equipment utilizing electronic systems is in the development stage and is expected to do more or less automatically the sorting, calculating, recording, and printing. The adaptation of such equipment to the proving function for use when circumstances warrant seems likely. Indorsing machines are used to stamp the bank's indorsement automatically on the back of each check.

The Teller's Cash Proof

At the end of the day, when all the deposits taken by a teller have been proved, the teller counts and balances his cash for the day. The process is simple: (1) He takes the amount of cash with which he started the day, (2) adds any additional cash received from the vault during the day, (3) adds the cash received over the counter (he uses the figure on the receiving teller's proof or on his batch sheets, depending on the system used in his bank), (4) subtracts the total of cash items paid, and (5) arrives at a figure which should be equal to his actual cash count. He then counts his cash

CURRENCY		CASH PROOF	
1 _____		Cash on hand from previous day	$_____
2 _____		Cash from Vault during day	$_____
5 _____		„ „ „ „ „	$_____
10 _____		„ „ „ „ „	$_____
20 _____		Total Cash from Vault	$_____
50 _____		Cash rec'd over counter	$_____
100 _____			
500 _____			
1000 _____			
Mutilated, etc., _____			
TOTAL CURRENCY _____			
		Cash paid	$_____

COIN

Dollars _____			
Halves _____			
Quarters _____			
Dimes _____			
Nickels _____		Cash to Vault during day	$_____
Pennies _____			
TOTAL COIN _____		NET CASH SHOULD BE	$_____
		ACTUAL CASH TO VAULT	$_____

RECAPITULATION

Currency _____		SHORT	$_____
Coin _____			
TOTAL CASH _____		OVER	$_____

FORM 3. TELLER'S CASH SHEET

30

and compares the figure with that shown on his cash proof. If his
figures balance, he is ready to place his cash in the vault for the
night. Form 3 illustrates a typical teller's cash proof sheet.

THE MAIL AND MESSENGER DEPARTMENT

Every bank has a large volume of correspondence, and many
deposits reach the bank by mail. As a consequence, the process of
properly sorting and distributing incoming mail is extremely important, and the collection and dispatching of the outgoing mail
is equally so. In small banks one individual is usually charged
with this responsibility, and it may be that only a part of his working day need be spent in this occupation. The volume of mail in
larger banks is frequently so great that a special mail department is
needed.

Sometimes one division of the department may be occupied in
proving incoming mail deposits. Speed is essential in this operation, as it is necessary to process the clearings items in time to meet
the clearing house deadline.

In addition to personnel who sort and distribute mail, this
department may have a messenger division. Messengers deliver
checks and other items, present items received by the collection
department, and make daily trips to the clearing house and to
local banks. Usually the following duties are performed by the
mail and messenger department:

1. The sorting and distribution of incoming mail
2. The collection and dispatch of outgoing mail
3. The maintenance of adequate messenger service
4. The exercise of receiving teller duties when mail deposits
are handled by the department.

In many banks the mail can be handled by a part-time force;
the employees work the incoming and outgoing mail when they
can be spared from their other duties. If an hour or two each day
suffices to collect and dispatch incoming mail and to handle outgoing mail, then probably a single employee can perform these
duties. Each day he sorts the incoming mail before banking hours
and distributes it early in the morning. He gathers and sends out
the outgoing mail in the afternoon.

Equipment of the Department

The equipment of the mail and messenger department depends on the volume of mail, the volume of items handled in mail teller work, the peak periods during the day, and the amount of registered and special delivery mail.

A small volume of outgoing mail can be sealed and stamped by hand; a larger volume may require the use of one or more machines for the sealing of the envelopes. A metered postage machine is generally used in larger banks. This machine, which imprints on the envelope the amount of the postage and the number assigned to the user of the machine, has the double advantage of dispensing with the handling of stamps and of providing an accurate check on postage through the meter total. If a large volume of mail must be handled at a peak period during the day, the metered postage system works with rapidity and ease.

Usually, a cage must be provided for registered and special delivery mail. But if the number of registered pieces is small, the paying teller or the collection teller may handle this outgoing mail.

Messenger Service

There are many operations that require messenger service. The return of unpaid clearing items to the sending banks, the presentment of items for the collection department, the delivery of statements to customers, the mailing of letters that must reach the post office at definite times, and many other tasks must be performed by the members of the bank's messenger force.

Coordination with Other Departments

The mail and messenger department works closely with all other departments. Its work is essential to the smooth operation of the bank.

The mail division begins working earlier each morning than other bank departments so that the sorting and distribution of incoming mail to the officers and departments may be completed before regular working hours. Mail is obtained from the post office at frequent intervals in order to speed up the work of other departments.

Outgoing mail is handled on a schedule to conform to the requirements of the entire bank staff. The work of collecting and dispatching the outgoing mail begins, as a rule, in the early afternoon. Letters are collected at regular intervals from officers' desks and from departments. They are stamped, sealed, and often delivered to the post office hourly until all the day's mail is dispatched. The department may be divided into groups for handling the different classes of mail—regular, special delivery, insured, and registered.

In large banks, an important part of the procedure established for the collection of out-of-town checks and other transit items is the routing, both as to collection points and as to train and airplane schedules. If the outgoing mail makes certain connections, a day can often be saved in the time required for the collection of transit items. The responsibility for maintaining special routing schedules is frequently assigned to one or more members of the mail and messenger department.

Prompt and accurate handling of mail deposits enables the clearing house department to have the items drawn on other local banks ready for the day's clearing. If all the departments concerned receive the items from the mail division before the counter deposits begin to come in, the result is a more even and steadier flow of work.

Questions Based on Chapter II

1. What are the principal channels through which deposits enter a bank?
2. Distinguish between cash items and collection items.
3. List the six steps taken in the process of receiving a deposit, and in a few words, explain the importance of each step.
4. What are (a) checks on us? (b) clearing items? (c) transit items?
5. Describe four principal systems used in receiving teller work. What do you think are the advantages of each system?
6. What is meant by individual deposit proof? By group deposit proof?
7. What are the methods used to prove deposits and to route items? Discuss.
8. How is the teller's cash proof made?
9. What are the four main duties of the mail and messenger department?

10. What factors determine the organization of the mail and messenger department?
11. What bank operations require messenger service? Why is it important?
12. Assume that the items listed below are received on a deposit slip. Using the batch system, describe how each item is received, proved, and distributed.

Currency	$ 104.00
Coin	29.18
Check on a New Orleans bank	1,227.11
Check on a Los Angeles bank	433.96
Check on a Chicago bank	22.13
Check on a local bank	53.32
Check on a local bank	100.00
Check on your own bank	42.30
Check on your own bank	98.47
TOTAL	$2,110.47

Questions for Investigation

1. How is the mail and messenger department in your bank organized?
2. Which system of receiving teller work is used in your bank? Why do you think your bank uses it?
3. How are deposits proved in your bank? If by the batch system, how does your system differ from that explained in the text?
4. What method does your bank use in handling incoming mail deposits?

CHAPTER III

THE PROBLEM OF COLLECTING LOCAL ITEMS

The Purposes of This Chapter:

1. To explain how checks drawn on other local banks are collected.
2. To discuss the purpose and nature of a clearing house association.
3. To describe what happens at the clearing house when checks are exchanged.
4. To indicate the methods of settling the net balances.
5. To point out the value of a clearing house association.

How CHECKS drawn on other banks come into your bank is discussed in the previous chapter. Some checks are taken in by the receiving tellers in the deposits made by the customers at the windows, others are in deposits received by mail, still others are received by the collection department in payment of collection items (Chapter IV). Checks are cashed by the tellers, and checks are received by various other departments in the course of a day's business.

Checks which are drawn on other local banks are called clearing items. In most cases, cash or immediate provisional credit has been given to the bank's depositor. Checks to be cleared, therefore, should be presented for payment as soon as possible to the banks on which they are drawn.

Clearing means the daily exchange of checks between local banks. Clearing is accomplished either directly by presentation of the checks to the banks on which they are drawn, or indirectly by an informal exchange or through a clearing house association.

The Purpose and Nature of a Clearing House Association

In order to dispense with the costly and cumbersome process of presenting each check direct to the bank on which it is drawn and of receiving payment from that bank, a clearing house association may be formed by the local banks. The primary purpose of such an association is to facilitate the exchange of checks and the settlement of the net balances. A clearing association is voluntary, and the rules and regulations adopted by the participating banks are its only source of authority. These rules and regulations relate to (1) the qualifications which a bank must have in order to become a member, (2) the time and place of clearing, (3) the kinds of items that may be cleared, (4) the method of correcting and adjusting errors, (5) the return of items that are dishonored (Chapter IV), and (6) the procedure for settling balances. Clearing house rules are enforced by fines or by expulsion from the association.

In large clearing house associations, the work of clearing is performed by association officers (elected by the member banks) and by a hired staff, in quarters owned or rented by the association. In smaller associations, the banks contribute management and necessary clerical help. They also furnish a meeting place, which may be a room set aside for this purpose in one of the participating banks.

The revenue required to establish and maintain a clearing house association comes from three sources: (1) membership fees, (2) current assessments prorated on an equitable basis, and (3) fines imposed for violations of rules (for late arrivals at clearings, for delays caused by errors in computing balances on settlement sheets, for boisterous conduct on the part of messengers, and for similar offenses). The major source of income is, of course, the current assessments.

The spirit of cooperation used in solving problems related to clearing naturally leads the banks to use the association for other purposes of mutual benefit. In some associations, a trained staff is used to examine the condition of the clearing banks. The clearing house association may also serve as the medium through which the participating banks may discuss matters of interest.

The Assembling of Clearing Items

Clearing items in a bank are routed at frequent intervals to employees who prepare them for presentation through the clearing house association. If the volume of operations and the rate at which deposits are received just before the clearing hour are sufficient to warrant a special out-clearing staff, the clearing items are routed to that staff. Chart 3 presents graphically the course of items sent to and received from the clearing house.

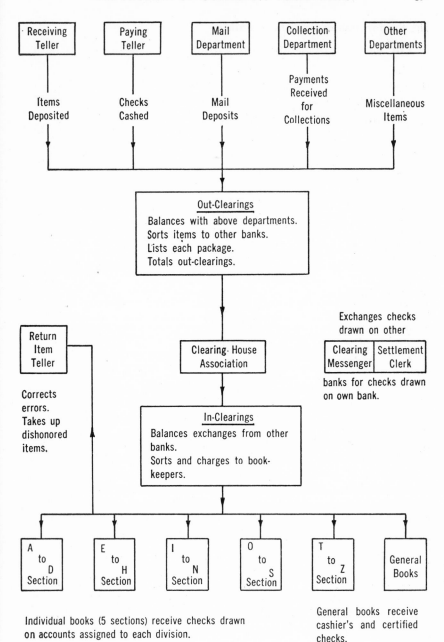

CHART 3. COURSE OF ITEMS SENT TO AND RECEIVED
FROM THE CLEARING HOUSE

The Preparation of Items for Clearing

The clearing items are sorted into groups; there are as many groups as there are other local banks. Each group contains only the checks drawn on one bank. A proof is obtained by totaling the amounts of the checks thus grouped by banks; this total must agree with the total of the amounts charged to out-clearings by the various tellers and departments. An adding machine with a carbon tape may be used for listing the checks. (Listing and totaling the amounts of the checks drawn on one bank is known as straight listing.) The carbon tapes are attached to the packages of checks that go to the clearing house. The listing on the original sheet or tape, which is retained by the out-clearings staff, serves for reference purposes in case items are returned. In lieu of an adding machine record, the checks may be photographed.

In some banks a special machine which is equipped with numerous compartments is used for listing and sorting items. The listing is recorded on individual tapes for each of the local banks as well as on the master tape. The total clearing figures also are automatically listed on the master tape.

A member of the out-clearings staff places the clearing house stamp on the reverse side of each item. This stamp is the equivalent of an indorsement; it bears the name of the presenting bank and the date, and it guarantees prior indorsements. In banks where the volume of clearings is fairly light, the stamp or indorsement is placed on the checks by hand; in other banks an indorsing machine is used. Form 4 illustrates a clearing house stamp.

PAY TO THE ORDER OF ANY
BANK, BANKER OR TRUST COMPANY
OR THROUGH
INSTITUTE CLEARING HOUSE

PRIOR INDORSEMENTS GUARANTEED
JANUARY 2, 1956

76-970   INSTITUTE NATIONAL BANK OF   76-970

INSTITUTE, NEBRASKA

FORM 4. CLEARING HOUSE STAMP

Proving, sorting, listing, and indorsing continues until shortly before the time set for the items to go to the clearing house. The deadline is generally twenty or thirty minutes before the clearing hour.

Every effort is made to include, in the day's clearings, large checks deposited just before the clearing. Instead of going through the ordinary proving and sorting procedure, these checks are routed to a designated staff member, who sees that they are added to the proper totals before the bank's representatives leave for the clearing house.

A summary figure for the dollar amount of checks to be presented to each bank is obtained by a recapitulation (recap) of the sheets or from the master tape. This figure is used in preparing the settlement sheet.

Preparation of Settlement Sheet

Shortly before the clearing hour, the checks (with the tapes) drawn on the other banks are enclosed in, or attached to, large envelopes. There is one envelope for each bank. On the face of the envelope is written the total dollar amount of the checks, the name or identifying number of the presenting bank, and the name or number of the bank on which the checks are drawn (drawee bank).

Assume that the presenting bank is The First National Bank (Bank 1) and that there are four other local banks: Third State Bank (Bank 2), Jones Trust Company (Bank 3), Farmers & Merchants State Bank (Bank 4), and Exchange National Bank (Bank 5). The five banks are members of the clearing house association. Four envelopes will be prepared by the First National Bank.

If the checks drawn on the Third State Bank amount to $1,026.33, the description on the envelope containing these checks will read:

Checks brought by

1. **First National Bank**

drawn on

2. **Third State Bank**

$1,026.33

Similarly, the descriptions on the other three envelopes might read:

Checks brought by

1. First National Bank

drawn on

3. Jones Trust Company

$5,631.01

Checks brought by

1. First National Bank

drawn on

4. F. & M. State Bank

$1,262.12

Checks brought by

1. First National Bank

drawn on

5. Exchange N/B

$3,246.09

These four envelopes, prepared by the out-clearings staff of the First National Bank, are handed to a member of the staff who will act as settlement clerk for that bank. From the information on these envelopes, he commences the preparation of the settlement sheet (sometimes known as the settling clerk's statement) of the First National Bank, filling in the left-hand column with the total dollar amounts of the checks drawn on the four banks, that is, *the checks brought.* (The information for the right-hand column is obtained after the exchange of the checks has taken place at the clearing house.)

Settlement Sheet

1. FIRST NATIONAL BANK

Debit (through C. H.) the banks listed hereunder for checks drawn on them and *brought* by us (1st N/B) to the clearing house

Credit (through C. H.) the banks listed hereunder for checks on us (1st N/B) which are *received* by us at the clearing house

$ 1,026.33	2. Third State Bank	$_____
5,631.01	3. Jones Trust Company	_____
1,262.12	4. F. & M. State Bank	_____
3,246.09	5. Exchange National Bank	_____
$11,165.55		

(Total claims against other banks)

This settlement sheet is partially completed; it shows that the First National Bank is presenting through the clearing house checks drawn on the other four banks in the total amount of $11,165.55. As the First National Bank desires payment or credit, the settlement clerk prepares a memorandum (first ticket):

First Ticket

1. FIRST NATIONAL BANK

To the Clearing House Association:

Please credit First National Bank (for checks on other banks brought by us to the C. H.):

$11,165.55

He writes in the same figure on another memorandum (second ticket).

The information needed for the completion of the second ticket (as in the case of the settlement sheet) is not available until the exchange of checks at the clearing house has taken place.

The Clearing Operation

A few minutes before the time established by the clearing house rules for the exchange of checks (the clearing), the representatives

Second Ticket
1. FIRST NATIONAL BANK

To the Clearing House Association:
Please credit First National Bank (for checks on other banks brought by us to the C. H.):

$11,165.55

Please debit First National Bank (for checks drawn on us received from other banks at the C. H.)

$_____

Balance due to Clearing House by First National Bank

$_____

Balance due to First National Bank

$_____

of the banks arrive at the place designated for the exchange of clearings. At the settlement clearing, (that is, the clearing at which the computations of the net balances due to and due from the participating banks are made), there are two representatives from each bank. One representative is the settlement clerk, who keeps a record of the dollar amounts of the checks exchanged between his bank and the other banks; the other is the clearing messenger, who brings the packages of checks drawn on other banks and makes delivery of these checks at the clearing house to the settlement clerks of the banks on which the checks are drawn.

Upon arrival at the clearing house, the settlement clerk hands the clearing house manager the first ticket which he has already prepared; he retains the partially completed settlement sheet and the second ticket. He then takes his place behind a desk or counter which bears the name of his bank or the identifying number assigned to his bank by the clearing house association. The clearing messenger who holds the packages of checks drawn on the other banks, stands by the desk or counter assigned to his bank, awaiting the signal for the clearing to commence. The same procedure is followed by the representatives of the other banks.

From the information on the first tickets, the clearing house manager commences the preparation of the clearing house proof (Form 5) by recording in the Bank Cr. column the amounts requested by the banks as shown on their first tickets. Form 5 shows that the amount requested by the First National Bank is $11,165.55. This figure is, of course, the same amount as the total of the left-hand, or debit (brought), column of the settlement sheet of the First National Bank which shows the amounts of the checks to be debited against the other four banks through the clearing house.

After the manager has recorded on the clearing house proof the credits requested by each bank, he totals the column, Bank Cr. The total, $43,700.70, is the clearings figure or *total exchanges* for the day, that is, the total of the checks being presented through the clearing house. (This figure is published in the financial pages of many newspapers for the information of those who find it an interesting indicator of day-to-day changes in the volume of business activity).

At exactly the time stipulated by the clearing house rules, the signal for making the exchanges is given by the manager. The clearing messenger of the First National Bank proceeds to the settlement desk for each of the other banks.

At the desk for Third State Bank, he hands to the settlement clerk the package of checks drawn on that bank, totaling $1,026.33. The amount, shown on the envelope, is recorded by the settlement clerk of the Third State Bank in the right-hand or credit (received) column of his settlement sheet opposite the name First National Bank (see Form 5).

Then the clearing messenger of the First National Bank proceeds to the desk of the settlement clerk for the Jones Trust Company, to whom he gives checks on that bank totaling $5,631.01. This amount is recorded by the settlement clerk of the Jones Trust Company in the credit (received) column of his sheet opposite the name First National Bank.

The clearing messenger next presents to the settlement clerk of the Farmers & Merchants State Bank checks on that bank totaling $1,262.12. This figure is recorded by the settlement clerk of the Farmers & Merchants State Bank in the credit (received) column of his sheet opposite the name First National Bank.

Finally, the First National Bank clearing messenger gives to the settlement clerk of the Exchange National Bank checks on that bank totaling $3,246.09. That figure is recorded by the settlement clerk of the Exchange National Bank in the credit (received) column of his sheet opposite the First National Bank.

At the same time, and in the same manner, the clearing messengers from the other four banks distribute the checks to the settlement clerks of the banks on which the checks are drawn. The settlement clerk of each bank thus receives checks drawn on his bank from the clearing messengers of the other banks. He records the total dollar amounts in the credit (received) column of his settlement sheet opposite the names of the presenting banks, since these amounts represent the credit being requested through the clearing house by each of the banks (Form 5).

Settlement Sheet

1. FIRST NATIONAL BANK

Debit (through C. H.) the banks listed hereunder for checks drawn on them and *brought* by us (1st N/B) to the clearing house

Credit (through C. H.) the banks listed hereunder for checks on us (1st N/B) which are *received* by us at the clearing house

Debit	Bank	Credit
$ 1,026.33	2. Third State Bank	$ 2,014.10
5,631.01	3. Jones Trust Company	5,716.30
1,262.12	4. F. & M. State Bank	498.17
3,246.09	5. Exchange National Bank	3,162.12

$11,165.55—Total claims against other banks
             Total claims against 1st N/B $11,390.69
      225.14—Balance due to C. H.
$11,390.69

The volume of the exchanges in many clearing houses is so large that the clearing messengers do not wait for a signal to be given by the clearing house manager. Instead, immediately upon arrival at the clearing house, they make a complete or partial delivery of the checks to the representatives of the drawee banks.

Thus, the settlement clerk of the First National Bank receives from the clearing messenger of the Third State Bank checks drawn on his bank totaling $2,014.10; from the Jones Trust Company, $5,716.30; from the Farmers & Merchants State Bank, $498.17; and from the Exchange National Bank, $3,162.12. Using the figures noted on the envelopes handed to him by the four clearing messengers, the settlement clerk of the First National Bank completes his settlement sheet by writing the figures in the credit (received) column. He then totals that column and, by comparison of the totals of the debit (brought) and credit (received) columns, determines whether there is a net amount due to First National Bank or due to clearing house.

From the information on the settlement sheet, the settlement clerk of the First National Bank now completes the second ticket.

Second Ticket
1. FIRST NATIONAL BANK

To the Clearing House Association:
Please credit First National Bank (for checks on other banks brought by us to the C. H.):

$11,165.55

Please debit First National Bank (for checks drawn on us received from other banks at C. H.):

$11,390.69

Balance due to clearing House by First National Bank:

$ 225.14

The settlement clerk hands the second ticket to the manager. From the information on this ticket, the manager records the figures for "debit First National Bank" and "Balance due to clearing house" on his clearing house proof opposite the First National Bank in Bank Dr. and Balances due to C. H. columns, respectively (Form 5).

In the same manner, the settlement clerks of the other banks complete their settlement sheets and second tickets and then hand the second tickets to the manager in order that he may complete his proof. This proof shows that three banks (First National Bank, Farmers & Merchants State Bank, Exchange National Bank) have received checks drawn on them which *exceed in dollar amount* the checks brought by them to the clearing house. Therefore these three banks have net balances due to the clearing house. The proof also indicates that two banks (Third State Bank, Jones Trust Company) have received checks drawn on them which are *less in dollar amount* than the checks brought by them to the clearing house. Therefore they have net balances due to them through the clearing house.

These net balances (due to clearing house and due to banks) are determined in each instance when the settlement clerks of the banks complete their settlement sheets. The clearing house manager, using the information on the first and second tickets for recording on his proof, verifies the accuracy of their calculations. The totals of the figures in the two inner columns of the proof agree because they are the *total of the checks exchanged.* The Bank Cr. column shows the amounts of the checks brought, for which the presenting banks ask credit; the Bank Dr. column shows the amounts of the checks received by each bank, for which the drawee bank (receiving bank) is to be debited. The figures in the two outer columns of the proof agree because they represent the net balances to be settled, resulting from the figures in the two inner columns.

If the figures balance when the proof is completed, the manager announces that fact; if the figures do not balance, the manager states the amount of the difference. The clerks then check over their work until the error is located and corrected.

As far as the clearing house is concerned, the first of its primary functions (the exchange of checks and the computation of the net balances) has been performed.

It should be noted here that the procedures are not the same in all clearing houses. For example, in the exchange at some clearing houses, the activities of the representatives of the participating banks are largely those of clearing messengers, who deliver checks to the clearing house and receive checks drawn on their own banks. Postings and calculations that would otherwise be performed by settlement clerks are done by a member of the clearing house staff, who completes the settlement sheet of each bank from information appearing on copies of the settlement sheets of the other banks.

Settlement of the Net Balances

Some banks, having brought to the clearing house a dollar amount of checks which is *greater* than the dollar amount of checks drawn on them and received through the clearing house, have net balances due to them. The clearings are said to be in their favor or *for* them; they have credit balances. Other banks, having brought to the clearing house a dollar amount of checks which is *less than* the dollar amount of checks drawn on them and received through the clearing house, owe net balances through the clearing house. The clearings are said to be *against* them; they have debit balances.

The next step in the collection process is the performance of the clearing house's other primary function—the arrangement for the settlement of the individual net balances. Payment of the debit balances (balances due to clearing house on the clearing house proof) must be made by those banks which have clearings *against* them, and the total of these payments must be distributed to those banks which have credit balances (balances due to banks on the clearing house proof). In former years, debit balances were usually settled by cash, but this is no longer a common practice. There are two simple methods of settlement that involve only bookkeeping entries. One is through a clearing house settlement account maintained by each of the participating banks on the books of a local bank. The other is through a clearing or reserve account on the books of a Federal Reserve bank. In either case, the clearing house manager addresses a memorandum to the bank which carries the clearing accounts for the participating banks.

CLEARING HOUSE ASSOCIATION

To the Federal Reserve Bank: Date_____

This certifies that the balances resulting from today's clearings are as shown below:

Debit		Credit
$ 225.14	1. First National Bank	$
	2. Third State Bank	819.09
	3. Jones Trust Company	314.98
313.71	4. Farmers & Merchants State Bank	
595.22	5. Exchange National Bank	
$1,134.07		$1,134.07

If the clearing accounts are maintained on the books of a Federal Reserve bank which is not located in the same city as the clearing house association, the clearing house manager may telegraph the amounts of the debit and credit balances and the names of the banks in code to the Federal Reserve Bank. This method of settlement is known as the wire clearing balance.

On the authority of the memorandum or the telegram, the bank that carries the clearing accounts for the participating banks *reduces* the accounts of those banks that have debit balances and *increases* the accounts of those banks that have credit balances. As the total of the reductions (debits) is the same as the total of the increases (credits), the grand total of the clearing accounts on the books of the Federal Reserve bank or the selected local bank does not change.

In-Clearings Procedure

When the clearing messenger of the First National Bank returns from the clearing house with the checks drawn on his bank, the in-clearings staff proves the batches of items and then sorts and delivers the checks to the appropriate people or departments (Chart 3).

The Handling of Return Items

Among the items exchanged through the clearing house there may be some that are "missorts" (checks drawn on banks other than the receiving bank) and some that cannot be paid because of improper or missing indorsements, insufficient funds, stop-payments, and so forth. Since the amount of these checks has been included in the day's exchanges and the receiving bank has paid for them, an adjustment or "reclamation" must be made. An adjustment can be made either by a return of the items direct to the originating bank, which reimburses the returning bank in cash, or by cashier's or treasurer's checks. If the volume of reclamations resulting from a day's clearings is so large that the handling of such items requires much time and messenger service, arrangements are often made for the return of the unpaid items to the originating bank, with provision for reimbursement in the next clearing settlement. The originating bank gives the returning bank a credit memorandum which is included among the items cleared and settled.

Provision is also made for the return of unpaid items through the clearing house, in accordance with the time schedule established by clearing house rules. Special settlement sheets, similar to those used for clearings, may be used for the return items (reclamations), and the net balances may be carried forward on the settlement sheets for the next day's clearings. A *return slip,* giving the reason for the nonpayment, is attached to each item or group if the same reason applies to all checks in the group.

The Value of a Clearing House Association

It is stated, at the beginning of this chapter, that the purpose of a clearing house association is primarily to dispense with the costly and cumbersome process of presenting each check directly to the drawee bank and of receiving payment from the latter bank. On seeing how the exchange of checks is effected through the clearing house, we can understand more clearly the benefits to be derived from a clearing arrangement. Form 5 shows the dollar amount that might be involved in a day's exchanges at a five-bank clearing house.

If there were no clearing house, First National Bank would have to send the checks by messengers for over-the-counter presentation to each of the other four banks. The bank might have to make not one but several presentations to each bank if the amounts of the checks were large and immediate payment were desired. Each of the other four banks would have to send its messengers to collect checks drawn on four banks. The result would be a steady stream of messengers going to and from each bank, and the banks would be engaged in the work of collection and settlement from the opening hour in the morning until the close of business at the end of the day. Payments would be made by the cumbersome process of issuing numerous cashier's checks or by cash which, if in large amounts, would require special protection when being carried through the streets. Furthermore, in the absence of a clearing arrangement, it would seldom be possible to offset the claims of one bank against another and pay only the net balance. The payments to be made by each bank would be the *gross total of all checks presented* against it.

Although the amounts shown in Form 5 are relatively small, it should be observed that, in the absence of a clearing arrangement, the five banks would have to pay a total of $43,700.70. With a clearing arrangement in effect, representatives of the five

INDIVIDUAL BANK SETTLEMENT SHEETS

Debit C. H. Brought	1 FIRST NATIONAL BANK	Credit C. H. Received
$ 1,026.33	2. Third State	$ 2,014.10
5,631.01	3. Jones Trust	5,716.30
1,262.12	4. F. & M. State	498.17
3,246.09	5. Exchange Nat'l	3,162.12
$11,165.55[1]		$11,390.69[3]
225.14[2]	Due C. H.	
$11,390.69		

Debit C. H. Brought	2 THIRD STATE BANK	Credit C. H. Received
$ 2,014.10	1. First National	$ 1,026.33
5,965.50	3. Jones Trust	6,210.02
410.05	4. F. & M. State	320.20
2,102.10	5. Exchange Nat'l	2,116.11
$10,491.75		$ 9,672.66
	Due Third State	819.09
		$10,491.75

Debit C. H. Brought	3 JONES TRUST COMPANY	Credit C. H. Received
$ 5,716.30	1. First National	$5,631.01
6,210.02	2. Third State	5,965.50
110.90	4. F. & M. State	205.40
1,042.10	5. Exchange Nat'l	962.43
$13,079.32		$12,764.34
	Due Jones Trust	314.98
		$13,079.32

Debit C. H. Brought	4 FARMERS & MERCHANTS STATE BANK	Credit C. H. Received
$ 498.17	1. First National	$ 1,262.12
320.20	2. Third State	410.05
205.40	3. Jones Trust	110.90
1,072.62	5. Exchange Nat'l	627.03
$ 2,096.39		$ 2,410.10
313.71	Due C. H.	
$ 2,410.10		

Debit C. H. Brought	5 EXCHANGE NATIONAL BANK	Credit C. H. Received
$ 3,162.12	1. First National	$ 3,246.09
2,116.11	2. Third State	2,102.10
962.43	3. Jones Trust	1,042.10
627.03	4. F. & M. State	1,072.62
$ 6,867.69		$ 7,462.91
595.22	Due C. H.	
$ 7,462.91		

CLEARING HOUSE PROOF

	Bank	Balances due to C. H.	Received Bank Dr.	Brought Bank Cr.	Balances due to Banks
1.	First National Bank	$ 225.14[2]	$11,390.69[3]	$11,165.55[1]	
2.	Third State Bank		9,672.66	10,491.75	$ 819.09
3.	Jones Trust Company		12,764.34	13,079.32	314.98
4.	Farmers & Merchants State Bank	313.71	2,410.10	2,096.39	
5.	Exchange Nat'l Bank	595.22	7,462.91	6,867.69	
		$ 1,134.07	$43,700.70	$43,700.70	$ 1,134.07

The superior figures relate the amounts shown on the settlement sheet of the First National Bank on the clearing house proof:

[1] Indicates the amount brought to the clearing by First National Bank.

[2] Indicates the amount due to the clearing house from First National Bank.

[3] Indicates the total amount of the checks received by First National Bank during the clearings from other banks.

FORM 5. BANK SETTLEMENT SHEETS AND CLEARING HOUSE PROOF

banks meet at a designated time and place to make their exchanges. To speed the presentation of the checks, there may be several preliminary exchanges before the settlement clearing; in such cases the debits or amounts brought are carried forward to the settlement exchange. After the exchanges are completed, the net result for each bank is determined at the settlement clearing, that is, whether the bank is required to pay a debit balance or whether a credit balance is due to it from the other banks. Thus the complicated procedure of collecting checks by messengers is reduced to this simple procedure.

The great advantage of a clearing arrangement is shown by a comparison of the amount which would be required for over-the-counter payment of all checks, $43,700.70, with the amount required to settle only the net balances, $1,134.07 (Form 5). This advantage is even more apparent when reference is made to the clearing position of the First National Bank which, in the absence of a clearing arrangement, would have had to pay $11,390.69 for checks drawn on it. Under a clearing arrangement, the amount of the checks presented by the First National Bank against other banks, $11,165.55, is offset against the $11,390.69. Then settlement is made by a convenient bookkeeping entry amounting to a relatively nominal reduction, $225.14, of the balance of the First National Bank on the books of the bank which carries the accounts of the clearing banks. Thus the exchanges and settlements are made easily, rapidly, economically, and with a minimum of risk.

Without a clearing arrangement it would be difficult, if not impossible, to handle the large volume of items which are interchanged between banks in many areas. During 1955, the clearings at the New York Clearing House Association (the checks exchanged or cleared) totaled $530,883,498,080.38, but the total of the net balances amounted to only $18,099,358,027.11. Payments of these balances were effected through clearing house settlement accounts maintained with the Federal Reserve Bank of New York.

Questions Based on Chapter III

1. How are clearing items assembled and prepared for presentation at the clearing house?

2. What part of the settlement sheet is prepared before the bank's representatives go to the clearing house?
3. What is the purpose of a clearing house stamp?
4. What is the source of the information written on the first ticket?
5. Define clearing.
6. What are the main objectives of a clearing arrangement?
7. Is a clearing house association required by law? Explain.
8. What kinds of rules and regulations should be established by a clearing house association?
9. What are the sources of revenue for the establishment and maintenance of a clearing house association?
10. How are checks exchanged at the clearing house?
11. How are the net balances due to or due from the banks computed?
12. How are these net balances settled?
13. What are return items? Why are they returned?
14. What is the value of a clearing house association?

Questions for Investigation

1. At what times do exchanges take place at the local clearing house?
2. What is the approximate total of daily clearings at your local clearing house? How are the net balances settled at your clearing house?
3. Has your local clearing house been of assistance to the banks in other ways than the clearing of checks? Discuss.
4. From the following information, construct the individual bank settlement sheets and the clearing house proof for the exchanges brought to the clearing house.

The First National Bank brought checks drawn on the

Security State	$1,017.05
Merchants State	2,810.15
Institute National	1,198.17

The Merchants State Bank brought checks drawn on the

First National	$2,815.16
Security State	1,531.10
Institute National	905.40

The Security State Bank & Trust Company brought checks drawn on the

First National	$ 926.31
Merchants State	3,105.04
Institute National	791.14

The Institute National Bank brought checks drawn on the

First National	$1,006.12
Security State	743.18
Merchants State	404.07

CHAPTER IV

THE PROBLEM OF COLLECTING TRANSIT ITEMS

The Purposes of This Chapter:
1. To explain the processes of converting cash items (not local) into cash or cash equivalents.
2. To describe the use of the Federal Reserve banks and of correspondent banks as collecting agents.
3. To consider aids in sorting, routing, and tracing items.

THE PREVIOUS chapter discusses the factors involved in obtaining payment for clearing or local items. This chapter considers the problem of collecting out-of-town items, called transit or remittance items. The handling of checks on us is treated in Chapters VI and VII.

We should recognize at the outset that there are numerous small banks throughout the nation whose operations do not require consideration of the various means available for the collection of checks drawn on out-of-town banks. In the course of a day, these banks receive only a small number of checks drawn on banks in distant places. Such a bank may group all its transit checks, regardless of the location of the drawee banks (the banks on which the checks are drawn) and forward them to one nearby sending point, either a correspondent bank or a Federal Reserve bank. There the checks are resorted, grouped with other checks being handled by that sending point, and dispatched toward their ultimate destination. The bank's true transit operation commences when its volume increases, and the number of its sending points must be increased to accomplish a faster, more direct routing and thus to speed the conversion of its funds from checks to cash.

Because of the varying distances involved, as well as the mailing schedules and train and plane time tables, it is necessary to give closer attention to the characteristics of the individual check in the transit function than is required in the clearing function. Primarily, the selection of the channel for the collection of transit

53

items is based both on the speed with which the task can be accomplished and on the cost of using that channel.

Basic Transit Considerations

Before considering the channels available for use and before evaluating the justification for basing our selection of any one channel on *speed* and *cost*, we should review some of the various factors that enter into the problem and should present some of the terms to be encountered in discussing transit considerations.

1. Cash items and collection items. Transit operations normally involve only cash items, the collection of noncash items (termed collection items) being handled separately. (See Chapter XIII.) Occasionally, certain kinds of drafts and warrants which require no special instructions for handling, are treated as cash items and are collected in the same manner as checks. Such items are generally handled through correspondent banks, since Federal Reserve banks do not handle them as cash items.

2. Par items and nonpar items. Although all banks that are members of the Federal Reserve System or of the par collection system must make settlement for checks sent to them for the full face amount of each check, certain state banks make a practice of deducting a fee for the payment of checks sent to them. For example, one of these state banks may settle for a $100 transit check with $99.50, thus levying an exchange charge of 50 cents per $100 of checks. Items from which such a charge is deducted are termed nonpar items, and the banks on which they are drawn are termed nonpar banks or nonpar points. Since the Federal Reserve System requires that all checks handled through its facilities must be settled at par, a sending bank is unable to use the Federal Reserve System for the collection of nonpar items. (The deposit volume of nonpar banks is a small percentage of the total.)

3. City items and country items. In the sorting and the mailing of transit items to any special point, it is common practice to include not only checks drawn on banks in that particular city but also checks drawn on banks anywhere in the vicinity, although normally the routing is confined to a natural geographic area. A bank sending only a small number of checks to a routing point would group them all under one total. But when sendings reach a reasonably large volume, the checks are usually sorted into two

bundles. The checks in one bundle are drawn on banks located in the collecting city and are called city items. The checks in the other bundle, being drawn on banks located outside that city, are called country items. By sorting large groups of checks in this fashion, the sending bank assists the collecting bank in speeding collection. Thus the collecting bank can immediately send the city items to its clearings division to be exchanged at the next clearing hour, without waiting to segregate and balance the country items. The country items in turn are forwarded by the transit division along with other checks received from various sources.

4. Instructions for handling. Uniform banking practices, developed throughout the years, have largely standardized the instructions which govern the handling of transit checks. Those instructions are set forth on a form resembling a deposit ticket, which is termed a *cash letter*. This letter may list all the items enclosed, or it may list only the totals of the adding machine tapes attached to the several packages of checks enclosed. Standard instructions are included in the cash letter, Form 6.

Occasionally it is necessary under special circumstances, perhaps at the request of a customer, to demand special treatment, such as "wire fate," in order that the sending bank may be positive that a certain check is paid. In this event, special instructions are contained in the cash letter, which must be sent to a correspondent bank or to the bank on which this check is drawn, since the Federal Reserve banks do not accept, for handling as cash items, checks accompanied by special instructions.

Elements That Determine Routing

It is important both to banks and to their customers that transit checks be collected speedily for two reasons:

1. All banks are anxious to know that the transit checks which have been credited to their customers' accounts are good, and they cannot be certain of that fact until the checks have been paid by the drawee bank. The faster a transit check is presented for payment, the less is the risk of loss incurred.

2. Before transit checks are presented for payment, they represent only claims to money; they do not represent usable cash or what is sometimes termed available cash. Since a bank's earnings

779 7-54 50M

THE INSTITUTE NATIONAL BANK
OF LOS ANGELES
LOS ANGELES 609, CALIFORNIA

THE BANK OF CHICAGO

CHICAGO 809 ILLINOIS

COUNTRY
AIRMAIL   9—

We Enclose for Returns Items as Listed Below

PROTEST all items over $500.00, except those drawn and payable in the State of California and bearing California indorsements only, or those bearing on face or back, this stamp or similar authority of a preceding indorser.

TELEGRAPH NON-PAYMENT of all items $1,000.00 and over except those being returned for Missing, Irregular or Unsatisfactory Indorsement.

N P
16-1

Please follow special instructions embodied in this cash letter or attached to the items.

FORM 6. CASH LETTER

are derived from the lending or investment of its available cash, it is vitally concerned with limiting the period that transit checks are in the process of collection.

It is also important to customers to know that they are receiving speedy collection services on transit items, since they are liable for the charge-back of any items that may be returned unpaid. Through rapid service, the likelihood of liability is reduced. Furthermore, in some methods of analyzing a customer's account for the purpose of levying certain types of service charges (discussed in Chapter XVIII), the bank reduces a customer's balance by the dollar amount of the transit checks which are in the process of collection. This practice is justified because the bank credits a customer's account immediately with transit items deposited, irrespective of the date the bank itself converts these items into usable cash. For the period of time between the deposit of a transit item and its collection, the funds represented by the check in process of collection are termed *uncollected funds*. The amount of uncollected funds which is deducted from the customer's average balance in figuring service charges is called *float*.

Although speed is obviously desirable and although it is equally obvious that the fastest way to collect a transit item would be to send it direct to the bank on which it is drawn, another element enters into the determination of the routing of transit items. This element is the cost involved. Even the smallest banks receive numerous checks drawn on remote banks, and large banks receive checks drawn on literally thousands of other banks throughout the country. The cost of mailing direct to each of these points, of accounting for checks which are in the mail, and of ultimately receiving funds in settlement would be far too heavy for banks to consider direct sending exclusively. As a compromise, banks normally develop a reasonable number of sending points to which they direct transit items. The number is determined by the volume that a sending point can handle in the interest of fast collection.

THE CHANNELS AVAILABLE FOR COLLECTION

The three channels available for presenting transit checks for payment are (1) the Federal Reserve System, (2) correspondent banks, and (3) direct presentation to drawee banks. Large banks normally use all three channels in varying degrees; very small banks may use only one.

Channel I: Transit Collection Through the Federal Reserve System

Through the banking system as a whole, the largest percentage of transit items to be collected are handled by the Federal Reserve System. This topic is more broadly discussed in Chapter XXII. The Federal Reserve System is divided into twelve districts, and each bank using the par collection facilities maintains an account with the Federal Reserve bank or branch of the district in which it operates. Banks using the Federal Reserve System customarily deposit transit checks in the nearest office of the Federal Reserve bank, in the same way that one of the bank's own customers deposits checks to his account with his bank.

A small or medium sized bank using the Federal Reserve System might deal exclusively with the branch in which it maintains its account. However, each Federal Reserve bank is unwilling to accept for deposit checks drawn on banks in another Federal Reserve district when a sizable volume has developed. Accordingly, when a bank's volume of transit checks drawn on banks located in another Federal Reserve district reaches 200 items a day, the bank is expected to segregate those items and transmit them direct to the Federal Reserve bank of the other district. The amount involved, however, is credited to the bank's account with the Federal Reserve bank in its own district. For example, a Chicago bank which has its account with the Federal Reserve Bank of Chicago separates its checks drawn on banks in the area served by the Los Angeles Branch of the Federal Reserve Bank of San Francisco and forwards those items direct to the Los Angeles Branch for credit to its account with the Federal Reserve Bank of Chicago.

Settlement by Federal Reserve Banks

In order to aid the Federal Reserve banks in making settlement for the tremendous volume of items handled through the par collection system, member banks segregate their transit items in accordance with an availability schedule set up by the Federal Reserve System. This schedule, illustrated in Form 7, indicates the period of time required by the various Federal Reserve banks before the funds deposited are considered as collected. It breaks down the settlement periods into three groups: (1) available for immediate credit, (2) one-day credit, and (3) two-day credit.

For settlement purposes all transit checks handled by the Federal Reserve banks are considered as being collected within two days, even though actual collection may take longer.

Checks classified for immediate credit are placed to the credit of the depositing member bank's reserve account on the date deposited and thus qualify as available funds in calculating the bank's reserve requirements. The one-day and two-day items are placed to the credit of its deferred account, which does not qualify as available reserves. Automatically, the deferred balances are shifted to the reserve account with the passage of time. When cash letters are dispatched by a bank direct to other Federal Reserve districts, Form 8 an appropriate notification, is sent to the local Federal Reserve bank. The local Federal Reserve bank uses this information for posting to the member bank's reserve or deferred account. To settle the transactions between the various Federal Reserve banks, a daily clearing (similar in function to the clearing function described in the previous chapter) is operated through the Interdistrict Settlement Fund of the Federal Reserve System.

To facilitate this clearing and settlement function and to give member banks further assistance in the nationwide exchange of funds, the Federal Reserve operates a leased wire system which connects all the Federal Reserve banks and their branches. It offers free use of this facility to all member banks for the purpose of transferring funds by wire.

Special Handling of Transit Items

It should be apparent that the nationwide scope of the Federal Reserve System and the widespread use of its par collection system by member banks necessitate the streamlining of its operations in order to permit the economic handling of a tremendous volume of items. Accordingly, the Federal Reserve banks have, through virtual necessity, clearly defined the types of items they will handle. In the course of processing items, they adhere strictly to uniform treatment. For example, small checks are not protested when they are not paid; large checks (over $500) normally are

FEDERAL RESERVE BANK
OF SAN FRANCISCO

CIRCULAR 90
SUPPLEMENT 3
EFFECTIVE JULY 15, 1954

Amending Supplement 3
Effective April 26, 1954

TIME SCHEDULES
AVAILABILITY OF CREDITS

CASH ITEMS DEPOSITED
at the office of the Federal Reserve Bank of San Francisco with which affiliated.

ITEMS [1]

AVAILABILITY [2]

When deposited in the office of the Federal Reserve Bank of San Francisco at

	San Francisco	Los Angeles	Portland	Salt Lake City	Seattle
Drawn on the office of the Federal Reserve Bank of San Francisco with which deposited.	Immediate	Immediate	Immediate	Immediate	Immediate
Drawn on the Treasurer of the United States—Government Checks, including checks payable "through" any Federal Reserve bank—if received prior to 3:00 P.M.‡ (12 noon Saturday at those offices open for business on Saturday).	Immediate	Immediate	Immediate	Immediate	Immediate
Postal Money Orders if received prior to 3:00 P.M.‡ (12 noon Saturday at those offices open for business on Saturday).					
Payable in Federal Reserve cities of the Twelfth District (†):					
Payable in San Francisco - - - - - - - - -	One day	Two days[3]	Two days[3]	Two days[3]	Two days[3]
Payable in Los Angeles - - - - - - - -	Two days[3]	One day	Two days[3]	Two days[3]	Two days[8]
Payable in Portland - - - - - - - - -	One day	One day	Immediate*	One day	One day
Payable in Salt Lake City - - - - - - -	One day	One day	One day	Immediate*	One day
Payable in Seattle - - - - - - - - -	One day	One day	One day	One day	Immediate*

60

Payable in Federal Reserve cities in other Federal
Reserve districts (†). - - - - - - - -   Two days | Two days | Two days | Two days | Two days

Payable outside of Federal Reserve cities (†) - -   Two days³ | Two days³ | Two days³ | Two days³ | Two days³

\# During the period when Daylight Saving Time is observed in San Francisco, the closing hour will be 2:00 P.M. at any office which remains on Pacific Standard Time.

† The right is reserved to decline to accept cash items for collection unless they are routed direct to the Federal Reserve banks or branches in the zones in which the items are payable when, in the judgment of the Federal Reserve Bank of San Francisco, the volume justifies.

* If cash letters are received too late to permit clearing on day of receipt, credit will be deferred one day.

CASH ITEMS SENT DIRECT to other Federal Reserve banks and branches, and to offices of the Federal Reserve Bank of San Francisco other than that with which affiliated.

ITEMS [1]	AVAILABILITY [2]
Payable in the Federal Reserve city to which sent.	Actual transit time to the Federal Reserve bank or branch addressed. Air transportation should be used whenever transit time can be reduced. If items will arrive too late for clearing, add one day. Maximum deferment, two business days.
Payable outside of Federal Reserve city in the zone of the Federal Reserve bank or branch to which sent.	Two days³

---

1 Member and nonmember clearing banks' own drafts on their commercial bank correspondents should be sent in cash letters separate from other cash items. Cash letters enclosing such items, and advices of direct sendings of such items, should be clearly marked by rubber stamp or other means with designation "Tranfer drafts." Credit for such items will be deferred on the basis of actual collection time, air mail or ordinary mail. Offices of this bank which are open until the next business day.

2 When the date of availability falls on Sunday, or a legal holiday, credit will not be passed on Saturday, notwithstanding that the collecting Federal Reserve bank or branch may remain closed on Saturday.

3 Business days. All other deferments are based on calendar days.

61

FORM 7. TIME SCHEDULES

protested. (For a discussion of protest see Chapter VIII.) A clearly defined policy governs the dispatch of advices by wire in the event of nonpayment of very large checks. The Federal Reserve banks accept deposits only on these uniform instructions and ignore any contrary instructions. Therefore, if a bank desires to receive notification of payment by wire or wishes to request some other special handling, the cash collection facilities of the Federal Reserve System cannot be used.

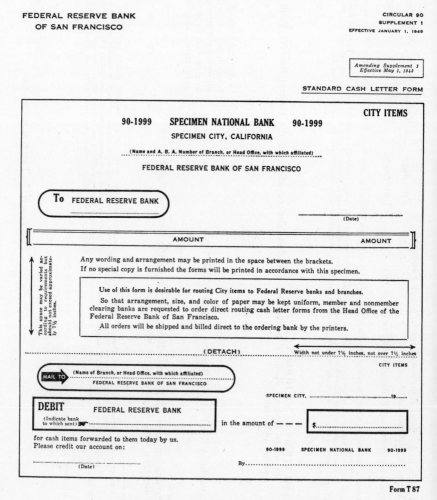

FORM 8. STANDARD CASH LETTER FORM

Channel II: Transit Collection Through Correspondent Banks

During the years before the establishment of the Federal Reserve System, banks relied almost exclusively upon a system of commercial banking relationships. A bank would select other banks in several financial centers to collect transit items, to furnish credit information, to assist in investments, and to participate in large loans. The term correspondent bank is used to describe a bank with which such relationships are maintained.

If a sending bank elects to use the facilities of a correspondent bank, either in addition to or instead of the Federal Reserve banks, it usually does so because the correspondent bank has worked out some special collection arrangement under which it agrees to follow special handling instructions to speed the conversion of checks to cash or to collect nonpar items. In many instances a small bank in an outlying community may consolidate all checks drawn on other banks and forward them to a nearby correspondent bank in a larger city. Thus it avoids the necessity of making several sorts, dispatching numerous cash letters, and accounting for a number of settlements. To compensate the city correspondent for the work involved in servicing the items forwarded for collection, the sending bank carries an account with the correspondent bank. The sending bank is expected to maintain a sufficient balance in its account to provide earnings that will at least offset the expense of handling the items forwarded for collection, just as a bank's customers are expected to carry balances commensurate with the work involved in handling their accounts.

Settlement Through Correspondent Banks

A bank carries all the accounts of its correspondent banks on its general books. These accounts as a group are usually called *country books* or *correspondent bank books*.[1] When cash letters are received by a correspondent bank, immediate credit for the items is placed to the account of the sending bank. Accounts of correspondent banks are subject to account analysis, in the same manner as those of individual customers. This analysis requires

---

[1] These books include two groups of accounts: (1) Due to Banks, that is, accounts other banks carry with us (included as a liability on our statement of condition, being grouped with Demand Deposits) ; (2) Due from Banks, that is, accounts our bank carries with others (included as an asset on our statement of condition, being grouped with Cash) .

the calculation of float covering the period during which items received in cash letters are being collected.

Occasionally the city correspondent bank sends transit items to the bank from which it normally receives items (the reverse of the regular procedure). In those infrequent instances, it obtains settlement for the items by arranging to charge the collecting bank's account for the amount involved rather than to request a remittance.

Channel III: Direct Presentation to Drawee Banks

In comparison with the other two channels available for transit collections, only a small volume of checks are handled by forwarding them direct to the bank on which they are drawn. This fact may appear strange since direct sending entails the least time, but the cost of mailing direct limits the use of this channel. Nevertheless, special circumstances, such as the following, may justify direct sending:

1. When the dollar volume is sufficient and the time saved warrants the expense and

2. When bank customers specifically request speedy collection of large checks.

The only disadvantage with this method of presentation is that the drawee bank is under no obligation to the sending bank and may impose a charge for making settlement.

Aids in Routing and Sorting

When new bank employees first contemplate the task of a transit sorter, who is charged with sorting checks drawn on banks all over the nation into proper groups to be forwarded for payment, they are usually amazed at the sorter's apparent familiarity with our country's geography. It appears that not only must he know the relative position of states but that he also must recognize the many instances in which portions of a state are served by different Federal Reserve banks.

Actually, familiarity with the numerous sorts is made possible through two numerical systems which enable the sorter, by observing certain numbers printed on all checks, to sort rapidly and accurately. These are known as the American Bankers Association numerical system and the check routing symbol. (For a description of these two systems, see the Appendix.) Not only are these systems helpful in sorting, but they also aid in identifying and tracing items in the event of loss in transit. Check routing symbols are assigned only to banks that are members of the Federal Reserve par collection system and necessarily settle for transit items at par. Therefore, any item is collectable at par if a check routing symbol is evident.

The Tracing and Accounting Function

One of the major elements of transit operations is the maintenance of an adequate control over the vast amount of transit checks which are continuously in the process of collection.

When cash letters are sent through one of the channels described, the dollar total is recorded in the general books section of the sending bank. Cash letters sent to the Federal Reserve bank are debited to either the reserve or the deferred account on the sending bank's books. The deferred account is credited, and the reserve account is debited as funds become available. Cash letters dispatched to correspondent banks are credited as of the date they should reach the respective banks. Every dollar outstanding in the process of collection must be accounted for.

Just as a depositor expects a receipt for a deposit he makes, so does a bank expect a receipt (called an advice) for a cash letter sent to a correspondent bank. Therefore, the transit division follows up each cash letter until an advice of credit is received. The transit division is also charged with promptly mailing an advice of credit for every cash letter received from a correspondent bank.

The correspondent bank's balance increases as cash letters are added to its account. The bank can draw down this balance by requesting remittance or transfer of funds through the Federal Reserve bank (just as an individual draws down his account through the issuance of a check), or it can place standing instructions with the collecting bank to make a transfer of all funds in excess of a predetermined amount.

The Handling of Return Items

As the items are processed through the various channels and reach the banks on which they are drawn, payment on some will be refused and these dishonored items will have to be returned to the sending banks indicated by the indorsements. The return of a dishonored item with a cash letter (and the recovery of the funds involved) is handled as though the items were a new cash letter consisting of only the dishonored item, with the exception that the letter is directed to the indorsing bank.

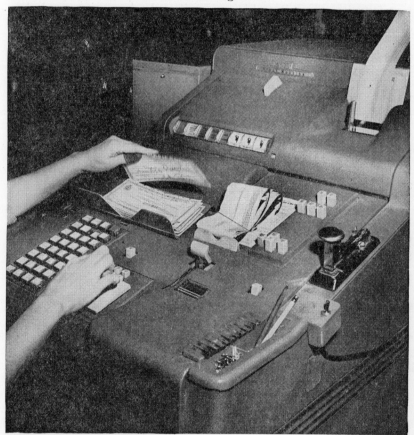

The First National City Bank of New York

MODERN CHECK SORTING MACHINE

Equipment Used

Complex proof machines have been developed in recent years to perform the listing, sorting, and indorsing of transit checks in one operation. They are normally used only when volume is heavy. Small banks and branches resort to simple adding machine listing of items which are forwarded to head offices or to nearby correspondent banks. Some banks photograph all transit checks, whereas others rely on city correspondents to provide this service. When feasible, specialized transit equipment is used for the identification of checks which might go astray in the mails. The use of this equipment has reduced the cost of operations and the likelihood of loss to a minimum.

Questions Based on Chapter IV

1. For the purposes of transit collection, what is the significance of being able to distinguish between (a) cash items and collection items? (b) par items and nonpar items? (c) city items and country items?
2. What is a cash letter? What standard instructions does it normally contain?
3. What are the factors which in general motivate the selection of transit routings?
4. What channels are available for the collection of transit checks?
5. What is meant by available cash? What uses are made of availability schedules?
6. In what way does transit collection by correspondent banks differ from collection by the Federal Reserve System?
7. What is meant by the American Bankers Association numerical system?
8. Briefly explain the salient features of the check routing symbol.
9. What type of equipment is used in transit collections to facilitate the tracing or identification of lost items?

Questions for Investigation

1. To what extent does your bank use the cash collection facilities of the Federal Reserve System?
2. How many nonpar points are there in the Federal Reserve district in which your bank is located?
3. What is the transit number of your bank? What is its check routing symbol?
4. What is the daily average number of transit items handled by your bank?
5. What arrangement does your bank have for the transfer of funds by wire?

CUSTOMERS DESKS

Customers desks are arranged at various heights to provide convenient writing levels for children of all ages. Both short and tall depositors appreciate this facility.

CHAPTER V

PAYING OPERATIONS

The Purposes of This Chapter:
1. To explain the significance of the paying function.
2. To discuss the qualifications of a paying teller.
3. To outline the considerations involved in paying checks.
4. To point out the problems involved in cashing checks.
5. To describe various methods of making payments from a depositor's funds other than by checks.

How BANKS handle the tremendous volume of cash, checks, and other financial instruments that flow into the banking system each day in the form of deposits is discussed in the preceding chapters. The bank receiving checks and other instruments on deposit has as its principal objective the conversion of these pieces of paper into cash as speedily as possible. The complex banking operations already discussed—the proof system, the transit system, and the clearing operations—are all a part of the means of achieving this objective. It is necessary that these pieces of paper be presented physically at the places of payment. In no other manner can these instruments be paid.

The paying and cashing of checks at tellers' windows is presented in this chapter, and the paying of checks through the bookkeeping department is discussed in the following chapter.

The Paying Teller's Window

Most checks reach their places of payment through bank collection channels and are paid by the bookkeeping department. However, a relatively small but important volume of checks is presented to the paying bank by the payee or holder. He appears in person and usually receives payment for an item in cash. The payment of checks at a teller's window involves a very important and delicate contact with depositors and the public. If a mistake is made in paying a check at a teller's window, it is most difficult

69

to correct the error. However, refusal to pay a check can produce very embarrassing and sometimes very costly results. A dishonored check (one not paid upon presentation) is a serious reflection on the drawer's (depositor's) credit and probably upon his integrity as well. If a bank should ever refuse payment of a check without proper cause, or through an innocent mistake, the depositor could bring suit and might be awarded damages by the court. In fact, the amount of damages would not necessarily have any relationship to the amount of the check that had been wrongfully dishonored.

What Is a Check?

What is a check? An examination of one shows that it is merely a simplified letter of instructions (Form 9). A vital part of the basic deposit relationship is the agreement between a bank and its depositor. From funds on deposit to the credit of the depositor, the bank agrees to pay any specified amount to any particular individual named by the depositor in the check.

```
_____19_____        No._____


                                                  60-1850
              THE INSTITUTE BANK                    313
                    INSTITUTE, PA.

   PAY
   TO THE
   ORDER OF_____ $_____

   _____DOLLARS


                        _____
```

Size 8¼ x 3⅟₁₆

FORM 9. A MODERN CHECK

A check is a streamlined letter of instructions which omits the nonessentials, such as the salutation and closing usually found in a letter. The check says tersely to the drawee, "Pay to the order of Bill Jones $65 00/100"; to this brief statement the depositor signs his name. Even the words "charge my account" are omitted because this part of the instruction is implied and understood by both parties. In addition to the brief facts stated, the check must bear a date. Other writing on the check is unnecessary. Even the number we frequently see on checks is placed there for the depositor's convenience and is not an essential part of the check.

A check is a written order which the bank is commanded to honor upon demand. The bank is fully responsible for the genuineness of the order. It must determine the genuineness of the order by a careful examination of the depositor's signature. If this signature is forged, no matter how cleverly, the bank is responsible. The bank is also responsible for seeing that the money is paid to the person named in the check as payee, or to another person or other persons to whom the check has properly been negotiated. If the payee alleges that he did not receive payment for an instrument which has been charged to the depositor's account, the drawer can compel the bank to refund the amount of money incorrectly paid.

Stop-Payment Orders

The bank is always bound by written instructions from its customer. Since a check is nothing more than a written order to pay funds to the payee, it is logical to assume that the depositor may rescind or revoke such an order in writing. Written instructions countermanding the instructions contained in a check are known as a stop-payment order. Banks are as responsible for the faithful observance of a stop-payment order as they are for the faithful observance of the original order to pay. A stop-payment order is illustrated in Form 10.

Qualifications of a Paying Teller

The payment of a check is a very serious business because it involves the handling of cash. For this reason, banks are very careful in selecting the individuals who will make such payments and who will thus come in direct contact with the bank's customers and the public.

A paying teller must be a person of unquestioned honesty and integrity, since the teller handles large sums of money daily. He

Form 76   **STOP - PAYMENT ORDER TO**
                        THE INSTITUTE BANK
        You are hereby authorized to stop payment on check described hereon

Maker		
Payable to		
Check Number	Date	Amount

From		Date Received	Time Received
		By	Examined

Maker		Date	Amount

FORM 10. STOP-PAYMENT ORDER (front)

STOP - PAYMENT ORDER

I/We hereby agree to hold you harmless for said amount and
for all expenses and costs incurred by you by reason of your
refusal to honor said check and in the event of a dispute
between the undersigned and the payee of said check, I/we
agree that every effort will be made to settle or adjust the
dispute between the immediate parties should this check be
paid by inadvertence or accident.

Date	Authorized Signature

FORM 10. STOP-PAYMENT ORDER (reverse side)

must possess an aptitude for getting along with people and for meeting the emergencies that always arise. A teller must be a fast and efficient worker, since the presentation of checks is often concentrated during lunch hours, closing periods, and regular pay days. A teller must be thoroughly familiar with the practical aspects of check handling, for he is a natural target for that small, but dangerous, section of the public who are content to make a living by fraud, deceit, and forgery. His decision to refuse payment of a check may lead to serious difficulties, but a careless willingness to honor all checks will certainly result in losses that are equally serious. Tellers play a vital part in a bank's customer and public relations program. A teller who is unfriendly, overly suspicious, or too dogmatic and adamant in handling customers can do a great deal of harm even though he is technically correct in his actions.

The Difference Between Paying and Cashing Checks

Although the terms *pay* and *cash* are used somewhat loosely in discussing bank operations, it is convenient and accurate to designate *pay* as meaning the exchange of cash for a check drawn on the bank that is doing the paying and to designate *cash* as meaning the advance of money on a check that must be collected from another bank. In the first instance, the bank is under legal obligation to pay checks drawn upon it if they meet all the requirements of being good, whereas the cashing of checks drawn on other banks represents a courtesy or an accommodation. A bank seldom cashes a check drawn on another bank unless it can recover from someone it knows if the check is not good or unless the responsibility of the drawer is unquestioned.

The bank teller is called upon to pay checks drawn on his own bank and to cash checks drawn on other banking institutions. Since a definite set of factors affects each of these situations, it is best to consider each type of transaction separately.

The Teller's Responsibility in Paying Checks

When a teller pays a check drawn on his own bank, he must apply seven different tests to the transaction confronting him. By these seven tests the teller determines whether the check is "good."

1. The signature must be genuine and authorized.

2. The check must neither be postdated nor bear a stale date.

3. The check must not have been altered in any way.

4. There must be no stop-payment order in effect.

5. The customer must have a collected balance sufficient to cover the check.

6. There must be no "hold" on the account because of attachment, bankruptcy of the drawer of the check, death of the drawer, or any other circumstance.

7. The check must be properly indorsed by the person entitled to receive payment.

How does the teller apply each of these tests to the instrument before him in the brief time at his disposal?

1. The signature must be genuine and authorized. A genuine signature is the true signature of the bank's depositor on whose account the instrument is drawn. The danger to the teller is that he may be confronted by a check bearing a forged signature. It is very difficult for the average person to comprehend the manner in which tellers avoid the payment of forged instruments. Obviously, it is part of a teller's training to become thoroughly familiar with the signatures of the depositors in his bank. On the other hand, no one can possibly expect a teller to remember accurately the thousands of signatures on which he is called to make payment. The truth of the matter is that a well trained teller, through experience, develops a sort of sixth sense which enables him, with surprising accuracy, to detect forgeries whenever they appear. Each bank maintains an orderly and well kept signature card file; the teller is expected to compare the specimen signature in the file with the signature appearing on any check which arouses his suspicion or with which he is unfamiliar. Most experienced tellers refer to the files very infrequently. As a matter of fact, if a teller were compelled to refer to the signature card file in the case of one-half or even one-third of the checks presented to him, his production rate would be exceptionally low. He would find a line of disgruntled customers constantly before his window.

An authorized signature does not involve forgery but does involve another important consideration. When a person draws a check as an individual, signing his name on an order for the withdrawal of funds deposited to an account in his name, the transaction is relatively simple. In many cases, however, individuals are signing for someone or something else; they may be acting as trustee, guardian, executor, administrator, treasurer, president, comptroller, or in some other legal capacity. In such cases, it is the bank's responsibility to see that the proper written authorization has been filed with the bank. The authority of the prospective customer is usually checked before the signature card is accepted. Thereafter, the teller must remember that this or that individual has the authority to sign in some capacity for the withdrawal of funds standing in the name of a beneficiary—an individual, a minor, or a corporation—and not in his own name. Well trained tellers develop an uncanny ability to recall accurately the relationship between such persons and the accounts from which they withdraw funds.

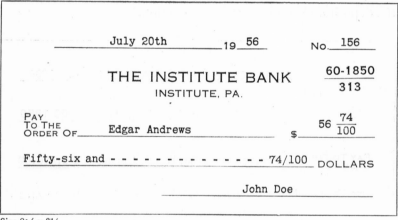

Size 8¼ x 3¹⁄₁₆

FORM 11. AN INDIVIDUAL DEPOSITOR'S CHECK

2. The check must neither be postdated nor bear a stale date. This condition is easily checked by examination of the date. A check dated in the future is not an effective order on the bank until that date arrives. A check bearing a future date is said to be *postdated.*

There are very few valid reasons for issuing a check dated ahead, and yet this is a practice too often indulged in by bank depositors. Whenever possible, banks attempt to discourage this practice.

If a teller honors a check bearing a future date, it is presumed that the depositor can refuse to permit the item to be charged to his account and that he has the right to issue a binding stop-payment order until the date appearing on the check has been reached.

A check that has been outstanding for an unusual length of time is said to have a stale date. Legally, the holder of a check is obligated to present it for payment within a reasonable time. There is no definite rule, and the length of time beyond which a check becomes stale varies in different states, sometimes in different banks within the same state. In some cases, a check ninety days old may be considered stale. In other cases, a check is not stale until a year has elapsed from the date of issuance.

The important point to remember is that a teller must be certain that checks paid bear current dates. When he pays postdated checks or stale checks, he exposes his bank to possible losses unless the depositor chooses to confirm his action.

A. B. C. CORPORATION   No. 1009

July 20   19 56   60-1850 / 313

PAY TO THE ORDER OF The Pennsylvania Railroad Company $ 1,470.62

One Thousand Four Hundred Seventy and - - 62/100 DOLLARS

To THE INSTITUTE BANK
INSTITUTE, PA.

John Doe
TREASURER

Size 8¾ x 3⅜

FORM 12. A CORPORATION CHECK

3. The check must not have been altered in any way. A bank is responsible for the payment of checks in strict accordance with the terms established by the drawer at the time his check is issued. If this were not so, no one would be willing to issue checks and deliver them in settlement of debts for fear that the amount or some other term might be changed before presentation of the

checks to the bank. Although this responsibility places a heavy burden on the bank, any other arrangement would place an even heavier burden on the drawer of a check.

The most common form of alteration is the raising of the amount of the check. Clever crooks have raised $10 checks to $110 or $100 checks to $400 in a manner that defies detection. The bank that pays such an item, obviously has no authority to charge the raised instrument to the depositor's account. It may charge only the original amount of the check, as issued and delivered by the depositor.

Another kind of alteration which is sometimes used to defraud a bank is changing the name of the payee. The date of a check also may be altered with the intent to defraud. Since many banks keep the file of stop-payment orders arranged according to the date of the check in question, alteration of the date may trick a teller into overlooking a known stop-payment order.

Although a bank is responsible for detecting any alteration in checks presented to it for payment, the public frequently makes the problem more difficult. Many people are very careless about the issuance of checks, and they do not hesitate to alter checks themselves at the time of issuance or to write checks in such a careless manner that they facilitate fraudulent alterations. Banks are constantly trying to educate the public to the need for care in issuing checks. A careless depositor should be informed that carelessness and negligence in the issuance of checks may have the effect of relieving the bank of its primary responsibility.

4. There must be no stop-payment order in effect. We have already learned that since a check is no more than a letter of instructions, the depositor has a right to cancel those instructions at any time before the check is paid. This right of a bank depositor has been upheld consistently by the courts. Despite the care exercised by bank tellers and bank bookkeepers, a check is occasionally paid after receipt of a stop-payment notice. Under most conditions, the bank cannot charge the depositor's account with a check so paid. Either it must recover the money from the person to whom payment was made or it must stand the loss. It is useless for the bank to claim that payment was made through an innocent clerical error or through inadvertence or oversight, or to point out that there was no negligence in the performance of the

bank's duties. As a matter of fact, even the insertion of an "escape" clause in the stop-payment request form does not serve to permit the bank to escape its liability. This very point has been tested in the courts time and again, and invariably the courts have held that the bank must suffer any loss involved.

5. The customer must have a collected balance sufficient to cover the check. If the amount of funds in a depositor's account is not sufficient to cover a check presented for payment, the item may be dishonored (returned unpaid).

It sometimes happens that the dollar amount of the balance is sufficient to cover the check in question, but a substantial part of the balance may represent recently deposited checks which have not had time to clear. It should be obvious that deposited checks cannot be considered cash until actual payment has been received. In such a case, the bank is justified in returning the item, giving as the reason "Drawn on uncollected funds" or simply "Uncollected funds." However, some banks will honor such checks as an accommodation to a responsible customer.

When a check is paid for an amount greater than the balance in a customer's account, a minus balance is created. This is called an *overdraft*. Overdrafts are not favorably regarded by banks, because they are, in effect, unauthorized loans for which the bank does not hold even a promise of repayment. Customers who consistently draw checks against insufficient and uncollected funds are usually requested to close their accounts.

6. There must be no "hold" on the account because of attachment, bankruptcy of the drawer of the check, death of the drawer, or any other circumstance. In banking terminology the word hold has a special meaning. A hold is simply a notation on a ledger card (frequently jotted down in pencil by the bookkeeper) which indicates that all or a part of the balance must be withheld because some situation has arisen. There are several such situations that banks meet and deal with every day.

For instance, if a paying teller pays a check for $5,000 late in the afternoon, he knows that several hours must pass before the check reaches the bookkeepers. In fact, the check may not be sorted and posted until the following morning. In order to protect himself, the paying teller may communicate with the bookkeepers and give them instructions to hold $5,000 of the depositor's balance until such time as the check he has cashed is duly processed and charged to the depositor's account. In another instance, an officer of the bank may be served with a *writ of attachment* or some other type of court order commanding the bank to freeze or impound a depositor's balance. In such a case, a hold is placed on the depositor's ledger card, and no payments are made until the funds have been released by the court.

In the case of accounts of individuals, the death of the depositor immediately revokes all outstanding checks that have been signed by him. In some states the law provides for the payment of certain items or it may allow payment of checks for a brief period of time after the depositor's death. In any case, as soon as the bank receives notice of the death of a depositor, it must act with considerable care and must scrutinize carefully all checks presented. This is accomplished by placing a notation or hold on the depositor's ledger sheet indicating the date of death. A notice of bankruptcy, of incompetence, or of some other circumstance which renders the depositor incapable of handling his own affairs is handled in the same manner.

7. The check must be properly indorsed by the person entitled to receive payment. Most persons presenting themselves at a teller's window are regular customers who are well known, and no question arises as to identity. In many instances, however, a check is presented by the payee or by an indorsee, and frequently such a person is a complete stranger to the bank and to the tellers. It is the responsibility of the teller to identify the person presenting the check and to satisfy himself that payment is being made to the proper person. Failure of the teller to identify the customer properly can result in a financial loss to the bank. As a practical matter, although the identification of a customer is fairly simple, it is by no means an exact science. There is no positive practical means of identification. Banks have not found it necessary or desirable to resort to fingerprinting. The average person identifies himself by means of cards, licenses, or documents of one kind or another, preferably bearing a specimen of his signature. Almost all of us carry such papers with us at all times. The teller who is passing on this evidence can never be sure, for identifying documents are frequently lost, stolen, or forged. Nevertheless, tellers with sufficient experience who exercise normal good judgment

can keep the instances of payment on faulty identification at a
minimum.

The Responsibility of the Teller in Cashing Checks

A teller must make decisions about more complicated situations when he pays a check drawn on his own bank than when he
is called upon to cash checks drawn on other banks. Normally a
teller does not cash a check drawn on another bank for a non-
depositor unless the responsibility of the drawer is unquestioned.
Therefore, in the majority of cases, the person presenting the
item to be cashed is either a depositor or a person well known to
the bank. There should be no question of identification, and the
financial responsibility of the indorser can easily be ascertained.

A moment's thought will make this point clear. In cashing a
check, a teller is not passing on the genuineness of the signature,
or whether there are sufficient (or uncollected) funds, or on the
existence of a stop-payment order; only the bank on which the
check is drawn can have any knowledge of these conditions.
Hence there is only one thing for which the teller is responsible
in the cashing of a properly drawn check and that is the ability
of the person tendering the check to return the cash if the check
is not good.

Other Methods of Making Payments From a Depositor's Funds

There are certain methods other than the paying of checks by
which a bank may be authorized to make payments from depositors' balances. As we have already noted, a check is nothing more
than a streamlined and simplified letter of instructions. It follows
that a bank is obligated to carry out written instructions given in
a more formal manner providing such instructions are clear and
complete.

Cashier's checks, treasurer's checks, and bank drafts. There are
situations when, for reasons of his own, a depositor may not wish
to use his own check in settlement of a transaction. In fact, the
person to whom payment is due may insist on receiving a bank
obligation rather than the check of his debtor. In such cases, the
depositor, by giving written instructions to the bank, may authorize the bank to debit his account for a certain amount and to
issue the bank's cashier's check (treasurer's check) or a bank draft

for a like amount, made payable to the person who is to receive payment. Instruments of this type are discussed more fully in Chapter VIII.

Certified checks. Sometimes a bank is requested to guarantee that it will pay a check at a later date rather than make a cash payment at the moment of presentation. To comply with this request, the bank may certify the check, although it is under no legal obligation to do so. For a more complete description of the nature of a certified check, the student is referred to Chapter VIII.

Transfer of funds. At the written request and authorization of a depositor, funds may also be taken from his account and transferred by wire, by telephone, or by mail to any designated payee through the Federal Reserve System or through a correspondent bank.

Control of Cash

A bank must have on hand at all times an adequate supply of both coin and currency in proper denominations in order to meet the needs of its customers. In fact, the services that banks furnish in this respect are indispensable to the proper functioning of our entire commercial system. This responsibility of those in charge of a bank's paying operations is particularly heavy. Sufficient cash is a necessity, but excessive cash is sheer waste since it represents unproductive funds. All banks seek to achieve the balance which enables them to avoid both the embarrassment of shortages and the stigma of wastefulness.

Excessive cash is not only wasteful; it is dangerous. A bank naturally provides a most attractive target for hold-up men. Armed guards and other protective devices discourage attempted robberies with surprising success. Nevertheless, it is tempting fate to permit unnecessarily large amounts of cash to be exposed to public view in the teller's area. The wisest course for a bank to follow is to keep as much of the cash as possible confined within the safety of its vault.

In order to control the amount of cash effectively, the bank must control the amount held by each teller. Ordinarily, the head teller sets a maximum amount of cash for each teller. This maximum will vary among banks, depending on the type and volume of business transacted. The amount will also vary according to the location of the teller's window. For instance, if a certain teller is selected to handle large transactions such as payrolls, he necessarily requires more cash than the average teller.

A teller sells (receives credit for) excess cash to the head teller, and he buys (is charged with) cash from the head teller when his supply needs replenishing. A teller starts each day with a certain amount of money, and at the end of the day he must have checks and cash equaling this same amount plus any additional amounts purchased and less any additional amounts sold.

SUMMARY

In concluding this discussion of a most important banking function, it seems proper to stress two very important points. First, the nature of this challenging and responsible duty requires that tellers be selected with great care and that they be given adequate training Second, the importance of the teller from a public relations standpoint cannot be overemphasized. It should be remembered that the only direct impression that many depositors have of a bank is through their dealings with tellers.

Questions Based on Chapter V

1. What is a stop-payment order?
2. What tests are applied by the paying teller in determining whether or not to pay a check?
3. What is the effect of a postdate on a check?
4. What is an overdraft?
5. Explain the meaning of the term uncollected funds.
6. Who is responsible for detecting alterations or forgery?
7. What is meant by the expression "genuine and authorized signature?"

Questions for Investigation

1. How is the teller's cash controlled in your bank?
2. Do the tellers in your bank receive any training in public relations?

CHAPTER VI

BOOKKEEPING OPERATIONS

The Purposes of This Chapter:
1. To describe the general function of the bookkeepers in a bank.
2. To discuss the duties of the individual bookkeeper.
3. To emphasize the fact that posted checks are paid checks.
4. To mention some widely used bookkeeping systems.

ALTHOUGH tellers have important responsibilities in handling and paying checks at their windows, the majority of checks are actually paid in *bookkeeping* operations. Even those checks that are paid at the tellers' windows eventually find their way to the bookkeepers for posting to customers' accounts. In this chapter attention is focused on bookkeeping operations.

Bookkeeping and the General Ledger

The word bookkeeping has developed a somewhat special meaning in banking circles. The actual bookkeeping operation of a bank, involving asset and liability and income and expense accounts, is usually referred to as the work of the general books or general ledger. In banking, when we say bookkeepers or bookkeeping, ordinarily we are referring to the personnel or the function of handling the detailed subsidiary records of the deposit liability accounts on the general ledger. For instance, the bank's liability to its depositors must be divided on the general books into two or more parts under such headings as Demand Deposits and Time Deposits. Each class of deposit liability is carried under a single total.

The Bookkeeping Function

The maintenance of the individual depositors' record that comprise the single totals appearing on the general books is the bookkeeping function. For example, in the case of the liability account Demand Deposits, the general books are concerned only with the total of deposits made each day and the total of checks paid each day. The bookkeepers, however, must record each individual transaction by posting each individual deposit ticket and each individual check to the proper customer's account. Sometimes this activity is known as keeping the *individual ledger*, but perhaps bookkeeping is the term most frequently used.

The Ledger Record and the Customer's Statement

The basic problem involved in the bookkeeping function can be simply stated. Naturally, it is essential for the bank to keep a permanent record of the transactions in all accounts. The record of each account is called a ledger. Each depositor is entitled to receive information from the bank relating to the transactions in his particular account. The bookkeepers, therefore, must furnish for bank use a complete permanent record of all accounts as well as a separate record of each account for the customer. Producing these two records is the basic problem of the bookkeepers.

In the early days of banking, one ledger record of a depositor's account was made, and the bank kept this record permanently in its possession. Huge bound books, known as Boston ledgers, were used for this purpose. It was not practical to provide the customer with a copy of his account for his own use; instead, he was requested to submit his checking account passbook to the bank periodically for balancing. The bookkeeper would add all the customer's deposits in the passbook, subtract from the deposit total the aggregate of checks paid since the last balancing, bring forward the new balance, and return the passbook, together with the paid checks, to the depositor. Thus, by means of the passbook, each customer was furnished with a record of all deposits made and of all checks paid, and he was given his current balance figure.

The passbook played a more important role in those days than it does today. It is now merely a receipt book and frequently is dispensed with entirely.

Mechanical or machine posting methods were introduced to banking primarily as the means of coping with a tremendous increase in the volume of bookkeeping transactions. However, this more modern technique also brought about a decided change so far as the customer's record was concerned. Mechanical posting proved so much faster than the older hand-posting methods that it became practical for a bank to go through the entire posting process twice (dual posting).

The record produced by the second posting, referred to as the statement, is delivered to the customer with his checks which have been paid and canceled. Dual posting dispenses with the tedious hand balancing of customers' passbooks, and the saving of time more than justifies the additional work. Moreover, the customer receives a current transcript of his account (usually monthly, but more or less frequently if requested).

Form 13 shows a typical bank ledger sheet designed for machine posting. The right-hand column repeats the account and gives a daily record of balances. This column may be detached and used for analysis purposes. The customer's statement sheet in dual posting is identical except that is omits the right-hand column that is shown in Form 13.

Name of Customer	In Account with THE INSTITUTE NATIONAL BANK			Name of Customer	
Debits	Credits	Date	Balance	Date	Balance

FORM 13. A TYPICAL BANK LEDGER SHEET (FOR MACHINE POSTING)

The double or dual posting method can be avoided and the same result can be obtained by the use of photography, carbon paper, special posting machines, or any device that simultaneously prepare the bank's record and the customer's record.

The Work of the Bookkeepers

In the discussion of the proof or distribution operation (Chapter II), it is pointed out that a bank receives checks on us from the clearing house and receives both deposits and checks on us from the receiving tellers. After these checks and the deposit tickets have been processed, they are sent to the bookkeepers. Each check is charged (debited) to the customer's account, thus decreasing his balance; each deposit is added (credited), thus increasing his balance. This bookkeeping process is known as posting.

The extreme importance of the posting process is apparent when it is realized that the customer's balance is affected by each debit or credit entry. In particular, the posting of checks involves the payment of the depositor's funds. Unless an error is detected within a reasonable time, it may be impossible for a bank to recover the funds thus paid out. For this reason, we must emphasize again that posting a check is paying the check.

In connection with the paying of checks, the work of the bookkeeper consists of the following duties.

1. Sorting checks and deposits to prepare them for posting.

2. Examining items to determine their eligibility for posting.

3. Paying checks and other debits by posting them to customers' accounts.

4. Posting deposits and other credits.

5. Proving and balancing with the general ledger deposit total.

The term sorting simply means the arrangement of all checks and deposits in alphabetical or numerical order according to account names or account numbers. This sorting process is usually the first bookkeeping step, because it facilitates the examining and posting procedures. However, certain phases of check examination may precede the sorting process.

A check that is eligible for posting is on its way to actual payment. The responsibility for the payment of checks or for the refusal of payment is an extremely important one, and the bookkeeper must perform this duty with the utmost care. The bookkeeper examines each check to be certain:

1. That it is drawn on the bank.

2. That it is drawn against a checking account.

3. That the signature is genuine and authorized.

4. That the check has not been altered.

5. That it is not postdated or stale.

6. That it is properly indorsed.

One or more of these duties may be assigned to personnel other than the bookkeepers.

Bank of America National Trust and Savings Association

ELECTRONIC CHECK SORTER

Erma (Electronic Recording Machine Accounting) can handle all the bookkeeping details of 50,000 checking accounts every working day. The sorter handles both checks and deposits.

Bank of America National Trust and Savings Association

MONTHLY STATEMENT PRINTER

Erma's printer searches in its reliable electronic memory for the items which appear on the statements. Erma can print 600 lines a minute.

Bank of America National Trust and Savings Association

CONTROL PANEL

Erma lets you know when she is in trouble. Engineers watch the overhead panel where Erma flashes lights when anything goes wrong in her complex innards.

A visual examination of the check will reveal whether the listed conditions are violated in any way. Of course, if the signature on the check is not known to the bookkeeper, reference to the signature or authorization file may be necessary. If the check fails to meet any of these conditions, however, it requires special handling by the bank.

There are certain other conditions requiring investigation by the bookkeeper. These conditions cannot be determined by a visual examination of the check, but they must be determined by an examination of the record of the customer's account.

1. There must be a sufficient collected balance in the account to cover the check.

2. The bank must not have an effective stop-payment order on file.

3. There must be no hold on the account (see Chapter V).

Whether the balance is sufficient is usually determined by the bookkeeper during his posting operation. The existence of uncollected funds in an account can be ascertained by an examination of the more recent deposits. Reference to the bookkeepers' stop-payment record or to the ledger itself will reveal the existence of a stop-payment order or a hold. If a check fails to meet any one of these requirements, the bookkeeper must see that it is given special handling by the bank.

Certain debits in addition to the posting of checks may reduce a customer's balance. Among them are debits representing service charges and out-of-pocket expenses, such as insurance, postage, and interest payments. Credits other than deposits may increase a depositor's balance. These credits may include the proceeds of loans made to the depositor, the proceeds of special collection items, the proceeds of funds from the sale of securities, or the proceeds of some other transaction.

When the entire posting operation has been completed, the bookkeepers must determine whether the individual ledgers are in balance with the general ledger. This balancing operation is usually accomplished by taking the previous day's deposit total, adding to it the total postings of all deposits and other credits, and subtracting from this figure the total postings of all checks and other debits. The resulting figure should balance with the new general ledger total.

Other Bookkeeping Duties

The bookkeeper has important duties and responsibilities in addition to the actual posting of debits and credits. They include the following:

1. Canceling checks.
2. Photographing checks and ledgers as required.
3. Filing canceled checks.
4. Filing deposit tickets and other record material.
5. Forwarding or delivering statements and canceled checks in accordance with customers' instructions.
6. Supplying information on customers' accounts.
7. Notifying tellers and other interested personnel of new stop-payment orders and holds.
8. Preparing reports that may be required, such as the listing of unusually large daily withdrawals and deposits and the providing of weekly or monthly balances of large accounts and of unsatisfactory accounts.
9. Assisting in the analysis operation by making a partial or complete compilation of activity as a basis for determining the amount of a service charge.

After checks have been posted, they are canceled. In other words, to prevent possible fraudulent rehandling, they are marked to show that they have been paid. The customary method of canceling is perforation of a check by a machine that cuts holes in the check, spelling out the date, the numerical symbol of the paying bank, and the notation "paid."

The rapidly increasing use of punch card checks may require the development of new methods of cancelation. Punch card checks are rendered ineffective by perforation, spindling, or mutilation of any kind. This should not present a serious problem since a check may be effectively canceled by means of a stamped impression across its face.

Depending on the type of system used, a bank may wish to photograph ledger sheets or canceled checks, or both. This task is usually performed by bookkeeping personnel.

In some banks, canceled checks are filed in drawers in the bookkeeper's desk or in the statement clerk's desk; in others, checks are kept in a special filing division until their delivery with the statements to the customers. From a customer relations standpoint, accuracy in filing is of great importance. A bad impression is created when a customer receives another person's canceled checks or when he finds some of his own canceled checks missing. Accuracy of filing is equally important to the bank, since bank employees must make frequent reference to deposit tickets, canceled checks, and other bookkeeping records in the course of their daily operations.

Forwarding or delivering customer's statements with their canceled checks is another important duty of the bookkeepers. In many cases, the only contact a customer has with his bank is through the regular receipt of his statement. The neatness and accuracy of the statement, or its lack of these qualities, form a vivid picture of the bank's effectiveness in the mind of the customer.

Canceled checks should always be checked against or compared with the statement before its delivery to the customer. The verification of statements is a most important duty, as this verification is the last opportunity the bookkeeper has to detect any posting errors before the statement reaches the customer.

Each customer feels, and rightfully so, that his balance and his transactions with the bank are confidential. Information regarding any account should be given only under unquestionably proper circumstances. Requests for vital information are frequently received from other departments of the bank, and these requests are necessary to complete routine transactions. Many requests for such information are also received from outside sources. In such cases, the information should be given only after absolute identification of the inquirer and after establishment of his right to receive the information. Considerable judgment must be exercised in this connection, since information properly given to responsible persons can help the customer in his business dealings.

In most banks the bookkeepers not only keep records of accounts but also act as a nerve center. They collect and relay important instructions and special notices in connection with accounts. For instance, stop-payment orders and holds resulting from death, court orders, or bankruptcy must be relayed promptly to all tellers. It is obvious that failure to handle this particular duty promptly and accurately could lead to embarrassment and financial loss.

The cashier and the top executive officers of a bank should always have their fingers on the pulse of deposit balances, and naturally they follow the movement of large transactions very closely. They could not carry out these responsibilities without the assistance of the bookkeeping personnel. In addition to reports of large accounts and large transactions, the bookkeepers furnish daily reports on overdrawn accounts, regular reports covering unsatisfactory conditions in any account, and periodic reports covering the transfer of accounts from active to inactive (dormant) status, or vice versa.

Finally, the bookkeepers must cooperate closely with the analysis department in compiling statistics of activity in connection with service charges. This cooperation is discussed more completely in Chapter XVII, in which the function of general bank accounting is presented.

Return Items

In the discussion of the examination of checks by bookkeepers, it is stated that a check which fails to meet certain requirements must have special handling. When a check cannot be properly charged to the depositor's account for any reason, payment must be refused. The item must then be separated from the great majority of checks to be paid, and it must be sent back to the person who presented it. Such an item is known as a *return item*. Return items require careful handling by experienced personnel, and this is termed special handling.

The drawee bank has a limited time, depending on how the item is presented, in which to make a decision regarding payment or nonpayment. If payment is to be refused, the item must be re turned as quickly as possible to the person who presented it. Therefore, the bookkeepers (or other personnel involved in the examination of checks) separate such items from the main volume and send them immediately to the *return teller* with all pertinent information. In small banks, return items are handled by a single individual; in large banks, they receive attention from as many persons as the volume requires.

Ordinarily, the return teller attaches to each item a printed slip on which is indicated the reason for dishonor. Form 14 illustrates such a slip.

The name of the bank, business concern, or person to whom the item is to be returned can be determined by a careful examination of the indorsements appearing on the reverse side of the check. Illegible, overlapping, and carelessly inscribed indorsements increase the difficulty of this task, but an experienced return teller rarely has much trouble deciding to whom such items are to be returned.

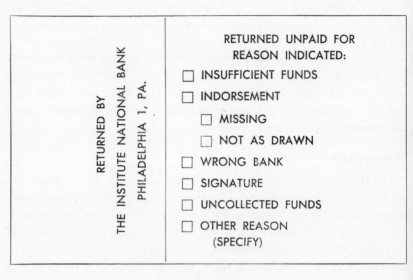

RETURNED BY

THE INSTITUTE NATIONAL BANK

PHILADELPHIA 1, PA.

RETURNED UNPAID FOR
REASON INDICATED:

☐ INSUFFICIENT FUNDS

☐ INDORSEMENT

☐ MISSING

☐ NOT AS DRAWN

☐ WRONG BANK

☐ SIGNATURE

☐ UNCOLLECTED FUNDS

☐ OTHER REASON
(SPECIFY)

FORM 14. RETURN SLIP

If the item is to be sent back to a depositor, the return teller prepares a debit memorandum which is used to offset the credit given when the deposit was posted to the ledger. If the item is presented by another bank, it is returned and settlement is made in accordance with banking laws and customs. For instance, items presented through the local clearing house must be returned in accordance with the local clearing house rules. In all cases, it is necessary to reverse the provisional credit given at the time of the original presentation of the item. Then the item must be returned physically, either by messenger or by mail.

Form 15 illustrates a typical multicopy form used by return tellers. The original is sent to the customer. The first carbon is used as a debit memorandum; the second carbon serves as a permanent record.

PERMANENT RECORD	THE INSTITUTE BANK
DEBIT	THE INSTITUTE BANK

THE INSTITUTE BANK

Institute, Pa.

Payable   Amount

⌐   ⌐

L   ⌐

CASH ITEMS RETURNED
For Reason, Refer to Check
or Attached Memorandum

FORM 15. CASH ITEMS RETURNED

Posting Systems

It is not the purpose of this text to detail the technical aspects of modern bookkeeping systems. However, it may be helpful at this point to summarize the methods and objectives of some of the principal systems in use today and to explain some of the more commonly used bookkeeping terms.

Dual posting. Although one of the oldest systems, dual posting is still a widely used system of bookkeeping operation. In dual posting, the bookkeepers make all postings both to a ledger and to a separate statement. Thus the statement is always prepared and ready for delivery to the depositor with his canceled checks. This posting system involves a duplication of all entries since everything must be posted twice. It is customary for one bookkeeper to make the ledger posting and for another bookkeeper or a statement clerk to make the statement posting. This procedure is followed for accuracy, on the theory that it is not likely for two individuals to fall into the same posting error. Some banks claim that dual posting provides more accurate settlements and eliminates the necessity of a reproducing process, such as carbon paper or photography, in order to obtain the customer's statement. However, the system does require that each entry be handled twice.

Single posting. Many banks use a single posting system, thus eliminating the duplicate posting process of the dual system. In single posting, all items are posted once to the ledger record. The customer's statement may be prepared in several ways, some of which have already been mentioned. Carbon paper may be used to produce a duplicate record, or the ledger sheet itself may be sent to the customer as a statement after the bank has made a photographic record for its own file. Under the single posting system, it is usually necessary to provide some accurate method for verifying the correctness of entries. This verification may be accomplished by a visual inspection of each entry.

The single posting system is frequently combined with a sight posting (visual paying) process. This process means determining through mental calculations whether the account's balance is sufficient to cover the checks in question. After the items have been sorted, the bookkeeper visually checks the debits and credits against the existing balance of the affected account in order to determine as soon as possible whether an overdraft is involved. This visual checking may be made *after* as well as *before* the actual posting. At the time of inspection, the accounts affected by the posting run are offset (extended an inch or so in the ledger tray) so that they may be distinguished from accounts that are not affected by the day's work. This offsetting makes it possible for the bookkeeper to prepare a total of the old and new balances of all affected accounts and helps materially in checking the accuracy of the settlement.

Machine pay system. The proof pay or machine pay method of bookkeeping operation attempts to combine the advantages of dual posting with the economy of single posting. In this system, two posting runs are made; but the first run is made on a proof tape, which usually carries four columns. In the first column, the old balance is picked up from the ledger card. The debits are next posted in the second column and the credits in the third column.

The new balance is then extended to the fourth column. This proof run is substantially the same as an ordinary posting run except that the bookkeeper does not post on a ledger or statement record; thus the time required for inserting and withdrawing the ledger or statement sheet is eliminated. This operation is estimated to run from 25% to 40% of the posting time. In the second run, debits and credits are posted directly to the ledger. Balancing of the second run and the proof run is facilitated, as in dual posting, because total debits, total credits, and new balance totals are provided. With this method the use of carbon paper or photography is necessary in order to produce either the customer's statement or the bank's record.

Post-to-check system. A comparatively recent bookkeeping system which has attracted considerable attention is the post-to-check system. This system eliminates daily posting to either a statement or a ledger because the new balance is carried forward on each item as it is posted. Between statement periods, checks and deposit tickets are filed in a cellophane envelope, with the most recently posted item in the front. Instead of referring to a ledger record, the bookkeeper merely refers to the envelope and finds the old balance on the last item posted. All checks as well as the statement are photographed before they are mailed to the customer.

All the systems described have been used successfully by one bank or another. There is no indisputably correct system of bookkeeping operations. Each bank adopts and refines the system or the operations best suited to its individual needs and to the ability and experience of its personnel. However, regardless of the system used, it is essential to remember that the bookkeeping operation of a bank is of the greatest importance and requires the utmost in accuracy of posting and settlement. Economies may prove to be false in the long run if they are achieved at the expense of accuracy or if they endanger the effectiveness of the records.

Deferred and Delayed Posting

Until very recently, it was the practice of the majority of banks to attempt the posting of most checks on the day of presentation. This practice was followed particularly for clearing items when the local exchange was held during morning hours. In most cases, clearing house rules required that dishonored items be returned to the clearing house by 3 p.m. on the same day, either by messenger or in an afternoon return item exchange, thus compelling the banks to make two posting runs. Clearing items had to be posted in order to meet the time limits for returns. Late counter items and "us" checks received in deposits were prepared for posting on the morning of the day following presentation.

Immediately after World War II, it was strongly urged that banks be permitted to take advantage of a delayed or a deferred posting schedule. With such a schedule, all items, *including clearing items,* could be returned up to late afternoon or even midnight on the day *following the day of presentation.* Under the impetus of an energetic campaign by leading bankers, the necessary legislation was obtained (the program required a change in Federal Reserve regulations as well as enabling statutes in each state) and deferred posting was generally adopted. This delayed posting schedule permits banks to eliminate the double run, and now practically all checks are posted in a single posting run on the morning following the day of presentation.

Cycle Statements

Many banks throughout the country still adhere to the practice of settling accounts as of the last day of each month and forwarding statements to customers on, or shortly after, the first day of the following month. In order to eliminate the unavoidable pressure and after-hours work involved in the giant task of mailing thousands of statements, with canceled checks, in a concentrated operation, banks are tending to adopt a cycle system. Under a cycle system, a group of accounts (roughly, one-twentieth of the total number of accounts) is settled each day and the corresponding statements are mailed. Thus, every account receives a statement at some time during each month; but the work of preparing statements is spread over as many working days as there are in the month, instead of being concentrated within one or two days. The average person usually has no objection to cycle statements so far as his personal affairs are concerned. However, most corporations and large business concerns insist on having their accounts settled and on receiving statements and canceled checks as of the end of each month in order that they may facilitate their own accounting process.

Inactive and Dormant Accounts

Over a period of time, a number of inactive or dormant accounts will appear among the bank's ledger records. Many banks separate such inactive accounts from active accounts. There are two good reasons for this action: (1) The constant handling of inactive and dormant accounts during the course of settlements places an unnecessary burden on the bookkeeper; (2) such accounts, if unprotected, sometimes become the target of dishonest bank personnel. To guard against this danger, many banks place inactive and dormant accounts under strict audit control.

SUMMARY

The bookkeeping function is a critical phase of bank operations. It is an activity usually associated with tremendous work volume, difficult peak periods, and considerable pressure made necessary by the imperative demand for accuracy. The satisfactory performance of this function requires not only an effective system of operation but well trained personnel with a clear understanding of their responsibilities.

Questions Based on Chapter VI

1. Explain the meaning of the term bookkeeping in its relationship to the term general ledger as it is used in banking.
2. Why is it necessary in the bookkeeping process to produce two separate records?
3. In what way does the bookkeeper's responsibility in posting a check differ from the responsibility of a teller in paying a check at his window?
4. What are some of the bookkeeper's responsibilities in the examination of checks?
5. What important conditions cannot be determined by a mere visual examination of a check?
6. Name some of the duties and responsibilities of the bookkeeper in addition to the payment of checks.
7. Distinguish between dual posting and single posting.
8. What are cycle statements?

Questions for Investigation

1. What posting system is used by your bank?
2. How are inactive or dormant accounts handled by your bank?
3. How are return items handled by your bank?
4. To what extent does your bank use deferred or delayed posting? Does your bank have two posting runs?

CHAPTER VII

LEGAL RELATIONSHIP WITH DEPOSITORS

The Purposes of This Chapter:
1. To describe the nature of the relationship between a bank and its depositors.
2. To explain the importance of obtaining identification.
3. To classify and describe the various types of accounts found in most commercial banks.

A BANK and its depositors have a very definite contractual relationship. In a legal sense, the relationship is ordinarily that of debtor (the bank) and creditor (the depositor). Sometimes the contract is expressed by a written agreement; but sometimes it is unwritten, and banking law and custom supply the framework of rules and regulations within which transactions are handled.

Most of the obligations in this type of contract rest upon the bank. It is right and proper that the obligations should so rest because the bank is selling services for a fee. However, certain obligations rest upon the customer as well. For example, among these customer obligations is the responsibility of examining all statements of account promptly and of reporting forgeries or irregularities without unreasonable delay.

A deposit is a sum of money or credit left with a bank to be used according to banking practice. A contract is a business agreement which is enforceable in law. Generally speaking, a contract is enforceable only if the parties to it have the legal power to enter into the agreement. A bank's authority to enter into contracts is established and limited by the provisions of its charter. Its authority may be limited further by the by-laws and the board of directors. The persons who exercise this authority to make contracts on behalf of the bank are designated and appointed by the board or by executive officers empowered to act on its behalf.

When a person enters a bank and deals with an individual seated in official quarters at a desk bearing a nameplate designating his title, he can assume that this person has authority to bind the bank in ordinary contracts having to do with the business of banking.

The bank officer finds himself in a slightly different position. Many of the people who approach his desk are complete strangers. A person may represent himself to be a certain individual, a partner, a corporation treasurer, a trustee, or an executor. Before entering into a contract with such a stranger, the bank officer should satisfy himself concerning the identity of the person. Furthermore, if the person is not dealing for himself as an individual, the bank officer should be satisfied regarding that person's authority to act in a certain capacity.

It seems quite logical to ask, "Why should the bank require identification of an individual who is offering the bank his money?" This inquiry completely overlooks the fact that the bank, in accepting the deposit, also accepts instructions regarding the withdrawal of these funds. It is always important for the bank to know that the person with whom it enters into a deposit relationship and to whom it pays funds from the account is the person that he claims to be; otherwise fraud might be committed for which the bank might be held liable.

With this general background in mind, we shall now examine the various types of accounts and the authority requirements that must be satisfied in each case.

ACCOUNTS CLASSIFIED ACCORDING TO AUTHORITY

On the basis of authority, accounts may be classified as individual accounts, joint accounts involving two or more persons, partnership accounts, or trade or fictitious name accounts, corporation accounts, fiduciary accounts, club, church, or association accounts, and public funds.

Individual Accounts

The proper opening of an individual account is not very involved, for only the identification of the person presenting the deposit is required. The question of identification itself is by no means a simple matter. As banks operate today, there is no absolutely positive means of identification. Automobile registration cards, operators' licenses, draft registration cards, social security cards, membership cards, letters of introduction, and all other common means of identification have been forged at some time.

There is ordinarily no set procedure for a bank to follow. Bank officers and tellers establish identification satisfactorily every day by a combination of experience and judgment. The circumstances surrounding each particular case should reveal how far a bank can go in its efforts to establish the desired identification. Some bankers with long experience maintain that two separate evidences of identity issued at different times offer a more reasonable assurance of authenticity than a single piece of evidence. For instance, an automobile registration card currently dated, together with a draft registration card issued a number of years ago, may be considered good evidence of identity. On the other hand, a single newly issued and otherwise unsupported piece of evidence such as a brand-new social security card would be regarded with some suspicion. Naturally, the signature of the person presenting such evidence should be compared with the signature appearing on identifying papers.

Once the identity of a prospective individual depositor has been established, only that person has the authority to withdraw the funds deposited. By signing his name to a signature card (Form 16), the depositor accepts all rules and regulations printed on the card and authorizes the bank to honor orders for the withdrawal of funds, either in the form of checks or in some other form, providing that the checks or orders bear his genuine signature and that there are sufficient funds in the account.

Since an individual depositor has complete control of an account opened in his own name, he may confer full or limited powers on some other person or persons with respect to the account. Anyone so authorized is known as an attorney in fact. The depositor must give the bank written confirmation and explanation of the authority vested in the attorney. This document, which the bank keeps permanently in its file, is known as a power of attorney.

An attorney in fact acts in the name of his principal, the depositor. For instance, he signs checks, "John Jones, by William Smith, Attorney." The authority granted to him is effective only during the lifetime of his principal. The depositor's death automatically invalidates any and all powers of attorney. Therefore, when a bank receives notice of the death of a depositor who had previously filed with it a document of this kind, it can no longer regard the signature of the attorney as effective in connection with the deceased depositor's account.

In the case of joint accounts, which are discussed in the next paragraph, the power of attorney should be signed by each of the joint depositors.

Joint Accounts Involving Two or More Persons

There are two general types of joint accounts: (1) joint accounts which carry the right of survivorship and (2) joint accounts without the right of survivorship or which require all co-depositors to sign.

In an account carrying the right of survivorship, each of the joint co-depositors generally sign an agreement with the bank authorizing the bank to deal with each depositor during the lives of the signatories and with the survivor or survivors as the owner or owners of all funds on deposit. Thus, each depositor agrees that, upon his death, all his rights, title, and interest in the funds on deposit shall pass immediately to the surviving depositor or depositors and that neither his estate nor his heirs nor assigns shall acquire any interest in the funds. Many banks are reluctant to accept such accounts in the names of more than two persons. Although the joint account would seem to be an excellent means of transferring funds to others in anticipation of death, to avoid the payment of inheritance taxes, the laws of many states require that the bank notify the state department of revenue in the event of the death of any party to a joint account.

With respect to accounts in which there is no right of survivorship if one of the co-depositors dies, his share will not pass automatically to the survivors. Instead, the bank will be obliged to deal with an executor or administrator before disposing of the decedent's share.

As indicated previously, a joint account should be based on a written agreement (Form 17). Not only should this agreement clearly state the relationship between the parties and outline the procedure to be followed in the event of the death of one of the parties; it should also specify whether orders for the withdrawal of funds are to be signed by any one of the depositors or by all depositors signing jointly. Although banks ordinarily accept the

☐ MR.   NAME _____   ☐ INDIVIDUAL

☐ MRS. ADDRESS _____   ☐ PARTNERSHIP

☐ MISS   ☐ FIRM

To (Name of Your Bank), _____

    You are authorized to recognize any* _____ of the signatures subscribed below in the payment of funds or the transaction of any business for this account. It is agreed that all transactions between you and the undersigned shall be governed by the contract printed on the reverse side of this card.

_____
SIGNATURE

(*Indicate number of signatures required.)

AUTHORIZED SIGNATURE(S) OF _____

_____

_____

_____

_____

DATE OPENED _____   INITIAL DEPOSIT $ _____

SIGNATURE AUTHORITY DATED _____   ACCOUNT OPENED BY _____

FORM 16. SIGNATURE CARD FOR INDIVIDUAL USE (front)

DEPOSITOR'S CONTRACT

Items received for deposit or collection are accepted on the following terms and conditions. This bank acts as depositor's collecting agent and assumes no responsibility beyond its exercise of due care. All items are credited subject to final payment and to receipt of proceeds of final payment in cash or solvent credits by this bank at its own office. This bank may forward items to correspondents and shall not be liable for default or negligence of correspondents selected with due care nor for losses in transit, and each correspondent shall not be liable except for its own negligence. Items and their proceeds may be handled by any Federal Reserve bank in accordance with applicable Federal Reserve rules, and by this bank or any correspondent, in accordance with any common bank usage, with any practice or procedure that a Federal Reserve bank may use or permit another bank to use, or with any other lawful means. This bank may charge back, at any time prior to midnight on its business day next following the day of receipt, any item drawn on this bank which is ascertained to be drawn against insufficient funds or otherwise not good or payable. An item received after this bank's regular afternoon closing hour shall be deemed received the next business day.*

This bank reserves the right to post all deposits, including deposits of cash and of items drawn on it, not later than midnight of its next business day after their receipt at this office during regular banking hours, and shall not be liable for damages for nonpayment of any presented item resulting from the exercise of this right.

In case this bank is requested to stop payment on an item or items, the depositor agrees to hold this bank harmless for all expenses and costs incurred by this bank on account of refusing payment of said item, and further agrees not to hold this bank liable on account of payment contrary to this request if same occur through inadvertence, accident or oversight, or if by reason of such payment other items drawn by the depositor are returned insufficient. Request for stop payment is effective for 60 days, but renewals may be made from time to time. No stop payment request, renewal, or revocation shall be valid if oral or unless served at this bank.

It is agreed that this account, whether active or dormant (an account shall be considered dormant when no deposit shall have been made or checks drawn for a period of one year), shall be subject to service and maintenance charges heretofore adopted by this bank and now in effect, and to such charges as may hereafter be adopted by this bank. New service and maintenance charges and changes in existing charges shall become effective upon the posting of notice in the office of this bank for a period of ten days and the publication thereof in any local newspaper before the end of said period, or upon giving the depositor, not less than ten days notice in writing mailed to his last known address. Such charges may be deducted from the depositor's account and this bank shall not be liable for dishonoring checks, draft, notes, acceptances, or other instruments because of insufficient funds resulting from the deduction of such charges.

This bank may mail statements, canceled checks, and notices to the last address known to this bank.

*Note: Individual banks or banks in different states may wish to vary the last two sentences depending upon whether such banks themselves adopt deferring posting, or if they have individual shut-off problems or problems arising out of branch bank operations. Since the last two sentences apply only to internal operations of banks in dealing with their own depositing and drawer customers, the need for uniformity is not the same as in the case of all prior sentences in the agreement.

FORM 16. SIGNATURE CARD FOR INDIVIDUAL USE (reverse side)

106

instructions of customers, calling either for any one or for all of the signatures, a good many banks take more than casual interest in these instructions because of past experience.

Normally, a bank would prefer to be instructed to honor withdrawals on the signature of any one of the depositors. Difficult situations sometimes arise in connection with joint accounts which do not permit withdrawals except on the signatures of *all* depositors. Sometimes one of the joint depositors becomes critically ill or suffers a stroke which leaves him alive but incapable of acting; or, as has happened, one of the joint depositors may simply disappear and never be heard from again. Without the signature of the ailing or missing depositor, the deposited funds are completely and effectively frozen. There is no immediate possibility of anyone qualifying to sign for such a depositor in the absence of proof of incompetency or satisfactory proof of death. To attempt to unfreeze the account through legal process would be tedious and time-consuming. These situations do arise from time to time, much to the discomfort and inconvenience of the remaining joint depositors and oftentimes to the extreme embarrassment of the bank, which is without authority to accept any instructions from the remaining depositors.

Partnership Accounts

A partnership account is a business account carried in the names of two or more partners. A partnership is based on a mutual agreement, usually in writing, between the various partners. For the purpose of setting up a bank account in a partnership name, many banks require the partners to sign a form or statement which covers the authority relating to banking transactions, such as the signing of checks and the making of loans.

Many states have adopted the Uniform Partnership Act, which is a special body of law dealing with partnership affairs. Banks situated in these states must be familiar wth the general principles of partnership law so that they may properly handle situations that may arise. Among other things, partnership law provides that each partner is responsible for the business contracts of the other partners and that one partner can bind all the other partners by his contracts. To be enforceable, the contracts entered into by a single partner must be within the scope of the partnership business.

NAME

ADDRESS

JOINT ACCOUNT

TO (Name of Your Bank),

You are authorized to recognize any of the signatures subscribed below in the payment of funds or the transaction of any business for this account. It is agreed that all transactions between you and the undersigned shall be governed by the contract printed on the reverse side of this card.

The undersigned, joint depositors, hereby agree each with the other and with you that all sums now on deposit or heretofore or hereafter deposited by either or both of said joint depositors with you to their credit as such joint depositors with all accumulations thereon, are and shall be owned by them jointly, with right of survivorship, and be subject to the check or receipt of either of them or the survivor of them and payment to or on the check of either or the survivor shall be valid and discharge you from liability.

Each of the undersigned appoints the other attorney, with power to deposit in said joint account moneys of the other and for that purpose to endorse any check, draft, note or other instrument payable to the order of the other or both said joint depositors.

Payment to or on check of the survivor shall be subject to the laws relating to inheritance and succession taxes and all rules and regulations made pursuant thereto.

Your rights or authority under this agreement shall not be changed or terminated by us or either of us except by written notice to you which shall not affect transactions theretofore made.

DATE

MR.
MRS.
MISS

☐
☐
☐

(1) SIGNATURE

DATE

MR.
MRS.
MISS

☐
☐
☐

(2) SIGNATURE

DATE
OPENED

INITIAL
DEPOSIT $

ACCOUNT
OPENED BY

FORM 17. JOINT ACCOUNT SIGNATURE CARD (WITH RIGHT OF SURVIVORSHIP)

108

The death of a partner ordinarily terminates the partnership. However, the law gives the surviving partners the right to carry on the business during liquidation, and this right carries with it the power to handle all assets, including funds on deposit in banks. Thus, the estate of the deceased partner ordinarily is without power to step in and claim or seize control of bank deposits which are in the partnership name. The surviving partners, however, are required to render an accounting to the estate and to disclose fully the financial data incident to the liquidation.

Trade Names

In business, people frequently find it advisable to use a trade or an assumed name (sometimes known as a fictitious name). Though a common business practice, the use of a trade name is a privilege which could be abused. Most states have laws designed to regulate the use of trade names to legitimate purposes. Usually the law provides that the name must be registered with the proper department of the state.

The principal purpose of statutes requiring registration of trade names is to identify the person or persons who wish to do business under the assumed name, thus fixing responsibility with respect to contracts or liabilities incurred in the name of the business.

Banks are frequently requested to open accounts in assumed or trade names. To repeat, it is always important for a bank to know the identity of the depositor. A check payable to the order of The Acme Fence Company may be used to open an account in the name of that company. But other than the word of the person presenting the check, this name would leave the bank with no definite clue to the real owner or owners of the money represented by the check. In states in which registration is necessary, a person opening an account with such a title must furnish the bank with a certificate issued by the state authorities, showing that the trade or assumed name has been registered and indicating by whom the name has been registered. With this document or a copy in its possession, the bank knows the name or names of the person or persons with whom it is dealing. After identifying the person representing himself to be the registrant, the bank may safely open an account in the name of The Acme Fence Company.

A single individual may register a trade name or an assumed

name. In many states this form of doing business is known as a proprietorship. When two or more persons register a trade name, the bank generally is dealing with a partnership account.

The use of the word "company" generally makes a name a trade name, as does the omission of the family name. For instance, Bill Smith's Machine Shop is not necessarily a trade name; Bill's Machine Shop is a trade name.

Although business corporations do not register under a law governing the use of trade names, or the equivalent, they must obtain a charter.

Corporation Accounts

A corporation is a legal entity to which life is given by law. It is obviously not a human being; however, it has in many respects the legal rights and standing of a human being. A corporation can do business in its corporate name, enter into enforceable contracts, bring suits against others in its legal name, and be sued. In fact, a corporation has one decided advantage over a human being—its life is not mortal and presumably it can continue its existence forever. A corporate charter can be revoked or rescinded, or the corporation can be dissolved, either voluntarily or through bankruptcy. The corporation receives its life with the granting of a charter through the power of the sovereignty. Ownership of a corporation is ordinarily evidenced by shares of stock, and the owners of these shares are called stockholders. The stockholders may adopt bylaws which limit the activities of the corporation. They elect a board of directors whose duty is to manage and direct corporation affairs, to appoint the active executive officers, and to approve contracts which the executive officers have no power to make under the bylaws.

The question confronting a bank, as well as anyone else doing business with a corporation, is the proper level of authority that must be sought in order to enter into contracts with the corporation safely. The stockholders are the real owners, but obviously it would be impossible to conduct business with what may be a large and scattered group. It is well established by law and by custom that the board of directors is the active governing body of a corporation, and when authority is given by the board of directors, this authority is normally sufficient evidence of the validity of any business negotiations carried on in the corporate name. Certain types of unusual contracts, such as merger agreements and the bulk sale of plants and equipment, must have stockholders' approval.

When a bank opens an account in the name of a corporation, the basis for all future dealings is a certified copy of a resolution adopted by the board of directors authorizing the opening of the account and empowering certain corporate officers and representatives to act for the corporation in the handling of ordinary business transactions. Banks use what is called a resolution form for the purpose of obtaining the required proof of authority and instructions for the handling of the account. The wording of this document contains an appropriate resolution, which is adopted by the corporation's board of directors at a regular or special meeting. After quoting the resolution, the document usually continues with a certification prepared for the signature of the corporation's secretary. This certification states that the resolution was duly adopted by proper action of the board of directors. In addition to inscribing his signature, the secretary affixes or applies an impression of the official corporate seal.

In some cases, the corporate bylaws go into great detail. Sometimes they may even confer on certain officers the power to handle bank accounts. When officers have this power, the bank obtains a certified copy of the section of the bylaws containing this specific authorization, instead of obtaining a resolution of the board of directors. It may then deal with the officer or officers so empowered.

It is important for a bank to examine each corporate resolution carefully, to make certain that it is in proper form and that it contains the necessary authority to cover completely the action of the corporate officers or designated representatives in their depositing and withdrawing of funds and in their performing of other acts necessary to conduct business pertaining to the corporation's account. The corporate resolution, Form 18, together with related papers (if any), must be carefully filed by the bank. In many cases, it is the basic evidence of proper authority covering the payment of many thousands and even millions of dollars of corporate funds.

Fiduciary Accounts

Generally speaking, a fiduciary is a person or a corporation authorized to handle property for the benefit of others. Circumstances often make it desirable or convenient for individuals or corporations to be given possession of the property of others and to act on their behalf in various ways. When an individual or a corporation has possession of and legal title to property but not equitable or beneficial ownership of it, the arrangement is called a trust and the individual or corporation holding the property is known as a trustee. Sometimes property is given by a court to a guardian, with instructions to administer the property for the benefit of a minor, an incompetent, or someone who does not enjoy the legal capacity to act for himself. When a person dies, an executor (who is named in the will) or an administrator (when the will mentions no name, when there is no will, or when the executor does not serve) becomes the decedent's legal representative. He administers the estate for the benefit of heirs and creditors. The term fiduciary is a broad one which includes all persons, such as trustees, guardians, administrators, and executors, who administer property for the benefit of others (see Chapter XIV).

Banks are frequently requested to open accounts in the names of trustees. In each case it is important for the bank to determine the validity of the trustee's authority and to obtain for its file proper evidence of his authority to act. Most accounts of this kind are formal in nature. A fiduciary may be appointed by a trust agreement which has been filed as a matter of public record; he may be appointed under a will which has been probated and made a part of the public record; he may receive his authority by court appointment, which is a matter of public record; or his authority may come from some other type of formal document which has been properly recorded in public archives. In each case, the bank should request and receive a copy of the document or certificate of appointment so that it may examine the authority vested in the fiduciary and may determine whether there are any important limitations which would affect the fiduciary's relationship with the bank.

Sometimes trusts are more or less informal in nature; either they are not evidenced by a formal document or, if a written agreement does exist, the document has never been recorded. Many banks follow the procedure established by their own experience in such cases. Banks may or may not require a copy of the particular deed or agreement if one exists. Some banks may have special signature

Certified Copy of Corporate Resolutions
—Opening and Maintaining a Checking Account

I, the undersigned, hereby certify to (name of bank) that I am the Secretary (Assistant Secretary) of (name of corporation), a corporation duly organized and existing under the laws of the state of_____; that the following is a true copy of resolutions duly adopted by the Board of Directors of said Corporation at a meeting duly held on the_____day of _____, 19____, at which a quorum was present; and that such resolutions have not been rescinded or modified.

RESOLVED, that (name of bank) is hereby designated as a depository of this Corporation and that a checking account be opened and maintained in the name of this Corporation with said Bank; that* [any (state number) of the following officers of this Corporation: (fill in names of offices, such as "President, Secretary, and Treasurer" and not the names of the present officers) is/are hereby]** authorized, on behalf of this corporation, and in its name: to sign checks, drafts, notes, bills of exchange, acceptances, or other orders for the payment of money from said account; to indorse checks, notes, bills, certificates of deposit, or other instruments, owned, or held by this Corporation, for deposit in said account, or for collection or discount by said Bank; to accept drafts, acceptances, and other instruments payable at said Bank; to waive demand, protest, and notice of protest, or dishonor of any check, note, bill, draft, or other instrument made, drawn, or indorsed by this Corporation; and

FURTHER RESOLVED, that (name of bank) be and it hereby is authorized to honor, receive, certify, or pay all instruments signed in accordance with the foregoing resolution even though drawn or indorsed to the order of any officer signing the same or tendered for cashing, or in payment of the individual obligation of such officer, or for deposit to his personal account, and said Bank shall not be required, or be under any obligation to inquire as to the circumstances of the issuance, or use of any instrument signed in accordance with the foregoing resolution, or the application, or disposition of such instrument, or the proceeds thereof; and

FURTHER RESOLVED, that the Secretary or Assistant Secretary shall certify to said Bank the names of the presently duly elected and qualified officers of this Corporation and shall from time to time hereafter as changes in the personnel of said officers are made, immediately certify

FORM 18. CORPORATE RESOLUTION (front)

113

such changes to the bank, and said Bank shall be fully protected in relying on such certifications of the Secretary or Assistant Secretary and shall be indemnified and saved harmless from any claims, demands, expenses, loss, or damage resulting from, or growing out of, honoring the signature of any officer so certified, or refusing to honor any signature not so certified; and

FURTHER RESOLVED, that the foregoing resolutions shall remain in full force and effect until written notice of their amendment or rescission shall have been received by said Bank, and that receipt of such notice shall not affect any action taken by the Bank prior thereto; and

FURTHER RESOLVED, that the Secretary or Assistant Secretary be, and he hereby is, authorized and directed to certify to said (name of bank) the foregoing resolution and that the provisions thereof are in conformity with the Charter and By-Laws of this Corporation.

I further certify that there is no provision in the Charter or By-Laws of said Corporation limiting the power of the Board of Directors to pass the foregoing resolutions and that the same are in conformity with the provisions of said Charter and By-Laws.

I further certify that the following are the names and official signatures of the present officers of this Corporation:

Name	Official Signature
President_____	_____
Vice President_____	_____
Vice President_____	_____
Secretary_____	_____
Assistant Secretary_____	_____
Treasurer_____	_____
Assistant Treasurer_____	_____

IN WITNESS WHEREOF, I have hereunto subscribed my name and affixed the seal of said Corporation, this_____day of _____, 19_____.

⌈CORPORATE⌉
⌊   SEAL   ⌋

_____
Secretary (Assistant Secretary)

*If officers are to sign in particular combinations, such language as the following should be substituted: "that the President or Vice President, together with the Treasurer or Assistant Treasurer of this Corporation."

**One of the following clauses, or a similar clause, may be used in place of the matter in brackets above:
   1. any one of the following officers of this corporation: the President, Vice President, Treasurer, Assistant Treasurer, Secretary, Assistant Sec-

retary is . . . (strike out any word not applicable and add name of any other office if desired).
   2. any two of the following officers of this corporation: the President, Vice President, Treasurer, Assistant Treasurer, Secretary, Assistant Secretary are . . . (strike out any word not applicable and add name of any other office if desired).
   3. the President, or Vice President, together with the Treasurer, or Assistant Treasurer of this corporation are . . . (modify as desired).

NOTE: In case the Secretary or Assistant Secretary is designated by the foregoing resolutions as one of the signing officers, this certificate must also be signed by a second officer of the Corporation.

FORM 18. CORPORATE RESOLUTION (reverse side)

cards or agreement forms, which give the bank the necessary authority to act if and when certain events affecting the trust take place. Many banks, however, accept such informal trusts without formal written authority, believing that they can meet any situation that is likely to arise. The most frequently encountered informal trust of this kind is the account opened by a parent, an aunt, an uncle, an older sister or brother, or some other relative in trust for a minor child.

Club, Church, or Association Accounts

Unincorporated associations formed for social or charitable purposes and not for profit usually have informal organization and few regulations. In such cases, a bank should exercise reasonable care to ascertain that persons dealing with it in the name of such a group or association have proper authority. However, for a bank to require of unincorporated associations the same letter-perfect authority and technical adherence to legal details that it requires of the modern business corporation obviously would impose unreasonable inconvenience upon the officers of the informal group. The procedure adopted by a bank may vary according to the circumstances confronting it. A large social or charitable organization with a substantial treasury probably would be expected to conform reasonably to the type of authorization furnished by a corporation. A small club or neighborhood group, with a modest treasury and with an entirely new slate of officers elected each year, may receive less exacting treatment.

Public Funds

Because of the variety of laws involved, the bank must be certain that it has obtained proper authority before permitting the withdrawal of public funds.

ACCOUNTS CLASSIFIED ACCORDING TO AVAILABILITY OF FUNDS

Accounts may also be classified according to the availability of funds deposited. In this case both the bank and the depositor assume legal obligations. On the basis of the terms of withdrawal, the accounts are classified as (1) demand accounts and (2) time accounts.

Demand Accounts

In the case of demand accounts, the bank assumes the obligation of meeting all requests for the withdrawal of funds immediately and without previous notice of any kind. Obviously, it is necessary that such requests be made during normal banking hours. A bank which is unable to pay demand deposits when requested in the usual course of business must close its doors. Thereupon, the proper state banking authority in the case of a state bank or the Office of the Comptroller of Currency in the case of a national bank takes charge of the institution's affairs. An audit by the Federal Deposit Insurance Corporation is conducted immediately in order to determine whether the bank is solvent (for the role of the Federal Deposit Insurance Corporation in such situations, refer to Chapter XXII).

1. Checking accounts. The most common form of demand deposit is the checking account. In this case, the depositor has the privilege of drawing checks up to the full amount of the balance standing to his credit, and he is under no obligation to notify the bank of his actions in drawing checks.

2. Certificates of deposit—demand. There are instances in which a customer wishes to place a sum on deposit with a bank and to retain official evidence of the deposit in his possession. Perhaps the most common instance is when the deposit is to be pledged as security for obligations undertaken in a contract. In such a case, the bank issues a certificate of deposit. The bank does not open a ledger account in the customer's name, as it does in the case of other deposits. This obligation of the bank is carried instead on its general books under the heading Demand Certificates of Deposit, since the instrument may be presented for payment by some person other than the one to whom it was originally issued.

Time Accounts

Banking laws prohibit the payment of interest on demand deposits, but banks, under certain conditions, may pay interest on time deposits when such deposits are subject to notice of withdrawal.

1. Savings accounts. The most common form of time deposit is the ordinary savings account. Savings accounts are usually

subject to a minimum of thirty days' notice of withdrawal. However, it is permissible and common practice for banks to waive the required notice of withdrawal, provided the same privilege is accorded to all depositors. The maximum rate of interest which may be paid is fixed by regulations of the Federal Reserve System, by regulations of the Federal Deposit Insurance Corporation, and by some state laws.

Society for Savings, Cleveland, Ohio

JUNIOR SAVERS

2. Time deposits—open account. The savings accounts described in the preceding paragraph are intended for the savings of individuals.

The banking system also provides interest-bearing accounts for corporations and others who may find themselves possessed of large sums of cash during temporary periods. In such cases, most banks have available time accounts. A time account may be subject to 30, 90, 180, or more days' notice before withdrawals are permitted. Federal Reserve and Federal Deposit Insurance Corporation regulations and some state laws restrict the amount of interest that may be paid in relation to the length of the notice required.

3. Certificates of deposit—time. The paragraph describing demand certificates of deposit also serves as a description of time certificates of deposit, except that a time certificate either requires notice before actual presentation may be made or has a definite date of maturity. These instruments are usually interest-bearing. A time certificate of deposit is illustrated in Form 19.

FORM 19. TIME CERTIFICATE OF DEPOSIT

4. The club account. A special type of time deposit—open account handled in the savings department is the club account, which offers a plan for the deposit of fixed sums at regular intervals and often for specified purposes. Such accounts run for varying periods, the most common being fifty weeks. At the end of the period the total is paid to the depositor, with or without interest,

depending on the policy of the individual bank. The object of such an account is to enable the depositor to build up a fund over a period of time to meet extraordinary or unusual expenses.

Questions Based on Chapter VII

1. What is the legal relationship between a bank and its depositor?
2. Why is it important for a bank to establish the identity of the depositor whose funds are on deposit?
3. Name at least six types of accounts found in most commercial banks.
4. What is the problem most likely to be encountered in connection with a joint account?
5. (a) Explain the nature of a corporation.
   (b) How does a bank establish authority for the withdrawal of corporate funds?
6. Give a simple definition of the word fiduciary.
7. Explain the difference between time accounts and demand accounts.
8. What is a certificate of deposit?

Questions for Investigation

1. Does the signature card used in your bank differ from Form 16?
2. Obtain a copy of the corporate resolution form used by your bank. Assume that you are the officer of a corporation, and complete the form supplying the name and other necessary details.

CHAPTER VIII

CHARACTERISTICS OF NEGOTIABLE INSTRUMENTS

The Purposes of This Chapter:

1. To describe briefly the development of negotiable instruments.
2. To introduce the broad classifications of negotiable instruments.
3. To discuss the principal kinds of indorsements.
4. To explain the functions of the more common negotiable instruments.

THE HUGE volume of items that flow through the business world and through the banking system each day is discussed in previous chapters, but little attention is given to the peculiar characteristics of these items, which are commonly referred to as checks, drafts, notes, or other types of negotiable instruments. These pieces of paper and the laws governing their use and circulation provide the basis for most of our modern business and banking functions. Each item has its own story to tell because it represents a specific transaction, such as the purchase and sale of merchandise, the purchase and sale of services, the payment of debts, the payment of interest on indebtedness, the payment of rent, or the payment of royalties or dividends.

Before discussing the legal character of these instruments, we should review the circumstances that made their use necessary and desirable.

Development of Negotiable Instruments

The development of civilization was directly responsible for the development of negotiable instruments. An irresistible thirst for more adventure and for greater profits encouraged ancient merchants to seek markets beyond the confines of their own communities and thus led to the development of international trade. Ever expanding commerce began to weave a network of commercial lifelines covering the face of the earth. The age-old system of barter was barely sufficient for community trade; it was wholly inadequate to meet the demands of an expanding commercial system. Merchants began to seek a satisfactory medium of exchange, that is, something having a relatively stable exchange value in terms of other commodities. Many items having fairly satisfactory qualifications to serve as mediums of exchange were discovered, such as precious stones and metals, cattle, sheep, beads, shells, salt, and gunpowder.

The chronic shortcomings of these items and other mediums led in time to the development of money (coin and currency) as an almost ideal medium of exchange. (The student will find a fuller treatment of this subject in the American Institute of Banking text Money and Banking.) But not even this ingenious device solved the problems brought about by the expansion of markets and commercial transactions covering wide areas and involving distant lands. First, a separate settlement for each purchase of merchandise resulted in an incredible amount of useless and unnecessary transportation of the medium of exchange itself. Second, trade carried on at a considerable distance was extremely hazardous when it became necessary for the seller to ship merchandise with only the bare assurance of the purchaser that payment would be made when the merchandise arrived at its destination. Similarly, it required an undue amount of trust on the part of the purchaser to make his payment to a seller many miles away when all he could rely on was the seller's assurance that the merchandise would be shipped promptly on receipt of the payment from the purchaser.

Credit instruments of some kind became necessary. Even in early times, merchants quickly discovered the desirability of keeping credit balances with other merchants located in the principal cities where trade was anticipated. For example, a merchant in Italy shipped a cargo of olive oil to a merchant in London for sale on the British market. Instead of having his payment immediately shipped to Italy by sailing vessel, the Italian merchant found it more convenient to leave the proceeds of the sale in the hands of the British merchant. In time, but not necessarily in the immediate future, the Italian merchant purchased from the British Isles commodities which he could sell in Italian markets. He made payment for these commodities by instructing the British merchant to use all or a part of his credit balance for that purpose. This method eliminated unnecessary transportation of money and unnecessary conversion of foreign exchange, that is, the conversion of Italian lire into British pounds.

Instructions to use credit balances for such purposes undoubtedly originated as simple letters explaining the wishes of the creditor. As time went on, these letters became streamlined and ultimately the bill of exchange came into being.

Bills of Exchange or Drafts

A bill of exchange may be defined as a written order addressed by one party, the creditor (drawer), to another party, the debtor (drawee), instructing that payment be made to a third party (payee). Today, a domestic bill of exchange, used in domestic transactions, is referred to as a draft. The term bill of exchange is still widely used in international transactions. The bill of exchange was the forerunner of the modern check. A check is a demand draft drawn on a bank. The only difference between a check and an ordinary draft is that the debtor or custodian of the money in the case of a check must be a bank rather than a merchant.

Bills of exchange or drafts have several convenient advantages in addition to their use for the payment of debts. For instance, the seller of merchandise, by attaching shipping documents to a draft drawn on (addressed to) the buyer and by delivering the draft through banking channels to his representative in the buyer's vicinity, has the assurance that his merchandise will not be delivered until the draft is honored or paid. Similarly, the buyer has the assurance that the merchandise is available for delivery to him.

Naturally, over a period of many years and in the course of countless business transactions, the development of these financial instruments has been beset with difficulties and disputes. Ancient courts of law were called upon quite regularly to settle differences between merchants. A vast section of the old Roman law and of the British law was concerned with cases and decisions involving such instruments. Whole sections of the British law were adopted by our courts in the development of our commercial practices, and these sections formed the basis for our present law of negotiable instruments, which has been adopted in some form or other in all forty-eight states.

At the outset, it became essential that the courts define carefully the exact type of document covered by the law of negotiable instruments. In order to qualify as a negotiable instrument, the document must have certain general characteristics:

1. It must be a contract only for the payment of money.

2. No conditions may be included in the instrument except those necessary to fix the time and place for payment of the money.

3. It must be possible for the instrument to pass readily from one person to another in such manner that the person receiving it can obtain the benefits set forth in the instrument without regard to transactions, agreements, or disputes between previous parties to the instrument.

This statement of qualifications does not mean that a merchant cannot deliver or receive in a business transaction an instrument which does not have these characteristics. If he does deliver or receive such an instrument, however, he cannot claim the benefits available under the law of negotiable instruments. His rights will have to be determined by other principles of law governing business transactions, which generally are less favorable to the holder of the instrument.

Orders to Pay and Promises to Pay

Negotiable instruments may be divided into two main classes: (1) orders to pay (checks and drafts) and (2) promises to pay (notes and acceptances).

In addition to the general characteristics previously described, a negotiable order to pay (a check or a draft) must have the following specific qualifications:

1. It must be in writing and must be signed by the maker or drawer.

2. It must contain an unconditional order to pay addressed by one party to another and requiring payment to a third party.

3. It must be an order to pay a sum certain in money.

4. It must be payable on demand or at a fixed or determinable future date.

5. It must be payable to order or to bearer.

Form 20 illustrates a typical form of draft.

The parties to a draft or a bill of exchange are: (1) the drawer (the party issuing and signing the order), (2) the drawee (the party to whom the order is addressed), and (3) the payee (the party to whom payment is to be made). These three—the drawer, the drawee, and the payee—are separate actors in a legal triangle. Each one has his own distinct role involving the peculiar rights and obligations assigned by law to a person in his position. One person may fill the shoes of any two of these actors in connection with a single instrument. In other words, the same person may be the drawer and the payee or the drawee and the payee, or he may be the drawer and the drawee. Indeed, in certain unusual cases, one person may be the drawer, the drawee, and the payee, although such an instrument would have to be drawn for purposes other than the consummation of a normal commercial transaction.

$_____   INSTITUTE_____19_____

AT SIGHT PAY TO THE ORDER OF

THE INSTITUTE NATIONAL BANK

_____DOLLARS

To_____

FORM 20. A TYPICAL FORM OF DRAFT

A promise to pay must have essentially the same specific qualifications as an order to pay:

1. It must be in writing and must be signed by the maker.

2. It must contain an unconditional promise to pay made by one party to another party.

3. It must be a promise by the maker to pay a sum certain in money.

4. It must be a promise to pay on demand or at a fixed or determinable future date.

5. It must be payable to order or to bearer.

It is evident that there are two main differences between promises to pay and orders to pay: A promise to pay involves two parties, the maker (promissor) and the payee; and it is essentially an undertaking on the part of the promissor rather than an order to another party requesting or demanding that he make payment. Form 21 illustrates a typical form of promissory note.

```
$_____                    _____19____

_____ AFTER DATE _____ PROMISE TO PAY

TO THE ORDER OF_____

_____DOLLARS

PAYABLE AT_____

VALUE RECEIVED.

NO._____ DUE_____  _____
```

FORM 21. A TYPICAL FORM OF PROMISSORY NOTE

Demand Instruments and Time Instruments

There is another broad classification for negotiable instruments, which also divides them into two groups: (1) demand instruments and (2) time instruments.

A demand draft or bill of exchange is an order addressed by one party to another party calling for payment to a third party on *demand*. In the case of a draft, demand is generally considered to be made when the instrument is presented to the drawee. Demand drafts may call for payment "at sight"; thus, they are called sight drafts.

A demand promissory note is a promise to pay whenever the holder of the note demands payment of the promissor. This demand usually must be accompanied by presentation of the instrument at the place of payment.

A time draft is an order addressed by one party to another party calling for payment on a fixed or a determinable future date. Such an instrument might read: "On August 18, 1956 pay to the order of....................." or "Thirty days after sight pay to the order of..............."

A time note is a promise to pay in which the promissor states that he will make payment on a certain future date or on a determinable future date, and he is not obligated to make payment before that date, regardless of demand made by the holder of the instrument.

Negotiation

With this background, we may now examine the manner in which negotiable instruments came into being and how they are negotiated or passed from one person to another. The instrument is created by the drawer or the maker, but it is not effective until it has been delivered to the payee. Upon delivery the payee becomes the holder of the instrument. Since the instrument is payable to his order, he may transfer his legal title in it to another person for value. To accomplish this transfer, the payee must deliver the instrument to the person to whom he intends to give his rights. If the instrument is payable to his order, he must indorse it by writing his name on the reverse side as it appears on the face of the instrument. Having done so, the payee assumes the obligations of an indorser. If the instrument is drawn to the order of "bearer," the holder may transfer it merely by delivery.

Note that *delivery* is an essential part of transfer and negotiation. By delivery is meant the physical tender of an instrument to another person with the intention of transferring good legal title in the instrument to that person. Thus, instruments which are not intentionally delivered, such as those that are lost or stolen, are not legally considered to have been negotiated properly. Despite this drawback, however, a future holder's rights may not be affected by such an event under certain circumstances.

It is characteristic of negotiable instruments that a subsequent holder who receives an instrument for value may obtain title to it with rights superior to those previously enjoyed by the payee. Presumably, the instrument came into being as a part of a transaction involving the payee and the drawer. In the event there is an argument or a dispute over a legal defect in the original transaction or in the event the instrument was not properly issued and negotiated, it is possible that the payee may lose his right to enforce payment of the instrument by the drawer. It is important to note, however, that regardless of a dispute or question involving the original transaction and the possible effect on the rights of the original payee, the rights of a subsequent holder are not affected under certain circumstances. This is true only when the subsequent holder (1) receives the instrument for value and (2) without notice or knowledge of any defect in the instrument itself or in the title of the person negotiating it. A person receiving an instrument under these circumstances is known as a *holder in due course* or a *holder for value*.

If it were not for this protective feature of the law, it would be exceedingly dangerous for anyone to receive a check, a draft, a note, or any other negotiable instrument without thoroughly investigating the transaction which gave origin to the instrument and without taking steps to make sure that all parties to the original transaction had completely and satisfactorily discharged their obligations under the instrument. For a more complete discussion of what constitutes a holder in due course and the rights of a holder in due course, reference should be made to the text of the American Institute of Banking entitled Negotiable Instruments, Chapter VI.

Indorsements

An indorsement is either the handwritten signature or the stamped or typed name of the payee or a subsequent holder of an instrument, usually placed on the reverse side, for the purpose of transferring the holder's rights in the instrument to someone else. A signature on the face of a negotiable instrument not designated as that of the drawer, drawee, maker, or payee is presumed to be that of an indorser.

There are five principal kinds of indorsements, each of which serves a particular purpose: (1) indorsement in blank, (2) special indorsement, (3) restrictive indorsement, (4) qualified indorsement, and (5) conditional indorsement.

1. Indorsement in blank. An indorsement in blank (also called a general indorsement) consists simply of the indorser's signature on the reverse side of the instrument. If the signature is the indorsement of the payee, it must agree with the name of the payee appearing on the face of the instrument. The effect of a blank or a general indorsement is to make the instrument payable to bearer; in this case, the instrument may be negotiated simply by delivery by the holder.

2. Special indorsement. A special indorsement names the person to whom the instrument is being negotiated. For instance, a check made payable to George Smith might bear a special indorsement reading as follows:

Pay to the order of
William Jones
(signed)   George K. Smith

The indorsement of the designated indorsee (William Jones) is necessary for further negotiation of the instrument.

3. Restrictive indorsement. A restrictive indorsement is one that imposes limitations on the transferee such as by naming the specific purpose of the transfer. There are several forms of restrictive indorsements, which are discussed more fully in the American Institute of Banking text Negotiable Instruments. The most common form of restrictive indorsement is the one used when the holder deposits a check in his bank for collection and for credit to his account in the bank. Such a restrictive indorsement might read as follows:

For deposit only in the
First National Bank
(signed)   George K. Smith

4. Qualified indorsement. A qualified indorsement is one in which the words "without recourse" or a similar expression appears above the indorser's signature. It has the effect of relieving the indorser of certain liabilities that usually accompany an indorsement. A qualified indorsement implies that while the party transferring the instrument has the right to do so, he does not guarantee payment. Such an indorsement may be acceptable when an instrument is drawn payable to a certain party in error. In order to obviate the necessity of creating a new instrument, the party erroneously designated as payee according to the writing may transfer the instrument to the correct payee by his indorsement. Obviously, this indorsement is for convenience, and the party so indorsing should not be charged with the usual responsibility of an indorser. Such a qualified indorsement might read as follows:

Without recourse
(signed)   George K. Smith

5. Conditional indorsement. A conditional indorsement imposes

upon subsequent indorsers the responsibility of determining whether the condition included in the indorsement has been fulfilled. Such an indorsement might read:

Pay to the order of

William Jones

if repairs on my house are completed by March 1

(signed)   George K. Smith

It should be fairly obvious that no one should accept an instrument bearing a qualified or a conditional indorsement unless he is fully aware of the circumstances surrounding the transfer of the instrument in this manner and unless he has full knowledge of the legal consequences of such an indorsement.

It may be noted that various combinations of the five forms of indorsements are possible. The example of a conditional indorsement is a combination of a special indorsement and a conditional indorsement. The following is a combination of a special indorsement and a restrictive indorsement:

Pay to the order of the

First National Bank

for deposit only

(signed)   George K. Smith

A qualified indorsement is often a combination of a special indorsement and a qualified indorsement.

Liability of a General Indorser

Most of us have at one time or another indorsed a check, but not all of us are fully aware of the responsibility assumed by an indorser when he signs his name on the reverse side of a negotiable instrument. Such indorser in effect guarantees all prior indorsements. This guaranty means that if any previous indorsement proves to be forged or unauthorized, subsequent indorsers assume full responsibility and can be compelled to reimburse the holder. An indorser also makes certain warranties or promises to the person who receives the check from him. For instance, the indorser warrants:

1. That the instrument is genuine
2. That he has a good title to it
3. That he has no knowledge of any defect in the instrument
4. That if the instrument is not paid upon proper presentment

he will pay it *provided* that he has been promptly and properly notified of the nonpayment.

These and other warranties of an indorser are discussed more fully in the Institute text Negotiable Instruments.

The liabilities of an indorser have been firmly established by law, and this fact makes possible the widespread use of negotiable instruments. It is certainly logical to assume that the holder of a dishonored check should have the privilege of recovering the money involved from the person who delivered the instrument and that this person should be able to recover from the indorser preceding him, and so on. If this were not the law, no one would be willing to accept indorsed checks, since in most cases there is no assurance that the check will be paid.

Banks are particularly interested in the liability of indorsers because of the huge volume of checks they handle daily. When a bank accepts checks and other cash items for deposit, it gives the depositor immediate credit, and the bank has the right to charge or debit the depositor's account with any item which is dishonored upon presentment.

When checks are cashed by a bank's tellers for customers, the situation is slightly different. Courts in some states have held that a cashed check which is subsequently dishonored may be charged to the depositor's account. Courts in other states have held that such items are not chargeable to the depositor's account. In the latter instance, however, there is no question about the customer's liability to the bank because of his indorsement on the check.

Presentment

Proper presentment of a negotiable instrument is exceedingly important. In the case of a draft or a note, the place of presentment is usually stated in the instrument, and the instrument must be presented at that place on the date it is due and within business hours. It should be noted that the liability of all parties to a negotiable instrument is conditioned on the proper presentment of the instrument. For example, if the holder of a note which is due on a certain day at a certain place is careless and misplaces the instrument, or for some other reason fails to make proper presentment on the due date, he cannot expect to retain his original rights against the indorsers. It is conceivable that the promissor may have been able to make payment on the due date but that subsequent financial reverses may have made it impossible for him to pay the note when it is finally presented by the careless holder. It would be neither fair nor equitable to penalize indorsers because of a situation which would not have arisen except for the holder's negligence.

In the case of a check, presentment must be made to the bank on which it is drawn within a reasonable time after issuance (see Chapter V). Here again, if the person receiving a check places it in his wallet and then forgets about it for six months or so, he may find that he has inadvertently relieved not only all prior indorsers of their responsibilities, but also the drawer of the check if the drawer has sustained a loss because of such delayed presentment.

Protest

The custom of protesting dishonored items is followed less frequently today than in years gone by. Before attempting to explain the term protest, we should examine the origin of the practice. As pointed out in previous paragraphs, the liability of an indorser rests on two conditions: (1) proper presentment of the instrument and (2) prompt notice of dishonor to the indorser. In many early lawsuits involving the liability of an indorser, the entire case hinged upon these two questions, and contradictory evidence made it very difficult to determine the true facts. The holder claimed that he had made proper presentment, but the indorser denied that this was so; or the holder claimed that he had dispatched proper notice of dishonor, and the indorser countered that such notice was never received.

The practice of protest has furnished a solution to this problem. When a negotiable instrument is dishonored, it is delivered by the holder to a notary public or other qualified public official. This official formally presents the instrument, and if payment is refused, he notifies the maker and all indorsers. He then attaches to the instrument an official statement bearing his official seal and relating all the facts concerning the nonpayment of the instrument and the action taken. Thus, when an original dishonored instrument with its attached official statement (sometimes called a jacket) is offered to the court in evidence (one form of protest jacket is illustrated in Form 22), it rather clearly establishes these facts:

(1) that presentment was properly made at the proper place and at the proper time and (2) that all indorsers as well as the drawer or maker of the instrument were duly notified by the public official.

Because of the development of our modern banking system and because the vast majority of negotiable instruments are presented for payment by banking institutions, it is exceedingly difficult in most cases today to deny that presentment was properly made. Moreover, the efficiency of our modern communication systems makes it equally difficult to deny that prompt notification was received . Twenty-five years ago, it was common practice to protest items of $20 and over, except those purely local in character. Today, it is the exception to protest items under $500, and it is possible that the present limit may be raised again in the near future.

In the chapters dealing with the ebb and flow of financial instruments, the student must have noticed that most items for collection are received by a bank with amazing optimism. When checks are deposited in a bank through a receiving teller's window, the acceptance of the deposit results in immediate credit to the depositor's account. The depositor is never informed that these items have been paid: he is notified only when an item is dishonored and his account is debited with the amount of the returned check. If it were not for this practice of accepting the vast majority of financial instruments on pure faith, in the belief that they would be paid, the handling of checks would be infinitely more complicated and expensive and the process of check collection would be greatly impeded. Actual experience by banks has completely justified this faith in the honesty of people issuing checks.

Cash Items and Collection Items

In effect, the banking system regards most deposited items as the equivalent of cash by accepting them at face value and by crediting the customer's account immediately. It is natural, therefore, that items handled in this manner should be referred to as cash items.

There are a considerable number of instruments, however, which banks are not willing to handle on this basis. Such instruments are known as collection items. For a full discussion of cash items and of collection items, see Chapter II.

United States of America

....
....
....
....
....
....
....

BE IT KNOWN, *That on the day of the date hereof, at the request of the*
....
the holder of the original.....................................of which
a true copy is above written, I, THE UNDERSIGNED, Notary Public for the
Commonwealth of Pennsylvania, by lawful authority duly commissioned and
sworn, residing in the City of Philadelphia, during the usual hours of business for such purposes, PRESENTED THE SAME AT THE
....
....

          and demanded the   thereof
which was refused, and answer made
....
....
....
....
....

     WHEREUPON, I, the said Notary, at the request of aforesaid, **have
protested and do hereby solemnly protest** against all persons, and every
party concerned therein, whether as Maker, Drawer, Drawee, Acceptor,
Payer, Indorser, Guarantee, Surety or otherwise howsoever against whom
it is proper to protest for all Exchange, Re-Exchange, Cost, Damages and
Interest, suffered and to be sufferd for want
of.........................thereof: Of all of which I duly notify
the...
Thus done and protested at the City of Philadelphia, aforesaid, the........
day of.....................19

....
NOTARY PUBLIC

Notarial Fee,
I hereby certify that I am not a Stockholder, Director or Clerk in the
Corporation for which I hereby act as Notary Public.

FORM 22. PROTEST JACKET

Some Common Types of Negotiable Instruments

Thus far in this chapter rather broad classifications of financial instruments have been discussed; orders to pay have been contrasted with promises to pay, time instruments with demand instruments, and cash items with collection items. These groups include many special items in current use which have been given distinguishing names. Some of the more usual of these items are named as follows: (1) acceptances, (2) certified checks, (3) cashier's checks and treasurer's checks, (4) bank drafts, (5) bank money orders, and (6) registered checks.

1. Acceptances. When a draft payable in the future is presented to the drawee before maturity, it is a common business practice for the drawee to acknowledge the right of the drawer to create the instrument by writing the word "accepted" across the face of the draft, the date on which the instrument is payable, and the place at which it is payable; then he adds his signature. By his acceptance, the drawee acknowledges his obligations under the instrument and promises to pay it when and where it is due. Thus it may be said that the instrument is transformed from an order to pay into a promise to pay. There are two general classes of acceptances. A trade acceptance is a draft drawn on the buyer by the seller of goods and accepted by the buyer. A bank acceptance is a draft drawn on a bank and accepted by the bank.

2. Certified checks. Another common form of bank acceptance, which is not generally regarded as such, is a certified check. A certified check is a demand draft drawn on a bank which the bank legally accepts but substitutes the word "certified" for the word "accepted." There are some important differences between certified checks and banks acceptances. A certified check is a check drawn by a depositor, and when certified by the bank, the amount of the check is immediately charged against the depositor's credit balance. The instrument is, of course, payable on demand. A bank acceptance is also drawn by a depositor on a bank and accepted by the bank, but usually this instrument is drawn under a credit arrangement. Instead of debiting the depositor's account, the bank sets up a loan which becomes an obligation of the depositor payable in the future.

3. Cashier's or treasurer's checks. A cashier's check is a draft

drawn by a bank on itself. In legal effect, cashier's checks are considered to have the qualifications of acceptances or promises to pay. Since the drawer and drawee are identical, acceptance or acknowledgment of the instrument by the drawee is implied. A cashier's check is illustrated in Form 23.

```
┌────────────────────────────────────────────────────────────────┐
│                                                                  │
│    THE  INSTITUTE  NATIONAL  BANK      12-345                     │
│              INSTITUTE,  U.S.A._____                   │
│                                         678                      │
│                                                                  │
│    PAY TO THE                                                    │
│       ORDER OF_____  $_____       │
│                                                                  │
│    _____DOLLARS         │
│                                                                  │
│                        _____         │
│                            AUTHORIZED SIGNATURE                   │
│    CASHIER'S CHECK                                                │
│                                                                  │
└────────────────────────────────────────────────────────────────┘
```

Size 8⅜ by 3⅜

FORM 23. CASHIER'S CHECK

A treasurer's check is essentially the same as a cashier's check. Cashier's checks are usually the instruments of national banks or any other banking institution in which the official who is responsible for the duties usually assigned to a treasurer is known as the cashier. The same official in many trust companies or state-chartered institutions is known as the treasurer, and instruments drawn by the State institution on itself are known as treasurer's checks.

4. Bank draft. A bank draft is a check drawn by one bank on a credit balance in another bank. A typical bank draft appears in Form 24.

5. Bank money orders. Bank money orders are bank obligations similar to cashier's checks and treasurer's checks. However, bank money orders are not drawn for official business purposes but are sold to depositors or anyone else to suit the purpose of the purchaser, usually for the payment of bills. The purchaser furnishes the name of the payee and the amount of the instrument, and the bank issues a money order. The purchaser pays a fee for this service. Bank money orders are frequently signed by tellers or clerks charged with the responsibility of handling such instru-

ments, whereas treasurer's checks and cashier's checks are commonly signed by officials of the bank.

No._____

INSTITUTE NATIONAL BANK

11-315
1210

ATLANTIC CITY, N. J.,_____19___

PAY TO THE
ORDER OF_____$_____

_____DOLLARS

TO

STANDARD TRUST COMPANY   _____
SAN FRANCISCO, CAL.

SIZE: 8⅜" x 3⅜"

FORM 24. BANK DRAFT

6. Registered checks. Registered checks are used for much the same purpose as bank money orders, but they are handled by the bank in a slightly different manner. When a registered check is purchased, the bank merely cuts the desired amount in a prepared check with a check writer, dates the instrument, and delivers it to the purchaser, who fills in the name of the payee and signs his own name as maker. These instruments, therefore, are not actually obligations of the bank. In effect, the purchaser obtains from the bank the right to draw a single check for a predetermined amount against a special account opened for that purpose alone.

Questions Based on Chapter VIII

1. Explain why negotiable instruments became necessary and desirable as trade and commerce developed.
2. What specific characteristics must a draft have in order to qualify as a negotiable instrument?

3. What specific characteristics must a promissory note have in order to qualify as a negotiable instrument?
4. Distinguish between a draft and a promissory note.
5. What is the purpose of an indorsement?
6. Name the five principal kinds of indorsements. Give an example of each.
7. Why is the proper presentment of a negotiable instrument considered important?
8. Explain in general terms the meaning of protest.
9. Distinguish between cash items and collection items.
10. What is an acceptance?
11. What is a registered check?

Questions for Investigation

1. Does your bank use registered checks?
2. Does your bank sell bank money orders?
3. In protesting checks, does your bank use a protest jacket?

CHAPTER IX

THE LOANING FUNCTION

The Purposes of This Chapter:

1. To point out the importance of the loaning function.
2. To discuss the loan limitations placed on the bank.
3. To explain primary factors affecting all loans.

ONE OF the oldest as well as one of the principal functions of a commercial bank is the lending of money to various individuals, businesses, and commercial enterprises. As a matter of fact, the interest a bank earns by making loans is usually the bank's largest single source of income.

Factors in Making Loans

It is in the performance of its loan function that a bank makes its greatest contribution to the economic well being, growth, and prosperity of the community it serves. Loans properly made to business and industry for worthwhile purposes help create employment and purchasing power that in turn contribute to the wealth, growth, and resources of the community, as well as raising its living standards.

When presented with an application for a loan, the bank must take into consideration many factors, all of which have some bearing on the application at hand. Some of these factors are discussed in subsequent chapters, because they are of a specific nature though they apply, in every instance, directly to the loan under consideration. In this chapter, we are concerned with basic loan principles and the more general factors which apply to all loan obligations.

The Deposit Obligation

At the moment it accepts a deposit in a checking account, every commercial bank assumes the obligation to pay back all or part of that deposit to the depositor upon demand. The depositor is not required to give, in advance, notice of his intention to draw on the money lying to his credit in the bank. Since most of the deposits held by a commercial bank are demand deposits, it follows logically that loans made by a commercial bank usually are of short duration. The reason becomes perfectly clear when we remember that it is for the most part the depositors' money, rather than its own, which the bank lends. The majority of the loans granted by commercial banks are made to mature within 30 to 120 days, the period most commonly used being 90 days. By using short maturities, in this manner, the bank assures itself of a constant flow of money being repaid to it on loans previously granted, with which to meet, if necessary, the withdrawal demands of its depositors. This obligation to pay back, *without prior notice,* which the bank assumes toward all its demand (checking) account depositors is an important factor when considering loan applications. If the ratio between deposits and loans becomes disproportionate, the bank would find it necessary to curtail its loaning activities.

Legal Limitations

The banking laws of the various states, as well as those laws enacted on the national level, place certain restrictions on the loaning activities of all banks. For example, the amount of money a bank may lend to any one borrower on an unsecured basis is limited by law; the limitation most frequently found being 10% of the bank's capital and surplus. The Board of Governors of the Federal Reserve System issued regulations, during the war years, limiting the amount of a loan permissible if the purpose of the loan was to aid in buying refrigerators, television sets, furniture, automobiles, electric stoves and washing machines, and many other consumer items.

Other national laws, which apply to all banks, limit the amount a bank may lend if the purpose of the loan is to purchase securities. The various limitations imposed by law are also important factors in considering loan applications, since no bank knowingly wishes to make an illegal loan. The bank may be able and willing to make a sound loan to a good customer but may be unable to do so because of the factor of legal limitations.

Local and General Conditions

The trend of business in general, with particular emphasis on local conditions, is an extremely important factor to be considered in determining the bank's loaning policies, as well as in arriving at a decision on a particular loan application. Certainly, a bank would be more likely to make loans to a company that is engaged in an active type of business and whose product is in demand than to make a loan to a company whose product is not in demand with the buying public. Because of the many and frequent changes that take place in an industry (such as a new type or product, improved methods of manufacturing, better methods of distribution, or any one of a dozen things that can take place which might adversely affect one or more of a bank's borrowing customers), bank loaning officers must be constantly on the alert. It is necessary for the banker, therefore, not only to have a thorough knowledge of economics and of money and banking but also to keep abreast of the changes which are constantly taking place. He must give particular attention to those industries or businesses to which the bank has loaned substantial amounts of depositor's money. Many banks actually set a limit on the amount they will lend in any one industry, regardless of the number of borrowers.

Policies of the Board of Directors

The board of directors of the bank constitute the governing body of the bank. As the duly elected representatives of the stockholders, who are the owners of the bank, it is the duty and responsibility of the board to take those steps which they feel are necessary to safeguard and protect the interests of the stockholders. As a matter of policy, in this connection, the board outlines the general field of loans, and it determines the types and kinds of loans the bank's loaning officers should consider. The board, through its committees, makes certain that the policies it establishes are carried out, and in addition, it requires that loans above a predetermined figure must have approval of a committee.

Primary Loan Considerations

The student should never lose sight of the fact that, in granting a loan, a bank is not lending its own money. The bank is lending stockholders' money to a limited degree when making loans. However, the bank makes most loans by using depositors' money. Therefore, the primary consideration governing bank loans is *safety of principal.* In view of the preponderance of demand deposits that exists in commercial banks, *liquidity,* or rapid turnover of loans, can also be considered of primary importance. Indeed, the object of all controls, whether they be external or internal in origin, is to insure the employment of the bank's funds without undue risk of loss and without tying up the funds for long periods of time. The rate of interest charged is largely determined by the relative safety and liquidity of the loan.

Safety of Principal

A loan is an advance of money or credit made upon the written promise of repayment by the borrower according to specified terms. Obviously, the bank does not grant a loan unless it is convinced that the borrower can and will repay the loan in accordance with terms agreed on at the time the loan is made. It is equally true, however, that every loan has a certain element of risk attached to it, and that despite every possible precaution, cases arise in which a loan is not repaid and the bank suffers a loss. It is only because the banks do exercise every possible precaution and because the loaning officers do not knowingly take any undue risks that the losses which do occur usually represent an extremely small percentage of the total funds which are loaned by the bank.

All the various states place a ceiling in one form or another on the rate of interest a bank may charge when lending money. The usual figure is 6%. Although the ceiling or maximum rate a bank may charge is 6%, the average rate for all banks is well below that figure. Thus the gross profit that may be realized by banks in the making of loans is definitely limited. This limitation of gross income provides another reason why safety of principal is so important, since all losses must be paid out of profits, and profits must obviously be greater than losses if the business is to survive at all.

The methods used to insure safety of principal are discussed in Chapter XII, Loan Processing, in connection with the work of the credit department.

Liquidity

When a banker speaks of liquidity, he really is discussing the need to have enough cash available to meet the withdrawal demands of the bank's depositors without any delay. Translated with regard to loans, this means short term loans that turn over rapidly. A bank may assure itself of liquidity in three ways: (1) short term self-liquidating loans, (2) eligible loans, and (3) loans that can be readily converted into cash in case of need.

Self-liquidating loans. A loan may be repaid from the proceeds of a transaction which was financed at its inception with borrowed money. A loan so repaid is a self-liquidating loan.

Assume that the Jones Manufacturing Company of Toledo, Ohio wishes to finance a shipment of goods to the Ajax Company of Newark, New Jersey. The Jones Manufacturing Company procures from the railroad company an order bill of lading covering the shipment, attaches it to a demand draft on the Ajax Company for the amount of the payment due, and then uses the draft as the basis of a loan from the bank. The bank advances a part of the amount of the draft, taking as security the bill of lading which the borrower indorses to the bank, and sends the draft, with the bill of lading attached, to a bank in Newark. The Newark bank presents the draft to the Ajax Company. The draft is paid and the proceeds remitted to the loaning bank. The Jones Manufacturing Company's loan is paid with these funds and the self-liquidating transaction is completed.

Eligible loans. A bank may be assured of liquidity by holding notes, drafts, and acceptances that it can rediscount with the Federal Reserve bank of its district. This ability to rediscount notes is one of the privileges of membership in the Federal Reserve System. Section 13 of the Federal Reserve Act, as amended, specifies what types of notes, drafts, and the like instruments are eligible for rediscount with the Federal Reserve bank. Further, under certain circumstances, the loaning officers of the reserve bank have the authority to make loans even if the notes offered are not eligible, provided that in their opinion the advance is necessary.

In a further effort to insure liquidity and still employ the bank's funds with a practical view toward earnings, many banks make a predetermined percentage of their loans in the form of advances collateralized by United States Government Bonds, securities listed on a stock exchange, or the cash surrender value of life insurance. These three forms of collateral have a high degree of salability, and under most conditions, the bank can dispose of them easily.

Questions Based on Chapter IX

1. Discuss the loaning function.
2. Explain the deposit obligation.
3. What is meant by safety of principal?
4. What is meant by liquidity?
5. How may a bank assure itself of liquidity?
6. What is meant by a self-liquidating loan?
7. What is meant by eligible loans?

Question for Investigation

What is the legal loaning limit for banks chartered by your state?

CHAPTER X

TYPES OF LOANS AND INVESTMENTS

The Purposes of This Chapter:

1. To develop the various classifications of loans.
2. To describe the main types of security for bank loans.
3. To consider the duties and the responsibilities which devolve on the collateral division.
4. To explain negotiable promissory notes and acceptances and their use in connection with bank loans.

As SHOWN in Chapter VIII, negotiable instruments are divided into two main classes, orders to pay and promises to pay. Included in the second main class are negotiable promissory notes, trade acceptances, and bank acceptances.

The basic contract into which a lender and a borrower enter each time a loan is granted is evidenced by the negotiable promissory note that the borrower signs and the lender accepts.

Promissory Notes

Negotiable promissory notes are the most widely used of all promises to pay. As evidences of debt they represent the largest portion of bank loans and discounts.

The signature of the maker of a note must be *genuine* and *authorized* for the same reasons that the signature of the drawer of a check must be genuine and authorized. Without exception, the bank must obtain full authority for the borrowing in every instance.

Acceptances

A trade acceptance is a draft drawn by the seller of goods on the buyer and accepted by the buyer. In other words, the buyer acknowledges the debt by writing the word "accepted" across the face of the draft and, at the same time, by designating the place of payment and the date of acceptance; the buyer then signs the

144

draft. Usually on the face of the draft there is a statement to the effect that the acceptor's obligation arises out of the purchase of goods from the drawer of the draft. Trade acceptances can be discounted by the seller of goods at his bank, under certain conditions, and they are also eligible for rediscount at the Federal Reserve banks. A trade acceptance is illustrated in Form 25.

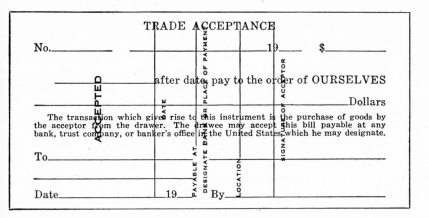

FORM 25. A TRADE ACCEPTANCE

A bank acceptance is a draft drawn on a bank and accepted by the bank. By accepting a draft, a bank lends its credit to the customer for whose account the acceptance is made. Bank acceptances appear in situations in which the seller is willing to accept the obligation of the bank but is not willing to accept the obligation of the buyer.

CLASSIFICATION OF LOANS

Loans basically fall into one of two classifications, either unsecured loans or secured loans. There are several other ways of classifying loans which are also discussed, but these classifications are, in reality, only a more detailed breakdown or division of the two main classifications. By means of daily summaries, the senior officers and directors are kept up-to-date regarding the loan portfolio of the bank.

Unsecured Loans

The majority of loans granted by banks are extended on the general credit standing of the borrower and are evidenced only by negotiable promissory notes. This transaction is called an unsecured loan and the note is referred to as an unsecured note, that is, one in which the borrower has pledged no specific asset to secure payment to the bank when the note matures.

The use of unsecured notes has its roots deep in American history. Much of our business has always been conducted on an *open account* basis. When a customer buys goods, no formal written promise to pay is given. The seller simply enters the sale as a memorandum on his book. At agreed periods, generally once a month, the seller sends the buyer a bill for the amount owing, at which time the buyer pays the amount that is due. The average business is operated on the basis of "flow of working capital." Merchandise is either purchased or manufactured. It is then resold on open account, and thirty or sixty days later it is paid for, completing the cycle or flow from merchandise to cash. American banks make many unsecured loans based on this flow of capital. They lend either for the manufacture or for the purchase of merchandise and are repaid when the merchandise is sold. This is another example of a self-liquidating loan. In making such an unsecured loan, the bank carefully investigates the financial condition of the borrower. It depends on the borrower's inventory, accounts receivable, and cash as protection for its loan.

Indorsed Loans

Although indorsed notes are usually classified as unsecured loans, they may be said to be "secured" because the bank relies on the signature of the indorser as its primary protection for the payment of the loan. When a loan applicant cannot fully meet the requirements for an unsecured loan and he has no specific property to pledge, the bank can grant the loan if one or more persons other than the maker assume responsibility for the repayment of the loan. By indorsing the note, the party other than the maker assumes the liability. Since the bank lends on the security afforded to it by the signature of the indorser, the loan is really a secured loan, even though no specific asset has been pledged to the bank. Form 26 illustrates an indorser liability agreement.

> FOR VALUE RECEIVED, the undersigned (who, if two or more in number, shall be jointly and severally bound) hereby unconditionally guarantee(s) the payment of the within note and all costs and expenses, including attorney's fees, incurred in the collection thereof and the enforcement hereof, and waive(s) presentment, demand, protest, and notice of dishonor and of any renewal or extension of said note, and consent(s) to any such renewal or extension and to the taking and disposition of any security for said note. Any money, credits, or other property belonging to the undersigned in the possession or under the control of the legal holder hereof may be appropriated and applied hereon at any time, without notice or demand, as well before as at or after the maturity hereof.

FORM 26. AN INDORSER LIABILITY AGREEMENT

Secured Loans

One of the most important words in a banker's vocabulary is the word *margin*. Margin is the value of collateral in excess of the amount of the loan for which the collateral is pledged as security. It is the lender's margin of safety. Although the loaning officer seeks to create a margin on all loans and the bank tries to have a margin of safety in all its activities, margin has a particular importance in connection with secured loans.

A secured loan is one in which specific property is pledged to secure payment of the loan. The note is referred to as a secured or collateral note. The collateral may consist of personal property such as stocks or bonds or documents giving legal ownership to or covering some article of property. A warehouse receipt covering marketable commodities, such as butter or eggs, would be an example of an instrument covering property.

The collateral form of note, in addition to the requirements and responsibility contained in a promissory note, authorizes the lender to sell the collateral pledged and to apply the proceeds to the loan. If the sale of the collateral does not provide enough money to pay the loan, the borrower is still liable for the unpaid balance. The note gives the bank wide powers in the matter of selling the collateral. A collateral note form appears as Form 27.

$............

City, State,................................, 19......

..........................after date............promise to pay

to the order of METROPOLIS TRUST COMPANY,...

....DOLLARS

at its main office, Main and Swede Streets, City, State, with interest thereon of.................
per cent per annum, without defalcation, for value received:

and............hereby empower any attorney of any court of record to appear and confess judgment against
............if this note be not paid at maturity, for the above sum, with costs of suit and an attorney's fee of............per cent for collection, all errors
therein being released hereby.

Exemption, inquisition, and condemnation required or which may be claimed, under any law now in force, or hereafter to be passed,
is hereby waived in execution proceedings against real or personal property hereunder.

As collateral security for the payment of this note and of any indebtedness of the undersigned, to the holder hereof, due or to become
due, whether absolute or contingent, now existing or which may hereafter be contracted, whether incurred directly or indirectly by the undersigned, including promissory notes, bills of exchange, and other evidences of indebtedness made, indorsed, or accepted by the undersigned and
purchased or owned by the holder hereof, the undersigned has deposited herewith the following:

....

....

....

....

The undersigned agrees to deposit with the holder hereof, within two hours after demand made upon the undersigned, such additional
collateral as the holder hereof may demand; and hereby gives to the holder hereof a lien for the amount of this note and of all liability of the
undersigned to the holder hereof as aforesaid upon all property of the undersigned and all right, title, and interest of the undersigned in any
property or securities in the possession or custody of the holder hereof for safekeeping or for any purpose whatever, as well as upon all proceeds
of said property or securities and also upon all deposit accounts which the undersigned may at any time have with the holder hereof; and all
remittances and property shall be deemed to be in the possession and custody of the holder hereof, when actually in the possession or custody of,
or in transit to, it, or any of its agents.

Additions to, reductions of, or substitutes for, any of the above collateral and payment on account of said loan, or increase of the same, or other loans made partially or wholly upon the said collateral may, from time to time, be made with the consent of the holder hereof without affecting or impairing in any manner the validity of this contract, all such collateral added or substituted being held with the same effect as if it had herein been originally pledged.

Upon the failure of the undersigned to perform the obligation herein, then the holder hereof is hereby authorized to sell, assign, and deliver the whole or any part of the said collateral or any substitutes therefor, or any additions thereto, or any other property or security of the undersigned and all the right, title, and interest of the undersigned in any property or security in the possession or custody of the holder hereof in any way for safekeeping or for any purpose whatever, at any brokers' board or at public or private sale at the option of the holder hereof without demand for payment or for additional collateral or for other performance and without regard to any such demand, if made, and without advertisement or notice of intention to sell or of the time or place of sale or otherwise, and at any such sales the holder hereof is empowered to become the purchaser, and all equity, rights, and interest of the undersigned in the said collateral or other property shall be divested thereby as fully as if such sale, or sales, had been made to a bona fide person other than the holder hereof.

Upon the failure of the undersigned to perform the obligations herein, then this note shall mature at the election of the holder hereof.

If this note be not paid at maturity, the holder hereof may recover all expenses incurred in the collection of this note or in the protection of the said collateral as well as all expenses incurred at any time by the holder hereof in the exercise of any of its rights hereunder, including taxes, premiums paid by the holder hereof on policies of insurance upon the life of the undersigned or upon policies of insurance upon property pledged hereunder.

If this note be not paid at maturity, the holder hereof is authorized to appropriate and apply any or all of the net cash receipts from any of the said property or securities and deposit accounts of the undersigned with the holder hereof and all moneys of the undersigned in the custody or possession of the holder hereof to the payment in whole or in part of this note or of the said liabilities or expenses, returning the surplus to the undersigned; and notwithstanding the retention by the holder hereof of said securities for the payment of this note and said other liabilities or any sale or exchange of the said property and securities, the undersigned shall remain liable for the payment in full of this note and of all said liabilities, including all expenses as aforesaid, except only to the extent that the same shall be reduced thereby.

If the undersigned or any indorser or guarantor of this note, or any maker, indorser, or guarantor of any of said security shall become insolvent or make a general assignment for the benefit of creditors, or if a petition in bankruptcy shall be filed by or against the undersigned, or any such maker, indorser, or guarantor, then this note and all of said other liabilities shall immediately become due and payable.

The holder hereof may rehypothecate any or all of the said securities to secure deposits or other obligations of the holder hereof, and shall be thereafter fully discharged from all liability therefor.

Any indebtedness due from the holder hereof to the undersigned may be appropriated and applied in payment of any debt or obligation of the undersigned to the holder hereof if this note be not paid at maturity.

The rights and remedies herein expressly specified are cumulative and not exclusive of any other rights which any holder hereof may have.

Signed, sealed, and delivered in the presence of

....(SEAL)

....(SEAL)

FORM 27. A COLLATERAL NOTE (front)

City, State, _____, 19____

In consideration of the credit extended, discount, loan, or extension of time granted upon the within note at the request of the undersigned, the undersigned hereby unconditionally guarantees to the METROPOLIS TRUST COMPANY, and every subsequent holder hereof irrespective of the genuineness, validity, regularity, or enforceability thereof, or of the obligation evidenced thereby or of any collateral therefor, or of the existence or extent of any other such collateral and irrespective of any other circumstance, that all sums stated therein to be payable thereunder shall be promptly paid when due in accordance with the provisions thereof, at maturity, by acceleration or otherwise, and in case of extension of time of payment all sums shall be promptly paid when due according to such extension or extensions at maturity, by acceleration or otherwise; and the undersigned hereby agrees that from time to time, without notice to the undersigned, payment of any sums due under the said note may be extended in whole or in part, or any of the said collateral may be sold, exchanged, or surrendered, and substitutions of collateral may be made, and the undersigned hereby waives presentment, demand of payment or protest or notice of any exchange, sale, substitution, or other disposition of collateral.

The undersigned hereby empower   any attorney of any court of record to appear and confess judgment against the undersigned, if this note be not paid at maturity, for the principal thereof, together with all sums stated therein to be payable thereunder, with costs of suit and an attorney's fee of _____ per cent for collection, all errors therein being released hereby.

Exemption, inquisition, and condemnation required, or which may be claimed under any law now in force, or hereafter to be passed is hereby waived in execution proceedings against real or personal property hereunder.

Signed, sealed, and delivered in the presence of:

_____   _____ (SEAL)

_____ (SEAL)

FORM 27. A COLLATERAL NOTE (reverse side)

TYPES OF LOANS AND INVESTMENTS 151

Because the value of any given piece of collateral can change rapidly, the loaning officer takes a margin of safety at the time the loan is granted in order to protect the bank against possible loss. For example, a wholesale dealer in eggs may purchase eggs in carload lots at fifty cents per dozen. He then puts the eggs in storage in a public warehouse to be withdrawn as he sells them. He requests a loan from the bank using as collateral for the loan the warehouse receipts covering the eggs. The loaning officer knows that, although the eggs presently are worth fifty cents per dozen, it is possible for the market price or value per dozen to decline. Therefore, to protect the bank against such an event, he lends only forty cents per dozen on the collateral that is worth fifty cents *at the time the loan is granted*. That differential of 20% is the margin of safety the loaning officer establishes to protect the bank from loss.

Direct and Indirect Loans

A direct loan is an advance made to a customer on his primary responsibility as maker of the note. For example, the John Smith Company desires to borrow $5,000 on an unsecured basis from the Institute State Bank. A note payable to the order of the bank is executed and is signed by the authorized officers of the company. The loan transaction is directly between the company and the bank. The responsibility for the repayment of the loan rests solely with the company.

An indirect loan is an advance in which the borrower's responsibility to repay the loan exists only if the party primarily responsible to repay the loan fails to do so. Thus, if the John Smith Company indorses a note payable to the company's order and borrows money from the bank on this note, the transaction is classed as an indirect loan. The John Smith Company is liable for payment only if the maker of the note does not pay.

COLLATERAL FOR BANK LOANS

The test of collateral acceptable for bank loans is its ready salability under adverse conditions. If business conditions are good, the value of the collateral usually increases. If business conditions are bad, and value of collateral is much more likely to decline.

Since a bank may be forced to sell collateral to protect itself when general conditions are poor, the kind of collateral originally taken and the margin originally established become very important. The following types of property constitute the chief sources of collateral acceptable to banks:

1. U. S. Government bonds (except savings bonds)
2. Stocks and bonds listed on recognized securities exchanges
3. Unlisted stocks and bonds actively bought and sold by brokers and others
4. Cash surrender value of life insurance policies
5. Warehouse receipts covering staple commodities
6. Bills of lading
7. Chattel mortgages and instalment contracts.

Many banks also make loans secured by assignment of accounts receivable, as well as loans secured by mortgages on real estate. Because of the legal complexities and the variety of state and of national laws that relate to accounts receivable and mortgage loans, loans secured by such collateral are considered in other texts.

The ability of the bank to sell collateral readily is the principal factor in determining the liquidity of collateral loans. Markets (places to buy or sell) for stocks and bonds are provided by stock exchanges. A stock exchange is an organization of individuals engaged in the business of buying and selling securities. Permanent quarters are equipped with facilities for the efficient execution of transactions. The part of the quarters where the actual buying and selling take place is known as the floor of the exchange, and the various locations where specific stocks and bonds are either bought or sold are called trading posts.

The members of the stock exchanges have adopted rules which regulate purchases and sales, the settlement of amounts due, and the commission charged for effecting a sale or purchase of securities. The commissions charged by the members of the exchange for effecting such sales and purchases are their main source of income. The members have also established rules covering the requirements for the listing of stocks to be traded on the exchange.

Bonds

A bond is an interest-bearing certificate under seal, which promises that the issuer (a government or corporation) will pay a certain sum in money to the holder of the bond at maturity. In effect, it is a long term loan by the bondholder (lender) to the issuer (borrower). Bonds may be either in bearer form or registered in the name of the owner. Attached to the bonds are coupons that call for the payment of interest at certain specified times. The holder simply detaches each coupon on the maturity date and either presents it to a bank for payment or deposits it for credit to his account, just as he would a check. In the case of a registered bond, the bond can be registered not only as to the principal but can be registered also as to interest. When it is registered as to both principal and interest, the issuer pays interest to the holder by checks at the specified interest dates.

Stocks

A *share of stock* is a claim which the owner, called the stockholder, has to share in the profits of the issuing corporation and in its net assets if the company is liquidated. A stockholder is, therefore, one of the owners of that corporation. This ownership is evidenced by a stock certificate, which is a document certifying that the person whose name appears on it owns a stated number of shares of stock in the issuing corporation.

There are two general classes of stock: (1) preferred and (2) common. Owners of preferred stock are usually entitled to dividends at a fixed rate before dividends are paid to owners of a common stock. In the event of liquidation of the corporation, preferred stockholders are entitled to be paid the full amount of their investment out of net assets before any amount is paid to the holders of common stock.

Common stockholders are entitled to dividends authorized by the directors, out of earnings, after the required dividend payments have been made to the preferred stockholders.

When an issue of a stock or bonds is accepted for trading on a stock exchange, it is said to be listed. The advantage of a listed security, from the standpoint of the bank accepting it as collateral, is that a buyer at a fair price is much more likely to be found through the facilities of the stock exchange than in any other way.

When a stock is not listed on any recognized exchange, it is referred to as an unlisted security. The market for such securities is created by commission houses and investment dealers interested in the securities. The dealers accept bids for the purchase and offers for the sale of securities at stated prices. This market is called the unlisted or over-the-counter market. United States Government bonds and the bonds of municipalities are traded in a substantial volume on the over-the-counter market.

Cash Surrender Value of Life Insurance

A life insurance policy is a contract in which the insurance company agrees to pay to a stated person or persons a certain sum of money in the event of the death of the insured during the life of the contract. In return for this promise the insured pays stated amounts (premiums) to the insurance company. As these premiums are accumulated by virtue of the payments made by the insured, they have the effect of giving a cash value to the policy which the insured can collect at any time during the life of the policy by canceling the contract with the insurance company. The cash benefits can be assigned to any lender, and in recent years, the volume of loans granted by banks secured by such assignments has been increasing steadily.

Warehouse Receipts

A warehouse company stores goods for their owner and charges a fee for the service. Upon receiving the goods, the company gives the owner a receipt known as a warehouse receipt. Warehouse receipts are of two kinds, non-negotiable and negotiable.

A non-negotiable warehouse receipt, sometimes called a straight receipt, provides for delivery of the goods *only* to the person named in the receipt, upon payment of the storage charges owing the warehouse.

A negotiable receipt, also known as an order receipt, provides for delivery of the goods to the person named in the receipt or to his order (anyone designated by the owner) on proper indorsement and surrender to the warehouse, together with payment of any storage charges due the warehouse. One form of negotiable warehouse receipt is illustrated in Form 28.

Loans, secured by commodities such as cotton, wheat, sugar, and canned vegetables, and evidenced by negotiable warehouse receipts or non-negotiable receipts issued in the bank's name, form an appreciable part of the loan portfolio of many American banks.

STORAGE WAREHOUSE COMPANY

ORIGINAL WAREHOUSE RECEIPT No.————————

NOT INSURED

RECEIVED EX.. DATE.....................

FOR STORAGE IN.. WAREHOUSE No.....................

LOCATED AT.. STREET,...

SUBJECT TO ALL THE TERMS AND CONDITIONS CONTAINED HEREIN AND ON THE

REVERSE HEREOF, FOR THE ACCOUNT OF AND TO BE DELIVERED TO...........................

.... OR ORDER

ONLY UPON SURRENDER OF THIS RECEIPT PROPERLY INDORSED

ITEM NO.	NO. UNITS	SAID TO BE OR CONTAIN
		NEGOTIABLE
		(DO NOT ACCEPT THIS WAREHOUSE RECEIPT IF ANY CORRECTIONS OR ERASURES APPEAR HEREON.)

SUBJECT TO LIEN FOR STORAGE, HAN-
DLING, AND OTHER CHARGES AS PER
CONTRACT AND LEASE WITH THE IN-
DUSTRY SERVED

STORAGE WAREHOUSE COMPANY

PER..

FORM 28. A NEGOTIABLE WAREHOUSE RECEIPT

Bills of Lading

A bill of lading is a document issued by a common carrier. It acknowledges the receipt of specified goods for transportation to a certain place, it sets forth the contract between the shipper and the carrier, and it provides for proper delivery of the goods. A bill of lading may be defined as a receipt for goods in transit. A bill of lading may be non-negotiable (straight) or negotiable (order).

A non-negotiable bill of lading provides for delivery of the goods only to the person named in the bill. The bill of lading may or may not be surrendered, but the carrier must be certain that the person to whom it delivers the goods is actually entitled to them.

A negotiable bill of lading provides for delivery of the goods to the person named in the bill or to his order and only on proper indorsement and surrender of the bill of lading to the carrier. An order bill of lading, like a negotiable warehouse receipt, has the effect of placing the goods under the control of the proper holder of the bill. Hence an order bill affords satisfactory security for a bank loan if it covers a sufficient amount of staple commodities.

Chattel Mortgages and Instalment Contracts

A chattel mortgage is an instrument by which the borrower gives the lender a lien on such personal property as machinery, equipment, crops or cattle as security for the loan. The chattel mortgage provides that if the borrower does not make payments in accordance with the agreement, the lender has the right to take the property, sell it, and use the proceeds to pay the loan.

An instalment contract provides much the same security as a chattel mortgage; the main difference is that under the instalment contract, the lender usually has title to the property until all instalment payments are made in accordance with the agreement. When all payments have been made, title to the property is transferred to the borrower.

These two kinds of obligations are used extensively to finance the sale of a variety of personal property, such as automobiles, home refrigerators and freezers, television sets, gas ranges, and air-conditioners. The purchaser is generally required to make a cash downpayment representing a percentage of the selling price; the remainder of the price is financed by the lender. The purchaser of the property repays the loan in equal monthly instalments. The difference between the cost of the article purchased and the amount loaned is the margin of safety taken by the lender.

DUTIES OF THE COLLATERAL DIVISION

Upon the collateral division of the loan and discount department rest certain responsibilities and duties with respect to collateral loans. These responsibilities impose certain well defined duties, four in number, which may be enumerated as follows: (1) verification of collateral, (2) safekeeping of collateral securing loans, (3) maintenance of adequate collateral, (4) maintenance of accurate collateral records.

Verification of Collateral

Although the primary responsibility for determining *good delivery* of collateral by the borrower to the bank rests with the loaning officer, that responsibility is also shared, in part, by the collateral division. Good delivery simply means that the stock certificate, bond, warehouse receipt, or other document bearing evidence of title being pledged as collateral is in proper form for the transfer of ownership. The correctness and presence of all the documents necessary for valid transfer of ownership must be verified.

Safekeeping of Collateral

Protection against loss and against misuse of collateral is an important responsibility of the collateral division of the loan and discount department. The collateral is verified, and a receipt is issued to the borrower. Then the collateral is placed in the bank's vault for safekeeping, where it usually remains until the loan it secured is repaid by the borrower. To prevent misuse of the collateral, the larger banks usually place it under dual control, that is, under the joint control of the collateral division and some other department of the bank, usually the auditing division or comptrollers department. Thus, when collateral either is placed in the vault for safekeeping or is removed from the vault to be returned to the borrower, a clerk from each of the two departments is present to confirm the deposit of securities in or their removal from the vault. The particular compartment in the vault in which collateral is stored requires either two keys or else two separate combinations, each department keeping its own key or combination and one being unable to open the vault without the other. By means of vault "in" and "out" slips both departments keep a record of collateral being stored in or withdrawn from the vault.

Maintenance of Adequate Collateral

When a banker speaks of adequate collateral and the maintenance of adequate collateral, he is referring to the maintenance of a satisfactory margin of safety by having an amount of collateral over and above the amount needed to equal the amount of the outstanding loan. As a matter of policy many banks fix the margin desired with relation to the collateral being offered. For example, one bank may decide on a policy of not lending more than 85% of the market value of bonds. In that case a borrower offering a bond having a market value of $1,000 could not borrow more than $850 against the security of that bond. From the moment the loan is granted, it becomes the responsibility of the collateral division to make certain that the margin is maintained at the percentage originally fixed when the loan was granted. The collateral division, therefore, checks the current market value of all collateral entrusted to it as frequently as is necessary to keep the record reasonably up to date. Whenever the current value of the collateral is not enough to cover the loan plus the desired margin, the matter is immediately referred to the officer who approved the loan. The borrower is then required either to reduce the principal of the loan by a cash payment or to bring in and pledge additional collateral acceptable to the bank. Thus, the margin is restored back to the desired percentage.

Maintenance of Adequate Records

From an accounting standpoint, collateral records are considered as supplementary records. When the volume of secured loans is small, or few types of collateral are handled, the records are comparatively simple. When the volume is large and a great variety of collateral is handled, the records must be complete and in great detail. Probably the most commonly used record is the loan card. This card shows the amount of the loan, carries a complete description of the securities held, and has columns for recording the market price and value of the collateral. Use of this record makes it possible to review loans quickly and accurately without actually withdrawing the collateral from the vault.

While the loan card provides information on the types of collateral securing loans and the nature of the customer's liability, the collateral register is the balancing record.

A Typical Collateral Department Operation

The collateral is first checked to see that it is complete and correct. If an important defect exists in the collateral the matter is referred to the loaning officer for decision.

When the security has been checked and approved, a receipt is issued to the customer. A memorandum is given to the posting division as its record. The next step is to check the margin. Each security is priced or checked for market value and the total value of the collateral is computed and compared with the loan to verify the fact that the desired margin is present. The proper entries are prepared, as are the collateral records, and then the collateral is lodged in the vault.

Funds or payments received by the bank are reported to the collateral division in order to keep the records accurate and to service or meet requests for release of collateral.

Questions Based on Chapter X

1. How may loans be classified?
2. What types of collateral are given for bank loans?
3. What is a warehouse receipt?
4. Distinguish between stocks and bonds.
5. What is meant by dual control?
6. Define the term margin, as used in banking.

Questions for Investigation

1. What precautions are taken by your bank against the misuse of collateral?
2. Does your bank make loans secured by chattel mortgages?

CHAPTER XI

LOANING PROCEDURE

The Purposes of This Chapter:
1. To mention the loaning staff of the bank.
2. To discuss the responsibilities of the loaning staff.
3. To consider the responsibilities of the credit department.
4. To describe the methods used by the credit department in the performance of its duties.

THE POSITION occupied by the loaning officer in the overall picture of the loan function of the bank is twofold. First, he is the final evaluator of the information assembled regarding the prospective borrower, and second, he is the interpreter of bank policy with respect to loans. On the basis of his judgment, loans are either granted or declined. To state his position as simply as possible, it is the loaning officer who either grants or declines a loan.

Although the policies are established by the board of directors, the primary responsibility for loans rests upon the loaning officers. It is not only the loaning officer's responsibility to make or reject loans, but it is also his responsibility to collect them, to make certain that they are repaid. The profitable and safe employment of the bank's funds depends upon the knowledge, the ability to appraise risks, and the sound judgment displayed by the bank's loaning officers.

The loaning officers are the senior and junior officers of the commercial department, namely, the vice presidents, the assistant vice presidents, and the assistant cashiers or the assistant treasurers. Each officer has under his direction a number of borrowing accounts with which he is expected to keep in close touch. He considers and passes upon loan applications made by customers.

In many banks the division of accounts develops in an informal way, since customers prefer to do business with officers whom they know personally. The board of directors of a bank usually places a limit on the loaning powers, dollarwise, of all its loaning officers.

The larger accounts, from the standpoint of dollars borrowed, are handled by vice presidents, because they have the authority to handle large loans. Assistant vice presidents handle smaller borrowers. In many cases junior loaning officers are assigned to work directly with and under the direction of senior loaning officers in the handling of the accounts assigned to the senior loaning officer. Informal division of borrowing accounts is usually found in small and medium sized banks.

Loaning Groups

In large metropolitan banks, the volume of loans, the many different kinds of businesses represented by the borrowers, and the number of loaning officers required to handle them all combine to require a more formal organization of loaning officers. This organization is usually accomplished by arranging borrowers by types of business and then assigning a group of officers to handle all the loan applications arising out of that particular category of business. A loaning group can and usually does handle several types of business. Each officer of the group becomes familiar with the borrowers handled by the other officers in the group; thus when an officer is absent, the others in the group can handle his loans. Chart 4 illustrates the organization of a loaning group.

The assignment of accounts by type of business or industry has an advantage in that the loaning officers assigned to a particular type of business become so familiar with the problems of the industry or industries that their specialized knowledge makes them better able to judge the merits of loan applications.

In the final analysis the problem of how best to organize the loaning activities of any particular bank varies somewhat from that of other banks, even in the same locality. The volume of business, the kind of business, and the experience and training of the loaning officers are all factors to be considered in determining how the particular bank should organize its loaning procedure.

Three divisions of the bank are frequently established and designated. Together they are responsible for the execution of the loaning procedure. Each of the three divisions has duties which are distinctly different from those of the other divisions. The loaning procedure, therefore, divides into the following arrangement of duties.

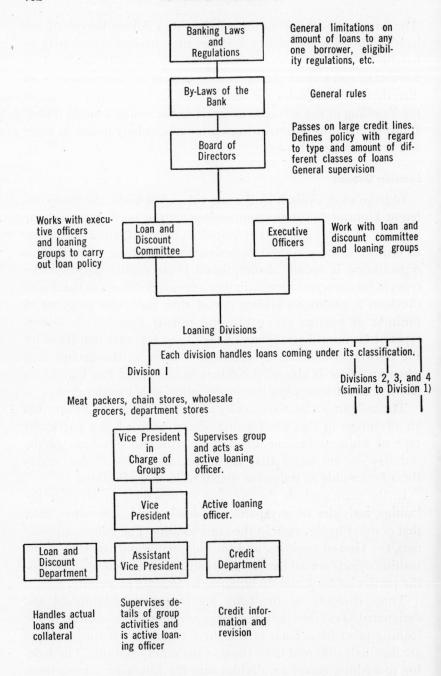

CHART 4. ORGANIZATION OF A LOANING GROUP

1. The proper application of the bank's basic policies by the loaning officers

2. The investigation, assembly, analysis, and recording of credit information by the credit department

3. The proper care and protection for notes and collateral, and the maintenance of the loan records by the loan and discount department.

In Chapter IX, brief reference is made to the responsibility of the board of directors in establishing loan policies. This phase of the loaning procedure constitutes an important problem of bank management, which cannot be discussed in detail here. It is treated at length in the Institute text Credit Administration.

The Credit Department

The main work of the credit department consists of investigating, assembling, analyzing, and recording credit information for the guidance of the loaning officers of the bank. The officers use the information in disposing of loan applications and in reaching decisions with respect to actions concerning loans already on the books of the bank.

The credit department also performs a valuable service for customers and friends of the bank by making credit information available to them under proper circumstances. This courtesy is often of value to nonborrowing customers, to other banks, and to business concerns. It assists them in making decisions on the applications for credit which they receive. From a public relations standpoint, the good will created by this service is incalculable. It is reflected often in new accounts or increased balances and by reciprocal courtesies from other banks.

The Investigation

There are a number of recognized sources of information which are available to the credit department in its work of investigation. The principal ones are:

1. The applicants themselves, through interviews with loaning officers or other members of the staff

2. Financial statements of the applicants

3. The bank's own records

4. Credit agency reports

5. Other banks and business concerns acquainted with the applicants.

The Interview

The best source of credit information is the applicant himself. The loaning officer interviews the applicant and learns from him the reasons for the loan request and the use to be made of the funds. Discussion is held regarding the present condition of the business—how sales compare with previous periods, how promptly the applicant is being paid by the people to whom he sells his products. Other information pertinent to the applicant's business is established. Lastly, provided the loan is granted, the method or schedule of repayment is discussed. If the application being discussed is a first application, that is to say, if this is the first time the applicant has requested a loan from the bank, the loaning officer uses this interview as a means of arriving at an estimate of the applicant's sincerity, capability, and general knowledge of his particular industry.

Some borrowers are conservative in their estimates of profits and in their ability to repay borrowed funds within a time limit; other borrowers are overly optimistic in their estimates, either because they do not know their business as well as they should or because they are knowingly trying to give the loaning officer a false impression. In any event the estimate the loaning officer reaches regarding the applicant as an individual is most important, since it is axiomatic that loans, in the final analysis, are made to people and not to financial statements. An individual can make figures appear better than they are; figures can never make an individual better than he is.

The Financial Statement

In the discussion of unsecured loans, it was said that the bank relies upon the assets of a company for the safety and repayment of its loan, even though these assets are not specifically pledged to secure the loan.

In order for the bank to know what these assets are and what their value is, the applicant is asked to submit a financial statement. A financial statement is a document that shows as of a given date, the applicant's assets and his liabilities. As the bank accumulates statements which reflect the condition of the business at various dates, it is possible to compare the trend of a business, that is, whether it is progressing and making money or whether it is regressing.

The financial statement also shows certain relationships between assets and liabilities which are important in gauging the soundness and strength of the company's financial position. Some of the more important relationships are: (1) as between total assets and total liabilities, (2) as between the assets of cash, accounts receivable, and inventory compared to the liabilities of accounts payable, notes payable, and taxes due, and (3) as between the assets of machinery and real estate as compared to the liabilities of mortgage and equipment loans. One form of financial statement appears in Form 29.

Whenever it can, the bank requires that the financial statements be prepared by certified public accountants. However, the statement can be prepared by the company itself and certified as correct by the authorized representatives of the company. It is not unusual for the bank's own representatives, on occasion, to prepare a statement gathered from the customer's books, for the use of the bank.

It is now the accepted custom, voluntarily or on the request of the loaning officers or credit department, for borrowing customers to supply the bank periodically with statements.

The Bank's Own Records

In every department of the bank, continuing records of transactions with customers are kept. From the records of the analysis department, it is possible to ascertain the average balance kept on deposit by the applicant and whether the account is profitable or not. The records of the bookkeeping department will disclose overdrafts (if any) and checks returned (if any). The credit file kept on each borrowing customer by the credit department will disclose previous borrowings, how they were repaid, and if the repayments were made in accordance with the promises made by the borrower. The bank's own records and its experience is thus assembled to reveal the value of the account to the bank and the manner in which the particular customer meets his responsibilities.

Credit Agency Reports

There are several credit agencies in the United States that are engaged in the business of assembling credit information on companies and individuals and furnishing reports at moderate cost. Such reports are used extensively in bank credit work. From the standpoint of the bank, probably the most important information contained in these reports relates to the background and business histories of the individuals and companies. These histories include all available information on bankruptcies, lawsuits, composition settlements with creditors, as well as other data, unfavorable as well as favorable. Agency reports also contain information obtained through trade checkings, which indicate the degree of promptness with which the borrower pays his bills. Some of these agencies cover the business field in general; others specialize in one or two particular industries.

Bank and Trade Checkings

Loan applicants are requested to furnish a list of the banks and business houses with which the company is dealing or has dealt in the past and to state the nature and extent of each business relationship. The credit department then verifies the information by checking with these references. These checkings are usually made by letter or occasionally by phone and the information obtained or a summary of it is placed in the credit file.

The bank, after stating the reasons for making the inquiry, requests other banks to state their experience with the applicant in such matters as loans made, promptness of repayment, average balances maintained, and whether the account was satisfactory. Business concerns are asked to indicate the amount of business done with the company, the arrangements for payment, and how payments have been met. Bank and trade references are consulted again from time to time to see if the relationship continues to be satisfactory and to give the loaning officers a current basis for review of existing loans or for consideration of new applications.

General and Specialized Information

There are many publications that specialize in the news and problems of particular fields or segments of business. These pub-

FINANCIAL STATEMENT

Corporation

STATEMENT OF...

ADDRESS...BUSINESS...

To: INSTITUTE NATIONAL BANK AND TRUST COMPANY,
EREWHON, ILLINOIS

For the purpose of procuring and maintaining credit with you, the undersigned makes and delivers to you the following as a complete, true, and correct statement of our financial condition as of the.....................................day of..., 19............ The end of our fiscal year, and the regular date for taking a physcial inventory, is.........................

Statement of Assets and Liabilities as of..., 19............ .

Cash on Hand and in Banks (see schedule A)...				
Notes Receivable and Acceptances of Customers (see schedule B)........................				
Accounts Receivable from Customers (see schedule B)..				
Inventory of Finished Goods (see schedule C)...				
Inventory of Work in Process (see schedule C)...				
Inventory of Raw Materials (see schedule C)...				
Goods in Transit and/or Advances on Merchandise (see schedule C)....................				
Stocks and Bonds (see schedule D)...				
Land (see schedule E)...				
Buildings before Depreciation (see schedule E)..				
Machinery and Equipment before Depreciation (see schedule F)............................				
Furniture and Fixtures before Depreciation (see schedule F)................................				
Automobiles before Depreciation (see schedule F)..				
Prepaid Items and Deferred Charges (see schedule G)..				
Amounts Due from Officers and/or Employees (see schedule H)............................				
Cash Value of Life Insurance Policies (see schedule I)..				
Other Assets (see schedule J)...				
TOTAL ASSETS				
Notes Payable to Banks and Brokers (see schedule A)..				
Notes and Trade Acceptances Payable for Merchandise (see schedule K)				
Accounts Payable for Merchandise (see schedule K)...				
Notes Payable to Others (see schedule L)...				
Accruals (see schedule M)..				
Amounts Due to Officers and/or Employees (see schedule L)................................				
Real Estate Mortgages and Funded Debt (see schedule E)...................................				
Chattel Mortgages Payable (see schedule F)..				
Other Liabilities (see schedule N)...				
Reserve for Bad Debts (see schedule B)..				
Reserve for Depreciation of Building...				
Reserve for Depreciation of Machinery and Equipment...				
Reserve for Depreciation of Furniture and Fixtures...				
Reserve for Depreciation of Automobiles..				
Capital (see schedule O)...				
Capital Stock—Preferred				
Capital Stock—Common				
Surplus—Earned				
Surplus—Paid in or by Revaluation of Assets...				
TOTAL LIABILITIES AND CAPITAL				

NAMES OF OFFICERS AND DIRECTORS. List here the names of all officers and all directors. If an officer is not a director, cross out the printed word director before his name.

Title	Name and Residence Address	Number of Shares Held	
President and Director..		Pfd........................	Com.
Vice President and Director................................		Pfd........................	Com.
Treasurer and Director..		Pfd........................	Com.
....		Pfd........................	Com.
....		Pfd........................	Com.

FORM 29. A FINANCIAL STATEMENT FORM (front)

If any of the officers or directors have other business connections or interests, name here. Als[o] list here the approximate worth of the indorsers or guarantors of your notes, aside from thei[r] interest in this business..
....
....

PROFIT AND LOSS STATEMENT FOR PERIOD BEGINNING....................................., 19........
AND ENDING........................., 19...........

Gross Sales ....
   Less Returns ....
   Less Discounts and Allowances.........................
Net Sales ....
   Inventory at Beginning of Period............, 19..........
   Purchases ....
   Labor ....
   Depreciation ....
   Other Manufacturing Expense ....

   Less—Inventory at End of Period............, 19..........
Cost of Sales..
Gross Profit ....
Salaries of Officers.......................................
Bad Debts Charged Off or Reserves Set Up...................
Other Expenses ....

Other Income ....
Net Profit or Loss...

Reconciliation of Surplus..................................
Surplus at Beginning of Period...................., 19..........
Add Net Profit or Loss (as above listed)...................
Adjustments (give explanation on line below)...............
Explanation : ....
Dividends Paid ....
Balance of Surplus (as per statement above)...............

Are your books periodically examined and audited by an independent accountant?..........................
Name and address...Date of last audit..........................
Do you maintain a full set of books of account?..(*)......................
To and including what year have your tax returns been approved by the U. S. Internal Revenu[e]
   Bureau? ....
Are any adjustments pending?...

We hereby authorize our accountants, banks, trade, and other creditors to supply you with suc[h] information as you may request. Your representative is hereby authorized to make examina[tion] of any or all of our books of account and all our records at any time.

All the foregoing statements, figures, details, and comments are truly and accurately tran[s]scribed from the books of account mentioned above (*) and represent our actual financia[l] condition on the date of the statement set forth above. This statement and all its details i[s] to be considered applicable and continuing until we advise the Institute National Bank an[d] Trust Company that there has been an impairment of our capital or reduction in our surplus[.] Such notice is to be given whether further application for credit is made or not.

All the foregoing information is intimately known to the undersigned. The foregoing state-ment has been carefully read, both printed and written parts, by the undersigned and is hereby represented to be true in every particular by the undersigned for the purpose of having the same relied upon in extending credit to us.
Name of corporation...
Date signed   Signed by (give title)...
.........................., 19...........   Signed by (give title)...

STATE OF   } ss.
COUNTY OF

....being duly sworn, on oath deposes and says
that he is the...of.. ; that he knows
the contents of the foregoing statement by him subscribed as such..................................., and that
he subscribed the same on behalf of said..., and that
said statement is true in substance and in fact to the best of deponent's knowledge and belief.
Subscribed and sworn to before me this........day of..............., 19...... ....
....
                          Notary Public

FORM 29. A FINANCIAL STATEMENT FORM (reverse side)

ications, known as trade journals, contain useful information in
their respective fields. Much information also is found in newspapers and magazines. In many instances pertinent information is
clipped and lodged in the credit files. Often trade journals and
financial publications are required reading on the part of loaning
officers and members of the credit department.

The Credit File

Over the years the credit files are the repositories of the bank's
experience with its borrowing customers. All the information
concerning a borrower that the bank has developed and accumulated during its dealings with the customer is chronologically
recorded in the credit files. The bank's credit files, if properly
prepared and kept, provide the loaning officers with much of the
information needed for making sound judgments concerning
loan applications.

Since the file is, in effect, the history of an account, the maintenance of the file is an important departmental activity. The
credit files may be withdrawn from the department only by
authorized persons, because much of the information in them is of
a confidential nature.

Credit files and their contents are reasonably uniform among
banks. The first section contains the various memoranda inserted
in the file from time to time by the officer handling the account
and by the credit department. The second section contains one or
more of the latest financial statements of the company bound to
the bank's comparative statement form. The third section contains
the correspondence with other banks and business concerns relative to the borrower, together with up-to-date reports from
agencies. In some banks, the records relating to average balances,
borrowings, interest rates, and the like are part of the credit file,
while in other banks these records are kept elsewhere in the credit
department.

CREDIT WORK IN BANKS OF DIFFERENT SIZES

The size of the bank naturally controls the loan volume to a
very large extent. The smaller the bank the smaller is the loan
volume; the larger the bank the greater is the loan volume. The

volume of credit work, in its turn, determines the number of officers and employees assigned to the various phases of the work.

The Small Bank

Although the volume of credit work in a small bank may not be enough to require the full time of even one individual, the usual investigations and other credit duties must be adequately performed. One officer, charged with the responsibility for loans, may not only handle all loan applications, but with the part time assistance of other employees may also handle credit inquiries and the other work requiring a full time credit department in a larger bank. The method used by the small bank is the one best suited to the bank's needs, but as in every other phase of banking it must be a method that covers the essentials of good banking.

The Medium Sized Bank

In medium sized banks it is usual to find a junior officer acting as manager of the credit department. He handles special credit investigations and general correspondence; the special correspondence is answered by the loaning officers. With the aid of a limited number of credit department employees, possibly two or three at most, the various duties of the credit department are performed under his supervision. Work is rotated as the need presents itself. Hence, all the members of the department are familiar with and capable of performing all the various phases of the work and the duties of the credit department.

The Large Bank

Just as the large bank because of the volume of its loan tends to create loaning officers who become specialists in certain industries and their loan problems, in the same way the credit department of the large bank develops employees who become specialists in certain duties of the credit department.

Chart 5 illustrates the organization of the credit department of a certain large bank, which is more or less typical of all large banks. This chart shows the division of credit work and the department personnel necessary to perform it.

The department consists of three officers and sixty employees. The vice president has overall charge and supervision of the de-

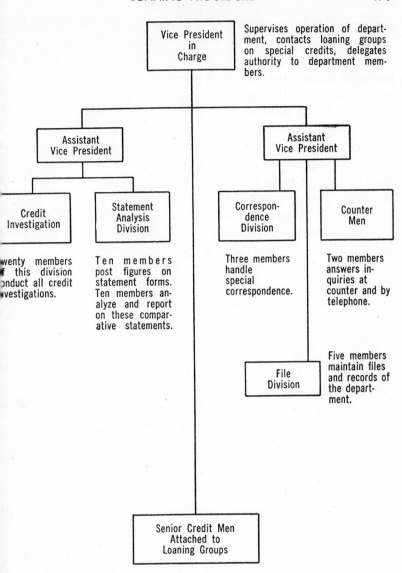

Vice President in Charge — Supervises operation of department, contacts loaning groups on special credits, delegates authority to department members.

Credit Investigation — Twenty members of this division conduct all credit investigations.

Statement Analysis Division — Ten members post figures on statement forms. Ten members analyze and report on these comparative statements.

Correspondence Division — Three members handle special correspondence.

Counter Men — Two members answers inquiries at counter and by telephone.

File Division — Five members maintain files and records of the department.

Senior Credit Men Attached to Loaning Groups — Ten men, each working directly with a loaning group, handle group credit correspondence, revision, reports, and prepare maturity schedule for consideration of loaning officers ten days prior to due dates.

CHART 5. ORGANIZATION OF THE CREDIT DEPARTMENT

partment. He is responsible for all contacts with the various loan
ing groups on special credit problems arising from loans handled
by any particular group. He holds the supreme authority on any
problems arising out of the department's work. The two junior
officers are responsible for directing the activity within the department and for so dividing the work that it is performed accurately
thoroughly, and promptly.

The credit investigation division, consisting of twenty em
ployees, conducts all credit investigations. It checks with other
banks and with trade references by mail, telephone, and persona
interview. It also summarizes information obtained from mercan
tile reports, newspapers, and financial publications. This division
has the responsibility of maintaining complete and current infor
mation about borrowers and prospective borrowers.

The statement analysis division has a force of twenty employee
who record and analyze all financial statements received from bor
rowing customers. Ten members of this group have wide account
ing experience and are thoroughly familiar with the bank'
methods in the classification of the items that appear on the
financial statement that is being posted on the comparative state
ment sheet. The other ten members are specialists in the
interpretation of significant items appearing on the statement
They analyze the figures carefully and prepare reports emphasizing
the important features of the financial statements.

Ten senior credit men are assigned to the loaning groups. It i
their duty to work with the loaning divisions on correspondenc
and reports. They assist in reviewing loans already on the bank'
books by preparing for the loaning groups all the records in con
nection with these loans, approximately two weeks before they ar
due. These senior credit men are considered to be in training fo
positions as junior officers in the loaning groups.

The correspondence division consists of three members, selecte
for their knowledge and ability in answering special inquirie
Correspondence that cannot be handled in the regular way by th
credit investigation division is referred to the correspondence div
sion.

The credit files are handled by the file division consisting of fiv
clerks who have the responsibility of properly filing all informa
tion received. The safekeeping of the credit files is the respons

bility of the file division; they can permit access only to authorized persons. They must know where every credit file is at all times so that it may be produced immediately when needed.

Lastly, there are two counter men who handle inquiries from customers and others when made either by telephone or at the counter.

Loans to Individuals

Loans granted to business and corporations, that is, to commercial enterprises that are operated for a profit are often referred to as *commercial loans*. In addition to making loans to business firms, many banks, however, also make loans to individuals who are employed by others at a fixed wage or salary. It can safely be said that our high standard of living in America is, to a very great extent, the result of the ability of the American people to use and enjoy a multitude of consumer articles. People take possession of these articles at once and pay for them later. The personal loan permits the customer to use the article while he is paying for it.

At first, banks would grant a loan to an individual only for a few purposes, such as the payment of medical or dental bills or tuition fees. As the banks gained experience with this type of loan, however, the purposes for borrowing that were acceptable to them increased in number. Purchases of all kinds of household appliances, such as gas ranges, refrigerators, vacuum cleaners, and television sets, are now financed by banks. It is now accepted practice to finance for individuals purchases of automobiles and swimming pools or to finance the remodeling of a room or part of a house. Insurance premiums of various kinds, furniture, and air conditioners, all may be purchased by individuals and paid for over a period of time. A form of application for a loan to purchase an automobile is illustrated in Form 30.

As the uses of this form of borrowing grew the name or classification given to this type of loan changed from personal loans to consumer loans to time sales loans. Nevertheless whatever name is used, it refers to loans made to individuals repayable in equal monthly instalments over periods of time ranging from twelve to thirty-six months. Personal loans have proven to be extremely attractive business to the banks, particularly to the metropolitan

CREDIT APPLICATION

AUTOMOBILE LOAN

Office _____

App. No. _____

Date _____

TO: THE INSTITUTE NATIONAL BANK

List dealer's name and address, or state purpose of loan: _____

New or used	Year	Make	Model	Serial No.	Motor No.

Car will be garaged at: _____

Name in which car will be registered: _____

	Private	Public	Parked on Street

Address: _____
City: _____

To be used for business ☐
Business and pleasure ☐

License No. and State _____

Drivers License No. _____

Trade-In (year, make, model) _____

Print name _____ Your age _____ Wife's name _____

Home address _____ How long _____ Phone no. _____

Landlord and address _____ Rent per month $ _____

Former address _____ How long _____ No. of dependents _____

Employer _____ Address _____

How long _____ Position _____ Name of Supervisor _____ Badge No. _____ Income $ _____ Week ☐ Month ☐

Former employer and address _____ How long _____

Wife's employer or other Income _____ $ _____ Week ☐ Month ☐

Name of your bank _____ Branch _____ Savings ☐ Special checking ☐
Loan ☐ Regular checking ☐

Do you own your home? _____ Do you own a car? _____ If you owe money on either, list below:

174

List all instalment accounts and debts you owe and places where you have used credit:

Name	Address	Purpose	Balance Due	Monthly Payments	Amount Overdue

Name of nearest relative not living with you:

Name	Address	Relationship

INCOME		FIXED EXPENSES	
Employment or business	$ _____ per ____	Rent or mortgage	$ _____ per ____
Wife's employment	$ _____ per ____	Automobile	$ _____ per ____
Other (list source)	$ _____ per ____	All other	$ _____ per ____
Total	$ _____ per ____	Total	$ _____ per ____

You are hereby authorized and directed to pay out of the proceeds of the loan, if and when made, the following amounts to companies and/or persons listed.

Name	Address	Amount
		$ _____
		$ _____
		$ _____

Draft status: classification _____   Veteran ☐   Reserve ☐   National Guard ☐

You are authorized to obtain such information as you may require concerning the statements made in the foregoing application, which are certified to be true and correct.

Due date preferred _____

Send mail to: Home ☐   Business ☐

_____
Signature

_____
Signature

Car inspection report attached, if not, why?

(Over)

Form 1146 4-54

175

FORM 30. APPLICATION FOR AN AUTOMOBILE LOAN (front)

WORK SHEET

INSURANCE

Agent's or broker's name _____

Address _____ Phone _____

Territory: Philadelphia ☐
            Suburban ☐
            New Jersey ☐

Driver classification   1 ☐   2 ☐   3 ☐

Age of car _____ Months

Insurance coverage _____ Months

   Fire & theft $ _____

   Comprehensive $ _____

   $ _____ Ded. coll. $ _____

   P.L. & P. damage $ _____

Total premium _____

Coverage confirmed by _____ Date _____

   By telephone ☐   By letter ☐

Low book _____ $ _____

Max. advance _____ $ _____

LOAN COMPUTATION

Cost of car $ _____

   Radio $ _____

   Heater $ _____

Total cash selling price $ _____

Trade-in allowance $ _____

Cash downpayment $ _____

Deduct: Total downpayment $ _____

   Unpaid balance due dealer $ _____

Add: Cost of insurance _____

Fees: $ _____

   $ _____

   $ _____

Balance to be financed $ _____

Interest charge $ _____

Amount of note $ _____

Terms: _____ Mos. _____ Payments @ _____

   Payment @ _____

176

FORM 30. APPLICATION FOR AN AUTOMOBILE LOAN (reverse side)

banks, since in large population centers it is possible to develop a large volume of loans. The large city banks have established entire departments to handle this business. The departments are staffed with loaning officers and personnel who are expert in this type of lending. These departments are complete and self-sufficient, since they do their own interviewing, investigating, disbursing, bookkeeping, and collecting. It is usual to find a large portion of the loan portfolio of metropolitan banks represented by time payment loans.

A more or less standard form of loan application is used in conjunction with the interview when the customer seeks the loan. The bank is particularly interested in obtaining information concerning the applicant's record of employment, salary, number of dependents, and real estate owned. Also pertinent to the application is the amount of money the applicant owes and his repayment record on previous loans. The information given by the borrower in filling out his application form is verified by the investigative section of the department, usually by telephone. If all the information received by the bank is satisfactory, the loan is either granted or rejected on the basis of the bank's judgment as to whether the applicant can safely devote the required amount of his income to making the monthly payments necessary to repay the loan within the specified time.

Since it is essential for the safety of the loan that the bank have accurate information concerning the applicant's obligations, methods have been devised to obtain this information. In a large eastern city, the consumer credit departments of all the banks doing a personal loan business created a central information agency. The banks listed with the agency all the personal loans then outstanding on their books, and as new applications for loans came to the member banks, the applicants were cleared through the agency. As loans were repaid, borrowing experiences were created and made available to the member banks. This agency has been in operation for twenty-six years; in its files are over seven hundred fifty thousand names, representing five hundred thousand active borrowers. Every five years inactive names are weeded from the files. The work of this agency has been of invaluable aid to installment credit departments of the banks in this city by making available previous loaning experiences and by preventing "overloaning," that is, it informs the bank processing the application of any existing bank loans the applicant may have. In this same city the banks work in close cooperation with department stores, specialty stores, and shops which have a similar agency for the immediate benefit of their own group. In this way the banks get information about charge accounts held by these stores and budget sales made by them. Banks in other large cities have similar agencies which they have created for the same purposes.

To eliminate the repeated handling of loans and economically to record payments as they are received, most banks give the borrower a coupon book, which contains detachable coupons equal in number to the total number of payments to be made on the loan. This book contains the borrower's name, his address, and the number of his account. As each payment is made, the stub and the coupon are stamped by the bank; the borrower retains the stamp stub as his receipt for the payment made. A coupon from a typical coupon book is illustrated in Form 31. On this type of

FORM 31. COUPON FROM AN INSTALMENT LOAN COUPON BOOK

loan the gross return to the bank is larger than the gross return on commercial loans, since it is customary to collect the interest in advance for the full period of the loan, even though repayment is made on a monthly instalment basis.

Personal loans have immeasurably increased the number of people who now have bank contacts which they ordinarily would not have. The personal loan department has been greatly aided in its development and in turn has greatly helped develop another bank service, namely the personalized or no-balance type of checking account.

Many of the Chapters of the American Institute of Banking now offer complete courses, using the Institute text Instalment Credit.

Questions Based on Chapter XI

1. What primary responsibility rests upon the loaning officers of a bank?
2. Discuss the principal duties of the credit department.
3. Name the principal sources of information available to the credit department in its work of investigation.
4. What are credit agency reports?
5. What is a credit file? What information does it contain?

Questions for Investigation

1. Who performs duties of the credit department in your bank?
2. How are credit inquiries handled in your bank?
3. Describe the organization of the loaning staff in your bank.

CHAPTER XII

LOAN PROCESSING

The Purposes of This Chapter:

1. To delineate the steps in the making of a loan.
2. To discuss briefly the loan and discount department.

IN A NARROW and restricted sense, from the viewpoint of the bank, a good loan is one that is repaid in full as to both principal and interest in accordance with the terms originally agreed upon by the borrower and the bank. The making of a good loan does not result from the application of some magical formula by the loaning officer. On the contrary, it results when that officer makes a complete and comprehensive investigation of all the facts presented to him. It results when he has learned by study and experience the meaning of the various assets and liabilities of the borrower and their relationship to each other. It results when he applies the experience gained through the years in the handling of all kinds and classes of loans. In addition to all these factors, a good loan results when the loaning officer approaches each application from a common sense viewpoint and backs his judgment with a thorough knowledge of the economic climate at the moment. Now we are ready to follow a hypothetical loan application through all the steps of its processing as shown in Chart 6.

The Interview

The Carbonation Manufacturing and Supply Company has been banking with your bank for the past three years. During this time the company has never requested any loan accommodation. Now, for the first time, they seek credit and are directed to a loaning officer. In the interview it develops that the company has, for the past eleven years, been engaged in the manufacturing business. Approximately eighty per cent of their sales are to wholesalers and jobbers of equipment, the remainder of their sales are made to retail or direct users of their product. The

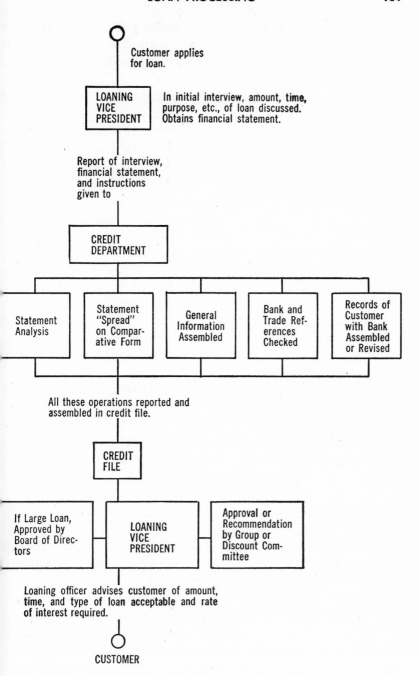

CHART 6. PROCESS OF MAKING A LOAN

company founder and president revealed that prior to opening an account with your bank, the company did its banking with the Institute Trust Company, which had extended credit to the company on several occasions.

The company has received an order for two thousand units of their product from a nationally known chain of stores. Partial deliveries will be permitted as the units are manufactured, and payments will be made thirty days after each delivery. The company president produced the order for inspection and requested a loan of $5,000 in order to buy materials to be used in the manufacture of the units. Further discussion develops the following facts: it will take thirty days to get all the materials and parts necessary, and when the company goes into production it can turn out fifty units daily.

THE CREDIT DEPARTMENT

Upon completion of the interview, the loaning officer sent to the credit department a memorandum of the interview and a financial statement of the company, together with instructions to check with the former bank of account, with the trade references, and with the bank's own records.

Statement analysis division: The financial statement presented by the applicant was "spread" on the comparative statement form; when analyzed, the division reported that the company had a satisfactory current position but that a somewhat frozen condition existed with regard to plant and equipment. The company earned reasonable profits during the year.

Investigative division: The investigative division contacted the Institute Trust Company and was advised by them that the company had maintained a satisfactory account with them for about eight years. They had granted loans on several occasions, and these advances had been repaid in accordance with their terms. The Institute Trust Company confirmed the statement, made by the company president during the interview, that the company had changed its bank when it moved into a larger building located conveniently near your bank.

Trade references were also contacted by telephone, and they reported satisfactory relations with the applicant, giving figures relating to the highest credit extended and the terms of sale in each instance. One of the firms reported occasional slowness, running to ten days, in meeting bills. However, they continue to sell to the company, and no bills are past due at the present time.

The credit agency report states that the company is a family-owned corporation, the father and two sons being the officers and stockholders of the company. The father founded the company eleven years ago, after having been employed in similar enterprises for a number of years. The background of the individuals is without blemish, and the company has never been the subject of a lawsuit or lien. Nor is there any record of bankruptcy or judgments against the company.

The bank's own records: Upon checking the bank's own records, the investigative section finds that the account is a satisfactory one, showing a profit to the bank every month with few exceptions. During the three years that the company has maintained an account there has been only one occasion on which a check has been dishonored because of uncollected funds.

All the information obtained by the various divisions of the credit department is assembled and recorded in the credit file and the file is turned over to the loaning officer. On the basis of the favorable information developed by the credit department, on the basis of the company's record of having successfully produced its product for eleven years, and on the basis of the order that the company holds from a company of known financial worth, the loaning officer decided to grant the loan on a ninety day note, with the privilege of reducing the note by fifty per cent at maturity and renewing the balance for an additional thirty days. The maturities granted were determined on the basis of the borrower's estimate, as stated in the original interview, concerning how long it takes to manufacture, deliver, and collect on the order received. The officials of the company are notified of the bank's decision; the proper promissory note is prepared. It is signed by the authorized officers of the company. On being initialed by the loaning officer, the note goes to the loan and discount department.

THE LOAN AND DISCOUNT DEPARTMENT

The loan and discount department does not have the authority to grant loans, that authority rests solely with the loaning officers.

Authorization of the loan is usually indicated on the note itself by the initials of the loaning officer. The officer also makes a notation as to the rate of interest to be charged. Upon the loan and discount department rests the responsibility for the physical protection of the notes and for the protection of the rights of the bank. To protect the rights of the bank, the department must properly present the notes when and where they are due and give notice to indorsers or guarantors when their liability becomes active. These responsibilities entail the following six well defined duties:

1. The safekeeping of notes representing loans
2. The proper presentation of notes when due
3. The calculation and collection of interest and other charges
4. The maintenance of accurate loan records
5. The safekeeping of collateral securing loans
6. The maintenance of adequate collateral.

The two duties last mentioned are discussed in Chapter X; the remaining four duties are briefly discussed in this chapter.

Safekeeping Duties

The protection of notes against loss or misuse is an important responsibility of the loan and discount department. When it is remembered that the note is the primary evidence of debt held by the bank (and in many instances the only evidence) this duty becomes doubly important. All notes are filed in steel cabinets and in many cases kept in the vault at all times. Even if it is the practice to keep notes in the loan and discount cage during the day, the notes are under the control of the manager of the department and can be withdrawn from the department only by authorized officers.

Presentment Duties

The place of payment is usually stated in a note, and the note must be presented at that place during business hours on the date it is due. If the place of payment is the bank itself, proper presentment is a simple matter. However, if presentment is at a place other than the bank, it is the department's responsibility to have the note presented for payment at the place designated in the note.

Calculation of Interest

Interest is the sum paid by the borrower for the use of money. Banks frequently discount notes, that is, deduct the interest from the total amount of the loan at the time the loan is made. In other cases interest is billed to the borrower and collected each month after it becomes due. Most states regulate by law the maximum interest rate that banks may charge on loans. The responsibility for calculating and collecting interest rests with the loan and discount department.

Loan Records

The records kept by the loan and discount department are characterized by their *completeness* and *permanency*. Long after the transactions have been completed, the bank may have to produce proof of them. For this proof the bank may have to depend on the records of loans made and repaid, of collateral received and returned, and of proper presentation of notes.

In the loan and discount department, the purposes of bookkeeping and accounting are (1) to provide a daily record of the work of the department, (2) to record the total liabilities of borrowers, and (3) to list the due dates of all notes and acceptances. The principal bookkeeping records of the department are the discount register, the liability ledger, and the maturity tickler. These three records represent the minimum records required for accounting and bookkeeping operations in loan and discount work. In a small bank where the loan volume is limited only these three records may be kept, since supplementary or memorandum records are not necessary. It is essential, therefore, that all loan records be complete and accurate.

The Discount Register

Each transaction on its occurrence is entered in the discount register, a book of original entry. This daily record of transactions provides the means for balancing the operations of the loan and discount department with other departments of the bank and for reconciling the new position of the department with its position on the preceding day. The total effect of loans made, loans paid, and interest collected is reflected each day in the balancing of the work of the department. In addition the discount register contains all the information required for the preparation of the other principal records of the department—the liability ledger and the maturity tickler. It is not unusual, however, for these latter records to be prepared from the notes themselves. A discount register is illustrated in Form 32.

The Liability Ledger

The liability ledger is also a permanent record used by the department. It can be compared to the individual ledgers used by the bookkeeping department for recording deposits, checks paid, and balances outstanding. The liability ledger has a separate sheet for each borrowing customer; on this sheet each loan transaction is recorded, together with its effect on the total owed by that borrower. The ledger also discloses whether (1) borrowings are on a secured or on an unsecured basis, (2) the balance owed is a combination of both types of loans, and (3) there are indorsers or guarantors. The ledger also records the type of collateral pledged with relation to secured loans.

The Maturity Tickler

The loan and discount department is responsible for the presentation of all notes and acceptances in its possession when and where they are due. Therefore, it must maintain a third record, the maturity tickler. This record is usually prepared in duplicate. The first copy of the maturity tickler card is filed according to the date on which the note matures. This file is used by the department as an additional check (additional to the notes themselves) on the notes falling due. It also acts as a check against the misfiling of notes. The second copy of the maturity tickler card is filed in a separate file arranged in such a way that the card appears ten days before the due date. It is then mailed to the customer to notify him that his note will be due and payable at the place designated in the note and upon the maturity date established when the loan was granted. Out-of-town notes are given to the collection department with full instructions. Notes payable locally are presented by messengers at the designated place. A maturity tickler is illustrated in Form 33.

DISCOUNT REGISTER

NUMBER	DATE	MAKER	COLLATERAL OR INDORSER	PAYABLE AT	DATE OF NOTE	TIME	DATE DUE	AMOUNT OF NOTE		RATE	INTEREST	NET PROCEEDS
								SECURED	UNSECURED			

FORM 32. DISCOUNT REGISTER

NUMBER	MAKER	PAYABLE AT	AMOUNT PAID	DATE PAID

MATURITY TICKLER
Unsecured
*Due Date*_____

FORM 33. MATURITY TICKLER

Questions Based on Chapter XII

1. What permanent records are used by the loan and discount department?
2. What is a maturity tickler?
3. How is interest on loans calculated?
4. How does the loan and discount department perform the duty of proper presentment of notes?

Questions for Investigation

1. Does your bank have both a loan and discount department and a collateral department?
2. What supplementary records are maintained by the loan and discount department of your bank?

CHAPTER XIII

COLLECTION SERVICES

The Purposes of This Chapter:

1. To show how collection services differ from other banking services.
2. To list the principal kinds of collection items.
3. To explain the collection operation.
4. To consider collection department accounting.
5. To describe the facilities provided by the Federal Reserve System for the collection of items.

IF YOU had recently moved from another city and wished to transfer the balance of your savings account from the distant city to a local bank, you would take your savings passbook and a draft on the bank you formerly used to the local bank. The local bank would give you a receipt for your passbook and the draft; it would mail them to the distant bank, asking that the balance of your account be sent to the local bank. When these funds were received the local bank would credit your account with the amount, but it might charge you a small fee for its *collection service.*

Assume that a broker bought a carload of potatoes for cash and that he sold them to a merchant in a distant city. To get his payment, the broker takes to his local bank a draft on the merchant together with the bill of lading covering the carload of potatoes. The local bank mails these documents to a correspondent bank in the merchant's city, requesting the correspondent bank to present them to the merchant (the buyer of the potatoes). The buyer pays the correspondent bank and obtains the bill of lading, which he takes to the transportation company to obtain the potatoes. Meanwhile, the correspondent bank remits the payment made by the merchant to the local bank. Finally, the local bank credits the payment (less the costs of making the collection) to the account of the broker. These examples illustrate typical kinds of collection services. The items thus handled are known as *collection items.*

189

By contrast, when you deposit a check in your bank, the teller either enters the amount in your passbook or issues a receipt. Your account is credited that same day, and the check is then forwarded for payment as a *cash item* rather than as a collection item. Cash items are explained more fully in Chapter IV.

Definitions of Collection

The words *collect* and *collection* may be defined in several ways, depending upon the concept of the person who is using the word. To the average person, the word collect means to demand and receive payment of a debt. This payment is ordinarily made in cash or by check.

In the broadest use of the terms, all types of checks, drafts, notes, coupons, bonds, and the like which pass through a bank are subjected to a collection process.

In the narrowest sense, the terms collect or collection are applied by a bank only to those items that the bank sends for collection, as indicated in the previous illustrations, and for which credit is given only when the items are paid. In this chapter, we are not concerned with the great volume of items that flow smoothly through the ordinary channels of a bank. We shall rather examine those types of items that require special procedures for their collection. For the sake of clarity, the following definitions are applied in this chapter.

1. A cash item is any item which the bank has cashed or for which the bank has given immediate credit and which will be paid or returned routinely through the normal banking channels.

2. A collection item is any item which the bank has received for collection and for which settlement with the owner will be made only when the item is finally paid or returned.

Collection Items Contrasted with Cash Items

Most items handled by a bank are checks. These checks are simple to handle. They are payable immediately and unconditionally, no other documents are attached to them, and instructions for handling them are uniform. Consequently, ordinary checks and other similar cash items can be processed readily, in batches or groups using mass production devices and techniques. The cost of processing them is low per item.

By contrast, collection items are relatively complicated to handle. They may be payable on demand or at a date in the future. Payment may depend on the happening of a certain event. Collection items are frequently accompanied by attached documents that vary in type. Each item requires special instructions. Such items, therefore, cannot be handled in batches; each item must receive individual attention. The cost of handling these items is much higher.

Another sharp contrast between the collection operation and other banking operations is found in the accounting methods used. In other operations most of the items are recorded merely by making an entry of the amount on a list or sheet; the entry is made by using an adding or bookkeeping machine. For example, when the customer deposits checks, the bank proves the deposit, thus balancing with the customer. Then the receiving teller should balance with the clearings, the transit, and the bookkeeping operations. The instant that cash, checks, or deposit tickets are "listed" or "posted" they become a part either of the bank's assets or of its liabilities and are accounted for automatically in balancing the books on that day.

After a receipt is issued by the bank to the customer for items left for collection, however, the items *do not go through any other department of the bank*; they *are sent directly* to a correspondent bank or to other collection agencies. Collection items are *not* credited to customer's accounts until *they are actually paid*. They do not appear either as liabilities to customers or as bank assets during the collection period; they are recorded only in the collection records or in supplementary or parallel records kept for control or audit purposes. For this reason collection records differ from those used in other operations. In our study of collection operations we must keep in mind this difference between the method of accounting for cash items and for collection items.

The instructions applicable to cash items may be contrasted with those applicable to collection items. The instructions applicable to various types of cash items are fairly standardized. Hence no instructions are needed for processing items within the bank because the items are merely enroute through other operations under which they are collected. The instructions governing clearing house items are so uniform that it is unnecessary to include them with checks sent to a clearing house. Even transit items are subject to uniform instructions that apply to the entire group, except when individual items are stamped or tagged for special treatment. The forms and records used even for transit items are, therefore, comparatively simple.

For collection items, however, there are many variations in the forms both in their number and in their application. What processes are used by the individual bank depend on the nature of its collection arrangements, on the extent of the collection operation, and on the kinds of collections handled. Although in most cases collection work can be handled effectively by the use of established forms, occasionally there are collections which require instructions so intricate or so unusual that the regular forms must be supplemented with special letters of instruction, written by the department manager or by an officer of the bank.

Kinds of Collection Items

Collection items vary greatly and are subject to instructions, ranging from those that are simple to those that are extremely technical and complex. It is this latitude of operation that makes collection services so convenient for the handling of any transaction that requires individual attention. Collection items may be classified in any one of several ways, that is, by destination, by type of item, by supporting documents, or by date of payment. The principal kinds of collection items are:

1. Classified as to destination:
   a. city collections—payable locally
   b. country collections—payable out-of-town
   c. foreign collections, export—payable outside of the United States
   d. foreign collections, import—originating outside of the United States
2. Classified as to type of item:
   a. drafts
      (1) to be paid upon presentment
      (2) to be paid after a designated number of days
      (3) to be paid upon the arrival of goods
      (4) with bills of lading attached, to be surrendered only upon payment of the drafts

(5) with bills of lading attached, to be surrendered upon acceptance of the drafts
(6) with warehouse receipts attached, to be surrendered only upon payment of the drafts
(7) with warehouse receipts attached, to be surrendered upon acceptance of the drafts
(8) with other documents attached, to be surrendered upon payment or acceptance of the drafts
(9) with securities attached, to be delivered upon payment of the drafts
  b. notes or acceptances
  c. real estate contracts or mortgages
  d. stock certificates
  e. bonds and coupons
3. Classified as to supporting documents:
  a. clean items—no documents attached
  b. bills of lading
  c. warehouse receipts
  d. securities
  e. mortgages or deeds
  f. savings passbooks
  g. miscellaneous
4. Classified as to date of payment:
  a. demand or sight—payable upon presentment
  b. payable upon arrival of goods
  c. single due date—payable after a designated number of days
  d. serial notes—separate notes bearing different due dates
  e. instalment notes or contracts—payable at specified intervals.

Certain other items may also be handled by the collection department (1) cash items, returned checks, and other non-collection items and (2) utility bill collections, or other special or unusual collection services. Many of the terms mentioned in this list are defined and explained elsewhere in the text.

THE COURSE OF A COLLECTION ITEM

A typical collection item might be handled in the following manner. The ABC Company in Institute City, dealers in automotive supplies, orders auto parts from various manufacturers or distributors throughout the country. The manufacturer, for example, delivers the parts to a transportation company and receives a negotiable bill of lading. This bill of lading and a draft drawn on the ABC Company are taken by the manufacturer to his bank, which sends them for collection to the Institute City Bank. This bank in turn notifies the ABC Company of the arrival of the draft and the bill of lading. The ABC Company pays the Institute City Bank and is given the bill of lading and the draft, stamped "paid." The bill of lading is presented to the transportation company, which then releases the auto parts to the ABC Company. The course of a collection item through the bank is presented graphically in Chart 7; the distribution of the proceeds of a collection item is presented graphically in Chart 8.

The Institute Bank follows this routine in executing the transaction. An acknowledgment is returned to the sending bank stating that the collection item has been received. A collection register form is prepared. The necessary steps are taken to collect the item, and the proceeds are sent to the drawer of the collection item. The flow chart, Chart 9, illustrates the collection procedure.

COLLECTION FORMS AND THEIR USES

Despite the variety of collection items, certain standardized forms are generally used in the collection process. The forms facilitate the handling of collection items and thus reduce operating costs.

Issuance of Receipts

A receipt or acknowledgment is given for each item entered for collection. For a collection item presented at the window, the teller may either issue a receipt on a form provided by the bank, or in banks using the method, he may enter the amount of the item in the collection section of the customer's passbook and initial this entry. The receipt is in triplicate form; on it the teller describes the collection item and lists the instructions. The original of this form is given to the customer as his receipt; one copy serves as the collection division's record and the other as the auditing department's record. These receipt forms are numbered consecutively and all must be accounted for.

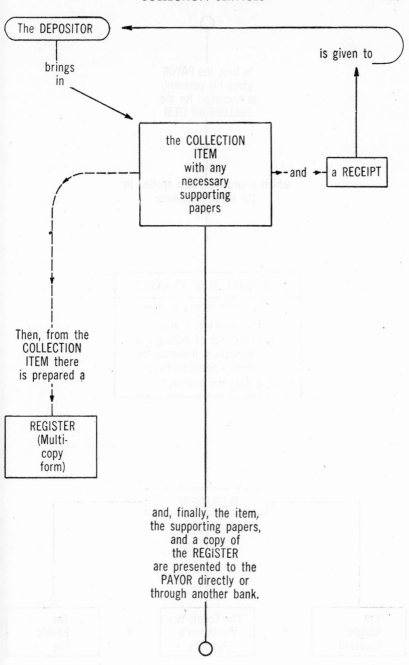

The DEPOSITOR

brings
in

is given to

the COLLECTION
ITEM
with any
necessary
supporting
papers

and → a RECEIPT

Then, from the
COLLECTION
ITEM there
is prepared a

REGISTER
(Multi-
copy
form)

and, finally, the item,
the supporting papers,
and a copy of
the REGISTER
are presented to the
PAYOR directly or
through another bank.

CHART 7. GRAPHIC PRESENTATION OF THE COURSE OF A COLLECTION
ITEM TO THE PAYOR

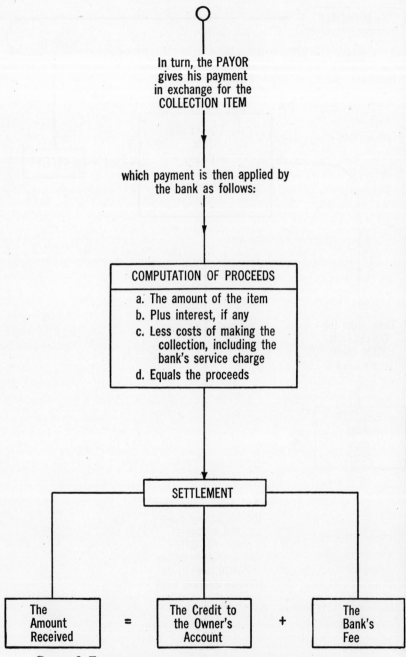

In turn, the PAYOR
gives his payment
in exchange for the
COLLECTION ITEM

which payment is then applied by
the bank as follows:

COMPUTATION OF PROCEEDS

a. The amount of the item
b. Plus interest, if any
c. Less costs of making the
   collection, including the
   bank's service charge
d. Equals the proceeds

SETTLEMENT

| The Amount Received | = | The Credit to the Owner's Account | + | The Bank's Fee |

CHART 8. FLOW CHART ILLUSTRATING THE DISTRIBUTION OF THE
PROCEEDS OF A COLLECTION ITEM

If the collection item is received from an out-of-town bank, an acknowledgment form (which is generally produced as a copy of the bank's multicopy register form) is mailed as a receipt.

Issuance of Acknowledgments

Some banks enclose an acknowledgment request form with collections that they send to their correspondent banks, particularly when the item is not collectable immediately. This form is stamped and initialed by some member of the collection division of the receiving bank and is mailed back to the sending bank. It serves not only as a receipt, but also as a notice that the item is in process of collection.

The Importance of Instructions

An important principle of collection procedure is that *complete instructions* must be obtained regarding every collection item, whether it is received from a customer at the window or through the mail and whether it is to be collected locally or in some other town or city. The item, of course, contains such information as the amount, the due date, the name of the maker, and the place of payment. The customer gives instructions regarding (1) the delivery of documents, (2) the collection of interest in case of delayed payment, (3) telegraphic advice, (4) whether the item is subject to protest, and (5) whether his account is to be credited or a cashier's check is to be issued in payment. Although general rules and regulations apply to all collection items, the treatment which is desired for items of the same kind varies so widely that definite instructions should be furnished with each item presented for collection.

In the case of cash items, a customer gives instructions subject to the rules of the bank simply by depositing the items. It is understood that if there is to be any variation from regular and routine handling of cash items, the customer must inform the bank exactly what he wishes.

Most of the collection items received by mail come from other banks, and full instructions are given in the accompanying letters.

After complete instructions have been obtained and a receipt has been issued to the customer for a collection item, a record of the item is prepared. The type of record prepared depends upon the kind of item received by the bank.

COLLECTION OPERATION

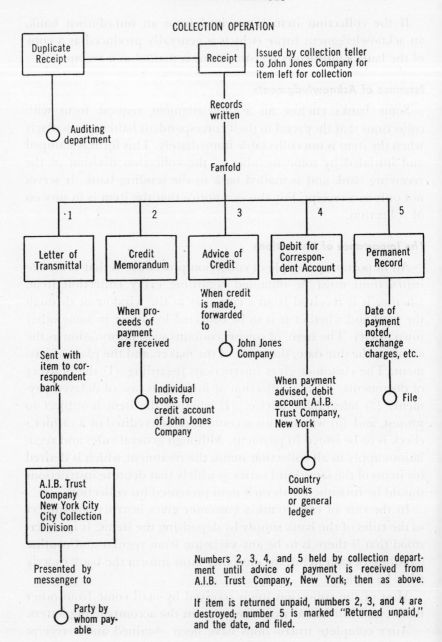

Duplicate Receipt

Receipt — Issued by collection teller to John Jones Company for item left for collection

Records written

Auditing department

Fanfold

1 — Letter of Transmittal

2 — Credit Memorandum

3 — Advice of Credit

4 — Debit for Correspondent Account

5 — Permanent Record

Sent with item to correspondent bank

When proceeds of payment are received

When credit is made, forwarded to John Jones Company

When payment advised, debit account A.I.B. Trust Company, New York

Date of payment noted, exchange charges, etc.

File

A.I.B. Trust Company New York City City Collection Division

Individual books for credit account of John Jones Company

Country books or general ledger

Presented by messenger to

Party by whom payable

Numbers 2, 3, 4, and 5 held by collection department until advice of payment is received from A.I.B. Trust Company, New York; then as above.

If item is returned unpaid, numbers 2, 3, and 4 are destroyed; number 5 is marked "Returned unpaid," and the date, and filed.

CHART 9. COLLECTION OPERATION

The Collection Register Form

The collection register form is so arranged that the information is duplicated on from two to seven carbon copies, thus giving a complete set of records for various purposes. Form 34 is an illustration of a typical multicopy form of collection record. A complete description of the collection item and full instructions are entered on the form, and it is then carefully checked.

The original of the multicopy form serves as the *letter of transmittal* (collection letter), to accompany the item.

The first copy is the bank's *permanent file* record. It contains such information as the maturity date, a notation showing the documents attached, the amount of the item, the name of the bank through which the collection is being sent, special instructions, and the name of the customer who left the item for collection. Each collection item is given an identifying number, which is used in correspondence and in telegraphic communication if necessary. The number is also useful in the audit procedure of the bank, since each collection can be checked by this means. Thus a complete record of the item is provided from the time it enters the department until it is disposed of by payment or return. While the item is outstanding, this copy is kept in a current or open file. When the item has been paid or returned, this copy is transferred to a closed file. All necessary details, such as paid or returned, and the computation of the proceeds are entered on this copy of the collection register form.

The second copy is often used as an *audit* form and is sent to the auditing department to aid in verification.

The third copy may be used as a *tracer,* if a prompt report on the disposition of the collection is not received. The form is so worded that it may be sent to the collecting bank as a tracer without further processing.

The fourth copy is the *debit* form, which is used for charging the correspondent bank's account on receipt of *an advice* (a notice) that the correspondent bank has obtained payment and has credited the sending bank's account. This arrangement frequently is used when one bank carries an account with another bank. If payment is made by check, the debit copy of the form is not needed and may be discarded.

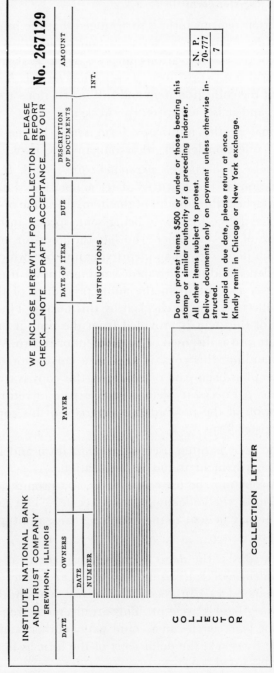

FORM 34. COLLECTION REGISTER FORM (Multiple copy)

The fifth copy of the form is designed to be used as a *credit memorandum* (credit ticket) after the item has been paid. This copy serves the same purpose as a deposit ticket in crediting the customer's account.

The sixth copy serves as an *advice of credit* and is sent to the customer at the time the proceeds of the collection are credited to his account.

There may also be a seventh copy which is used as a *customer cross file* copy and is filed alphabetically according to the name of the customer.

COLLECTION PROCEDURE

The transmittal letter, the collection item, and attached documents, if any, are mailed to a correspondent bank in the vicinity of the payor to effect collection of the item, as indicated in Chart 7.

Should an item remain outstanding longer than is ordinarily required to collect it, the tracer copy is mailed to the collecting bank to determine the cause of the delay. This tracer is returned by the correspondent bank with an appropriate explanation written thereon.

In due course payment is made or the item is returned. Payment may be made either in the form of an official check, in the form of a draft of the collecting bank, or in the form of an advice of credit to the sending bank's account in the collecting bank.

Deductions are made to compensate the collecting bank and the sending bank for out-of-pocket expenses incurred by them for postage, insurance, and the like, and a service charge is made to compensate the banks for their work in effecting collection of the item.

The sending bank then turns over the proceeds to its customer. Such payment may be made by a credit to the customer's account or by issuance of an official check, depending on the arrangement between the customer and the bank at the time that the item was entered for collection. Payment in cash is not customary.

If the collection item is returned unpaid, the customer's account is not credited, but the customer must pay a nominal charge to recover costs of collection and must also pay the bank's service charge. The unpaid item is returned to the customer.

Acceptability of Payment

The responsibility of the collection division may be readily understood when the basic difference between cash items and collection items is considered. Although a cash item is credited to the customer's account immediately, it is stated in the rules and regulations to which the customer agrees that the credit for a cash item is subject to final payment. A collection item, however, is not credited to the customer's account until it has been paid, and the customer is entitled to regard the payment as final. Therefore, the collection division must be certain that it does not report the item as paid or give credit for a collection item until payment has been received.

Technically, in accepting payment in any form other than cash, the collection division assumes responsibility for the final payment of the check (or other instrument) accepted in lieu of cash. In actual practice, therefore, only cash or certified checks are accepted, unless the credit standing of the payer is unquestioned. This requirement is usually stated on any notice sent to the payer of the item. Occasionally, when the party on whom an item is drawn is a company or an individual known to be of unquestioned responsibility, the bank, knowing that the risk is negligible, accepts an uncertified check in payment.

Collection Charges

Service charges for handling collection items vary with the kinds of transactions.

Drafts with securities attached are handled at rates based on the par value of the securities. Other transactions are handled at flat rates or at rates determined by agreement. In addition, a charge is made to recover any out-of-pocket expense incurred, such as postage and insurance.

In view of the ease with which customers can expedite many kinds of transactions by taking advantage of the collection division's services, the fees charged are moderate, and all types of customers make frequent use of these services.

Country Collection Items

The collection process varies somewhat according to the type of item being handled.

Country collection items are those payable outside the local area, that is, outside the area that can be reached easily by messenger service. In effecting country collections, extensive use is made of correspondent bank facilities. Extensive use also is made of the "Noncash Collection Service" maintained by the Federal Reserve System. This service is described at the end of this chapter. Furthermore, some items are sent to banks that are not correspondents of the sending bank; in such cases the collecting bank may be asked to make payment by means of a draft payable in the sending bank's city or some large center.

The collection procedure previously described applies particularly to country collection items.

City Collection Items

City collection items are items payable locally—within such a distance that the customer can come to the bank or can be reached by messengers (collectors). Most of these items (such as sight drafts) are payable on demand. Others (such as time drafts, notes, and acceptances which are due within a few days) are entered for collection in advance of the due dates, in order that ample time may be had to send out the usual notices to drawees, makers, or acceptors. Items immediately due and items due within a short time are usually called *regular* collections. Most city collections are received from out-of-town customers, particularly correspondent banks.

The method of processing city collection items is quite similar to the method of processing country collection items. Each such item is entered on a fanfold form similar to the country collection form. The original of the city collection form serves as a permanent record, one copy serves as an audit copy, a second as an acknowledgment of the collection, a third is used as a notice (to notify the drawee or maker that the bank is holding an item drawn on him which he must pay or refuse to pay), a fourth copy serves as a ticket for entering credit to the customer's account, and a fifth copy is an advice of credit.

The maturity tickler is another form commonly used in the city collection division. It is filed by due date and serves as a reminder of the maturity date of a time item.

In most cases, the payers of city collection items present their payment to the bank and at that time receive the items drawn on them. Sometimes collection items are delivered to customers by a messenger who receives acceptable payment or, if so authorized by the bank, takes a receipt.

Instalment or File Collections

In addition to "regular" collections (those payable at once), there are items that call for a series of collections to be made at stated intervals, generally monthly, for a period of a year or more. These continuing collections (real estate notes or contracts, equipment sales, and similar items) are called *instalment* or *file* collections.

In handling instalment collections, the following procedure is typical. The collection teller satisfies himself that it is proper for the bank to accept the item and that the item is in order. He then writes a receipt describing the item and stating the instructions to be followed. The receipt is signed by the bank and the customer. The original is given to the customer and the bank retains the copy. Some banks also keep a second copy for the bank's auditor.

A ledger sheet is prepared showing all necessary details. A simple tickler card is also prepared and filed under the next due date. A cross file card is typed to be filed alphabetically by *owners*. The ledger sheets are filed alphabetically by *payers*, as are also the notes.

A fee may be charged on acceptance of the file collection, and an additional small fee is usually charged for each payment handled.

About a week before the due date of the payment, a notice is sent to the payer showing the amount to be paid, that is, the principal, interest, and the taxes or insurance, if any. Some banks send a second notice as a reminder if payment is not received on the due date.

When payment is made, a receipt is given to the payer. Credit is given and an advice is sent to the owner. The collection division's record is posted to show the payment made.

Coupons and Bonds

Coupons and bonds are another type of item requiring special attention because of their small size and ease of negotiation.

Coupons and bonds of the United States Government, some municipalities, and a few others which the bank knows will be paid promptly, are credited to customers' accounts when deposited and are handled as cash items. Other bonds and coupons are customarily accepted by a bank for collection.

Since instructions applying to the collection of bonds and coupons are quite standardized, simple forms can be used to record them. A coupon envelope is used to hold the coupons. Such an envelope is illustrated in Form 35. This envelope is often attached to the bonds, too. A collection letter is prepared to accompany the coupons or bonds. The letter contains enough information to identify each item, that is, the *name* of the owner, description of the coupons, and the amount. A copy of this letter is retained by the bank.

```
                        No.....................

  Item.................................................    Payable at...............................

  ...............................due..................@................    $.................................

  ...............................due..................@................    $.................................

  ...............................due..................@................    $.................................

  Remarks...............................................  Total..........$.................................

                  INSTITUTE STATE BANK
                      Atlanta, Georgia
           Please Report Non-Payment Immediately
```

FORM 35. COUPON ENVELOPE

The coupon collection clerk ordinarily collects bonds and coupons for the various divisions of the bank such as the trust division, the loan division, and the investment division, in addition to those handled for customers. Coupon collection work is subject to extreme peaks of volume, as many bond and coupon maturities tend to fall on the same day, such as the first or last day of a quarter year.

Collection By Messenger

In some cases customers come to the bank to pick up and pay for collection items.

Other collection items are presented to other banks or business houses by bank messengers, who are given specific instructions by the bank as to what to do with each item. For example, it is common practice to require a certified check upon delivery of a collection item. If an uncertified check is to be accepted in payment, or if an item is to be left on receipt, definite instructions regarding variations from the general rule are always given to the messenger. Documents are not ordinarily left without receiving payment, although sometimes the bank is willing to assume the responsibility for leaving the documents on receipt or for waiving the action required by the attached draft.

A messenger should never permit any document to go out of his possession, nor permit any modification of instructions, without receiving authority to do so from his supervisor. He should never make an exception on his own responsibility. The bank must give definite instructions to its messengers, to assure correct handling of items.

The bank often informs the paying or accepting party by telephone that an item will be presented by a messenger. This courtesy enables the party to consult his records and have the check drawn, in case of payment, before the arrival of the messenger or to be prepared to refuse action on the item. Thus, the party to whom the item is to be presented is accommodated by the advance notice, and the messenger's work is expedited.

Collection Accounting

Collection work consists of receiving an item for collection from one party, presenting the item to the payer, receiving payment, crediting the owner's account, and receiving compensation for the services.

Such transactions necessitate several entries: (1) credits to customers' accounts, arising from final payment of collection items, (2) debits to customers' accounts, arising from collection items drawn against these accounts, (3) debits to accounts of correspondent banks, upon receipt of payment advices for collections forwarded to them, (4) credits to other bank divisions, arising from payment of items which they have entered for collection, (5) credits to the bank's income account for its fee, and (6) entries to offset any expenses which the bank has incurred in making the collection.

When final payment of a collection item is received, the bank determines the costs of collection and its service charge. It enters these amounts on the multicopy form pertaining to the collection item, deducts the amounts from the total amount of the collection items, and brings down the net amount. The various parts of the multicopy form are then distributed.

A copy of the credit ticket is used by the bookkeeper in crediting the net proceeds of the collection to the individual customer's account.

A second copy of the credit ticket is given to the general bookkeeper for crediting the proper income accounts on the general books.

Debits to customers' accounts arise from payment by the bank of collection items (drafts, notes, or acceptances) owed by customers, which they have authorized the bank to pay from their accounts.

Debits to accounts of correspondent banks arise upon authorizations by the other banks (advices) to charge their accounts for collections which have been paid and forwarded to them.

Other divisions of the bank also enter items for collection. These items are handled by the collection division in the same manner as collections for customers. Thus, the trust division enters bonds and coupons for collection; the loan and discount division enters acceptances and notes payable at other banks locally or in other centers. A collection receipt is given to the division entering items for collection, and that division is credited with the proceeds when the payment is received. Each day the totals of credits sent to the various divisions are verified by the means of interdepartmental proofs.

Audit of collections may be accomplished in several ways: (1) by requiring more than one person to handle each item, (2) by maintaining a running audit through the use of numbered forms, and (3) by frequent verification to determine that selected items are properly handled and accounted for.

Collection Work in Banks of Different Sizes

In some banks the volume of collections is so small that the work is performed by a teller in addition to his regular assignment. Suitable forms and records are used, the collection routine following much the same procedure as that previously described. In such banks, items are usually sent to city correspondents for collection or credit, or they are routed through the noncash collection division of the Federal Reserve bank or branch.

Somewhat larger banks generally employ a full-time teller for handling country, city, and coupon collections. He may also handle the issuing of certificates of deposit, cashier's checks, and bank drafts, and he may perform other miscellaneous functions not related to collection work.

In the largest banks, work is divided into country, city, and coupon collection divisions, with subdivisions if necessary, to handle country collection items, regular and instalment city collections, and coupons as previously described. Sometimes the city collection division is so named because it handles notes, drafts, and acceptances that are payable locally.

FEDERAL RESERVE NONCASH COLLECTION SERVICE

The noncash collection service of the Federal Reserve banks operates in much the same way as does the collection department of a large commercial bank. Multiple forms, maturity ticklers, tracers, acknowledgments, and advices of credit are used as in commercial banks.

Although the Federal Reserve noncash collection service is not so extensive as the par check collection service, the statistics compiled by the Federal Reserve System reveal that it is nevertheless of importance. Exclusive of the collection of United States Government bond coupons, the total number of noncash items (or pieces) handled annually is in excess of fifteen million, representing a dollar total in excess of five billion dollars.

Each Federal Reserve bank publishes and sends to its member and nonmember participating banks an operating letter or circular in which are listed the rules and regulations governing the collection of noncash items. Two sections from a circular appear.

Definition of Noncash Items

As used in Regulation G and in this operating letter, the term "noncash items" means any items of the following classes when payable in any Federal Reserve district:[1]

(1) Maturing notes, acceptances, bankers' acceptances, certificates of deposit, bills of exchange, and drafts with or without securities, bills of lading, or other documents attached;

(2) Drafts and orders on savings deposits with passbooks attached;

(3) Checks, drafts, and other cash items which have previously been dishonored or on which special advice of payment or dishonor is required (any check, draft, or other item which is normally handled as a cash item will not be handled as a noncash item unless special conditions require that this be done, and the Federal Reserve bank will decide whether such special conditions exist);

(4) Maturing bonds and coupons (other than obligations of the United States and its agencies which are redeemed by Federal Reserve banks as fiscal agents);

(5) State and municipal warrants, including both orders to pay addressed to officers of states and political subdivisions thereof and any special or general obligations of states and political subdivisions thereof;

(6) All other evidences of indebtedness and orders to pay, except checks and bank drafts handled under the provisions of Regulation J and checks and bank drafts drawn on or payable by a nonmember bank which cannot be collected at par in funds acceptable to the Federal Reserve bank of the district in which said nonmember bank is located. (Checks and bank drafts drawn on or payable by a nonmember bank which cannot be collected at par in funds acceptable to the Federal Reserve bank of the district in which such nonmember bank is located, and which may not be received under the terms of Regulation J, likewise may not be received as noncash items under the terms of Regulation G and this operating letter.)

---

[1] For the purposes of this operating letter Alaska, Hawaii, Puerto Rico, and any dependency, insular possession or part of the United States, outside the continental U.S. shall be deemed to be in or of such Federal Reserve bank district as the Board of Governors may designate.

This bank will not accept noncash items payable in the same city in which the sending bank is located.

Questions Based on Chapter XIII

1. What are the duties of the collection division?
2. What subdivisions are often found in collection divisions?
3. What is the difference between a cash item, a cash collection, and a noncash collection item?
4. In the handling of collection items, why is it necessary to adopt methods different from those used in the handling of cash items?
5. How does the cost of handling a collection item compare with the cost of handling a cash item?
6. What part do messengers play in collection division duties?
7. How does the accounting procedure of the collection division differ from that commonly used in other divisions of the bank?
8. What special forms and records are frequently used in collection division work?
9. How does the coupon collection division operate?
10. What advantages do customers obtain by using the facilities of the collection division?
11. Describe the noncash collection services of the Federal Reserve banks.

Questions for Investigation

1. Is there a separate collection division in your bank?
2. If so, does it have divisions similar to those mentioned in this chapter?
3. What forms are used in your bank's collection division?
4. What types of collections are most commonly handled by the collection division in your bank?
5. Approximately how many collections does your bank's collection division handle each month.

CHAPTER XIV

TRUST SERVICES

The Purposes of This Chapter:
1. To outline the trust services rendered by banks.
2. To explain briefly the organization and operation of a trust department.
3. To suggest some of the underlying principles of trust institutions.
4. To call attention to some of the safeguards for trust property and some of the distinctive features of the trust business.

ONE OF the highly specialized activities of banks is that of rendering trust services. Originally a trust company was founded to render trust services, it probably did not engage in the accepting of deposits and the lending of money. In contrast, a bank was founded to deal with money and did not engage in trust business. Today neither a trust company nor a bank necessarily engages in one activity to the exclusion of the other. Throughout this chapter the term bank, unless otherwise indicated, includes trust companies; and the term trust institution includes both banks and trust companies. The department of the bank through which trust services are rendered is known as the trust department, and the activity itself is known as trust business. Not all banks have trust departments; as a matter of fact, only about one bank out of five has a trust department.

In this country banks have been engaged in the trust business since 1822. Although national banks have been authorized to render trust services only since 1913, nevertheless at the present time they constitute more than half of the nearly three thousand banks with trust departments.

TRUST SERVICES RENDERED BY BANKS

The trust services rendered by banks fall under three main heads: (1) settling estates, (2) administering trusts and guardianships, and (3) performing agencies.

Settling Estates

Perhaps the best known of all trust services rendered by banks is that of settling the estates of deceased persons. When a property owner dies, his estate must be administered according to law; that is, his assets must be inventoried, his debts paid, death taxes, if any, must be paid, and the assets remaining must be distributed.

An individual has the privilege of making a will and naming the individual or the bank he desires to have settle his estate, or he may not leave a will. If he leaves a valid will, he is said to die *testate;* if he leaves no will, he dies *intestate.*

The one named in the will to settle the estate is known as the executor of the will. While the court actually makes the appointment of the executor, it will appoint the executor named in the will unless there are compelling reasons why it should not do so. If the executor named in the will is unable or refuses to serve or if the court declines to appoint the executor named in the will, the court must appoint some other individual or bank to settle the estate in accordance with the terms of the will. The individual or bank so appointed is known as the *administrator with the will annexed.*

If a property owner dies without having made a valid will, the court appoints an individual or a bank to settle his estate; the one so appointed is known as the *administrator* of the estate. When a property owner names (or the court appoints) more than one executor, the two or more executors are known as *co-executors.* Similarly, when the court appoints two or more administrators, as frequently happens, they are known as *co-administrators.*

The duties of a bank as executor or as administrator are substantially the same—namely, to take possession of the property of the deceased person, to pay the debts and other charges against his estate, and to distribute the remainder of the property as directed by the will if there is a will, or as provided by law if there is no will. An administrator has only the power given him by the law; an executor has the same power plus any additional powers the will may confer upon him.

Administering Trusts and Guardianships

The second main branch of trust services rendered by banks is that of administering trusts and guardianships.

1. Trusts. A trust exists when one person holds the legal title to property and another person is entitled to the benefits derived from the property. The person holding the legal title is known as the *trustee;* the person who derives the benefits from the property is known as the *beneficiary.* It sometimes is said that the trustee is the legal owner while the beneficiary is the equitable or beneficial owner of the property.

A trust may be created by will, by agreement, by declaration, or by order of court; or it may be an outgrowth of the relationship between the parties. A property owner may by will leave property in trust, or by agreement or by declaration he may place the property in trust with an individual or a bank. One who makes a will is known as a *testator;* one who creates a trust by agreement or by declaration is called a *settlor* or trustor. The court may order a property owner to place property in trust, as sometimes happens in divorce proceedings.

A trust may arise by operation of law because of the relationship between the parties. For example, a guardian buys real property with his ward's money but takes the title in his own name. The guardian holds the property in trust for the ward. This trust is known as a *resulting trust,* that is, resulting from the relationship between the guardian and the ward.

The best known types of trusts administered by banks are (a) trusts under wills, often called testamentary trusts, (b) living trusts, (c) insurance trusts, (d) corporate trusts, (e) employees' trusts, (f) institutional trusts, and (g) community trusts.

A trust under will, or a testamentary trust, is created when a testator leaves property in trust to be held and administered for the benefit of some one other than the trustee.

The following is an example of a *living trust.* Smith, during his lifetime, transfers and delivers property to the X Bank in trust directing the bank to pay the income to Smith during his lifetime, and after his death to pay the income to his wife during her lifetime, and after her death to pay over the principal to their children.

An *insurance trust* is created if Smith has his life insurance policies made payable to the X Bank as trustee, directing the bank to pay the income to Smith's wife during her lifetime and after her death to distribute the principal among their children. If Smith himself continues to pay the premiums, the trust is known as an *unfunded insurance trust*. If Smith places other property in the trust and the rents, dividends, or interest from that property is sufficient to pay the insurance premiums and if Smith then charges the trustee with the duty of paying the premiums, the trust is known as a *funded insurance trust*.

The White Company, desiring to borrow money by the sale of its bonds, conveys property to the X Bank in trust to secure its bonds. It thus establishes a *corporate trust*.

Employees' trusts are typified by the *pension trust* and by the *profit sharing trust*. Under the terms of a pension trust the employer (and possibly his employees) contributes under a predetermined plan, to a fund that is held in trust by the X Bank for the purpose of purchasing annuity contracts or for the making of payments direct to employees as they reach retirement age. If the employees make payments into the fund, the pension plan is know as a *contributory plan* and the trust is a *contributory pension trust;* if the employees make no payments to the fund, then the plan and the trust are *non-contributory*.

Under the terms of a *profit sharing trust* an employer contributes, under a predetermined plan, a portion of his profits (or all his profits over a given figure) to a fund which is held in trust by the X Bank for the purpose of distributing the accumulated contributions and any income therefrom to the employees of the business upon their reaching retirement age, or upon the termination of the plan.

Y College transfers cash, stocks, and bonds, which it owns outright, to the X Bank to hold in trust, invest, manage, and administer for the benefit of the college. Such a trust is an *institutional trust*.

Various citizens of a community may, from time to time during their lifetime, or by will, leave property with the X Bank to hold in trust and administer under the terms of a single declaration of trust for the benefit of the people of the community as directed by a committee of citizens. The trust is known as a *community trust*.

2. Guardianships. Banks serve as guardians of the property of minors and incompetents. In most states a minor is a person under twenty-one years of age. An incompetent is a person who, whatever

his age may be, is regarded by the law as being incapable of taking care of his property. Incompetents include not only persons who are mentally defective but also, in some states, those who are unable for other reasons to manage their own property. Although the guardian may be recommended by the family, the appointment is made by the court.

There are two main types of guardians; one of the property and the other of the person. The guardian of the property takes care of the property of the ward, while the guardian of the person takes care of the person of the ward—that is, looks after his home, his food, his clothing, his schooling, and the like. The guardian of the person stands in the place of a parent as far as the upbringing or protection of the ward is concerned. A bank seldom is appointed guardian of the person, but frequently, where there is no guardian of the person, the bank as guardian of the property performs many personal services for the ward.

In some states the individual or bank appointed by the court to take care of the property of an incompetent is known as a committee or conservator rather than a guardian.

Since World War I a special type of guardianship has developed, known as veteran's guardianship; that is, the guardianship of funds paid by the government through the Veterans Administration to or for the use of minor or incompetent veterans, or minor or incompetent dependents or beneficiaries of veterans. These veterans' guardianships are governed by the general state laws applicable to all guardianships and, in addition, by special laws adopted by all the states at the recommendation of the Veterans Administration which are applicable only to the estates of wards of the Veterans Administration. The number of such guardianships increased substantially after World War II, and events since that time have occasioned a continued growth in the number of such guardianships handled by banks.

The usual duties of a bank as trustee and as guardian are similar fundamentally. These duties are to receive, hold, and manage property for the benefit of the beneficiary in the case of a trust and for the benefit of the ward in the case of a guardianship. However, the duties of the bank as trustee cover a much wider range than its duties as guardian. As trustee, the work of the bank may range all the way from the mere holding of title to

the property, with no active duties whatever, to management of
the property as full and complete as that of an absolute owner.
In the case of a guardianship, whether of a minor or of an incompetent, the duties of the bank are for the most part defined
and limited by law.

Performing Agencies

The third main branch of trust services rendered by banks is
that of performing agencies for individuals, for business organizations, for institutions, for other fiduciaries, and for units of
government.

The term agent, in its broadest sense, includes any person who
acts for another by the authority of the latter. The person granting
the authority is known as the *principal,* the person receiving the
authority as the *agent,* and the relationship as an *agency.* The
fundamental difference between a trust and an agency is that in
a trust the trustee has the legal title to all the property, but in an
agency the title to the property is in the principal.

Agencies performed for individuals. The chief types of agency
services rendered by banks for individuals are (1) safekeeping,
(2) custody, (3) management, and (4) escrow.

1. Safekeeping. As safekeeping agent, the bank receives, holds,
and delivers the property upon the order of the principal; it has
no other active duties.

2. Custodian. As custodian, the bank performs the duties of
a safekeeping agent and such other active duties as collecting and
paying out income and buying, selling, receiving, and delivering
securities on the order of the principal.

3. Managing. As managing agent, the bank performs all the
usual duties of a custodian; in addition, to the extent specified
in the agency agreement, it engages in the active management of
the property. For example, as managing agent of securities, the
bank may analyze and review the securities in the account and
may recommend changes in the investment; or in some cases it
may make changes on its own initiative. As managing agent of
real property, the bank may rent, lease, or in some cases operate
the property for the principal. For practical purposes the basic
difference between a custodian and a managing agent is that the
custodian waits for and carries out the orders of the principal,

whereas the managing agent makes recommendations as to and participates in the active management of the property.

4. Escrow. An agency service rendered for individuals less frequently than any of the three preceding services, although well known in some sections of the country, is that of acting as escrow agent. For example, Brown owns a house which White is ready to buy and pay for as soon as the title is clear. Brown executes a deed and delivers it to the X Bank. White pays over the purchase money to the X Bank. The bank is instructed to deliver the deed to White and the purchase money to Brown as soon as it receives a certificate of title from a designated attorney. This arrangement is known as an *escrow,* and the bank is known as the *escrow agent.* This service greatly facilitates real property transactions.

Agencies performed for business organizations. The chief agency services rendered by banks for business organizations are those of acting as (1) transfer agent, (2) registrar, (3) depositary, and (4) paying agent.

1. Transfer agent. As transfer agent, the bank serves as agent of the corporation in the transfer of its shares of stock and registered bonds from one owner to another. The bank as transfer agent is agent of the corporation and not of the stockholder or bondholder.

2. Registrar. As registrar, the bank keeps a record of the number of shares of stock issued and transferred in order to prevent an overissuance of the stock. A bank cannot properly serve as both transfer agent and registrar of the same stock. It sometimes is said that the bank as registrar is agent both of the corporation and of the stockholders.

3. Depositary. The bank serves as depositary in connection with corporate reorganizations and changes in the capital structure and in many other cases in which there is need for an impartial and trustworthy stakeholder to hold cash or securities while financial transactions are being worked out.

4. Paying agent or dividend disbursing agent. The bank frequently serves as the agent of the corporation for the payment of dividends on its stock and for the payment of interest on and principal of its bonds.

These, however, are only a few of the agency services which banks render for corporations. The performance of corporate agencies, in fact, constitutes a substantial part of the trust business of many large metropolitan trust institutions.

Agencies performed for institutions. To an increasing extent banks are serving as agents for endowed institutions in the custody and management of their endowment property. For example, Y College delivers a part or all of its endowment funds to the X Bank under an agreement by which the bank is to render the usual safekeeping and custodian services (those mentioned in this chapter), making purchases, sales, and deliveries as directed by Y College through its board or designated committee or officers. Going a step further, Y College may arrange with the X Bank to analyze and review the investments in its endowment and to recommend changes.

Still another type of institutional agency which apparently is growing in favor is that of agent for the treasurer of churches, schools, hospitals, and the like. In this capacity the bank keeps the records and does the bookkeeping and generally serves as a financial secretary.

Agencies performed for other fiduciaries. It frequently happens that individual executors, trustees, guardians, and conservators desire to obtain for the benefit of the estates or trusts which they are handling certain of the services which a bank offers its trust department customers. In such cases the individual fiduciary may employ the bank to act as his agent in connection with the administration of the estate or trust, delegating to the bank some one or more of the ministerial duties of the individual fiduciary, such as custody of securities, collection of income and principal, the making of disbursements directed by the fiduciary, the keeping of records of receipts and disbursements, and the reviewing of the investments of the estate or trust with the objective of making recommendations relative to the retention of disposition of such investments. The discretionary duties of the individual fiduciary cannot be delegated, and a bank cannot assume to perform such duties for an individual fiduciary. Through an arrangement of this sort an individual who has undertaken to act as a fiduciary may relieve himself of many of the burdensome features of his undertaking with the assurance that the duties he has delegated to the bank will have the attention of its trained specialists.

Agencies performed for units of government. Units of government, such as cities and counties, make use of trust services in connection with their financial transactions. These units of government find the services of banks useful in connection with pension funds for superannuated employees (such as teachers, policemen, and firemen) and in connection with their sinking funds and their bond issues. It is thought that service to units of government may become an increasingly important part of the trust business of banks.

The foregoing is only an illustrative and by no means a complete list of the trust services offered and rendered by banks. A complete list might include over fifty different services. But even more impressive than the number is the variety and adaptability of these services. Banks have trust services designed for the special needs of persons in the prime of life as well as the very young and the very old, of the strong as well as the weak, of active business men and women, of corporations as well as individuals, and of public institutions and units of government as well as individuals and private corporations. Trust services are adaptable to the needs of persons in all walks of life and are not restricted to the needs of special groups of persons or special types of enterprises or institutions.

ORGANIZATION OF THE TRUST DEPARTMENT

There are four essential steps in the organization of a trust department: (1) obtaining trust authority, (2) establishing a separate department for the conduct of the trust business, (3) designating a trust officer, and (4) creating a trust committee.

Trust Authority

In only a few states is a bank, simply by virtue of its being a bank, authorized to render trust services. In these few states the issuance of the charter to the bank carries with it authority to engage in trust business. But in the vast majority of states, the bank, although long established as a bank, must obtain from some government authority a special permit or license to open a trust department. If it is a national bank, it must obtain this permit from the Board of Governors of the Federal Reserve System. If it is a State bank, it must obtain the permit from the bank commissioner or banking board of the state or from some other designated state officer or board.

In many states a bank desiring to open a trust department must make a special deposit of securities with the state treasurer or with some other state officer to guarantee the faithful performance of its duties. In some states the capital requirements are greater for a bank with a trust department than for a bank without one.

Although there is little uniformity of detail in the special requirements imposed upon banks desiring to engage in the trust business, there is one general requirement that applies in nearly every state, namely, that a bank must obtain from the appropriate government agency, state or federal, special authority to engage in the trust business.

Trust Department

The regulation (Regulation F) of the Board of Governors of the Federal Reserve System under which national banks carry on their trust business provides that, before undertaking to act in a fiduciary capacity (that is, to render any of the trust services previously mentioned), a national bank must open a trust department which must be separate and apart from every other department of the bank. The laws of several states make substantially the same requirement of state banks.

Aside from regulation or statute, a bank engaging in the trust business should, as far as practicable, have a specially designated trust department with its own space, equipment, and records because it is essential that the property of the bank be kept separate from the property of its trust accounts and that the property of each trust account be kept separate from the property of every other trust account. Consequently, the physical separation of the banking and the trust business and the conduct of those two businesses in separate departments make it easier to avoid the mingling of the property of the bank and the property of its trust accounts.

Trust Officer

The first step in the organization of a trust department is the election of an officer to be the head of that department. The regulation governing national banks requires that the trust department shall be under the management and immediate supervision of an executive officer or officers qualified and competent to administer trusts. A bank cannot carry on a trust business without having a trust officer, in fact if not in name.

Trust Committee

By regulation, national banks are required to have the acceptance of all new accounts approved and the closing out of all trust accounts approved or ratified by the board or by a committee of capable and experienced officers or directors of the bank. They are required also to have the making, retention, or disposition of all trust investments approved by a trust investment committee of at least three members, who must be capable and experienced officers or directors.

OPERATION OF THE TRUST DEPARTMENT

The operation of a trust department requires five types of activities: (1) executive, (2) administrative, (3) operative, (4) service, and (5) business development. The layout, equipment, and staff of the trust department must be developed to meet the requirements of these activities.

UNDERLYING PRINCIPLES OF TRUST INSTITUTIONS

The underlying principles of trust institutions have been set forth clearly by the Trust Division of the American Bankers Association in "A Statement of Principles of Trust Institutions." At least four of these statements should be common knowledge to students of banking as well as to students of trust business.

The Duty to Exercise Care

It is the duty of a trustee, in administering the trust, to exercise the care a prudent man familiar with such matters would exercise as trustee of the property of others.

The usual standard of care applied to a trustee is that of a man of ordinary prudence administering his own property under similar circumstances. By following this principle, the trust institutions of the United States have raised the standard from that of a prudent man handling *his own* property to that of a prudent man handling *other people's* property. The practical difference between the two standards lies in the fact that a prudent man might be justified in taking chances with his own property which he would not be justified in taking with the property of others. The point here is that trust institutions have set for themselves a higher standard of care than even the law imposes.

The Duty to Keep Trust Property Separate

The properties of each trust should be kept separate from those of all other trusts and separate also from the properties of the trust institution itself.

This principle was mentioned in the discussion of the need for having the trust department separate and apart from the other departments of the bank. The legal penalty for the mingling of trust property with the property of the bank is that, if any loss to the beneficiaries results from such mingling, the bank itself must stand the loss, whereas if any profit results, the bank must account for it to the beneficiaries. The practical effect of this separation is that the fate of any one trust account is not involved in the fate of the bank or in the fate of any other trust account. The failure of the bank would not jeopardize the trust property; nor would the termination or depletion of any one trust account affect any other trust account.

The mingling of trust property with the property of the bank would inevitably lead to confusion and ultimately to loss. The mingling of the property of different trusts, other than that resulting from the operation of a duly authorized common trust fund or trust investment, should be neither permitted nor practiced by any trust institution.

The Duty to Exercise Skill

A trust institution should devote to its trust investments all the care and skill that it has or can reasonably acquire.

It is the phrase *can reasonably acquire* that is the main point in this principle. It may be taken for granted that a trust institution devotes to its trust investments and, in fact, to all its trust work all the skill that it has, or else it would not be living up to the standard of the prudent man. But should it go further and try to acquire

additional skill and apply its ever increasing skill to the execution
of its trust work? The trust institutions of the United States have
given an affirmative answer to this question.

Upon this principle of self-improvement are founded the trust
educational programs of the American Institute of Banking and
of The Stonier Graduate School of Banking, the internal training
courses of trust institutions, and every other educational effort of
banks. Among the graduate courses of the American Institute of
Banking are two courses in trusts. The Institute texts, Trust Department Services and Trust Department Organization, used in
the respective courses, are authoritative texts, discussing in detail
matters that can only be mentioned in this chapter.

The Duty To Avoid Self-Dealing

*A trustee should not have any personal financial interest, direct
or indirect, in the trust investments bought for or sold to the trust
of which it is trustee, and it should not purchase for itself any
securities or other property from any of its trusts.*

While this principle refers to trust investments only, it applies
with equal force to every other phase of trust administration. It
rules out any and all dealings between the bank and its trust
accounts known as self-dealing, that is, dealings between the directors or officers of the bank and its trust accounts.

EXAMINING AND AUDITING

The supervisory authorities not only issue regulations for the
conduct of trust business by the banks under their supervison but
also examine the trust departments from time to time through
specially designated and experienced trust examiners to see that
the regulations are being complied with and that the trust departments are being conducted in a manner that is both thoroughly
safe and proper.

For national banks, Regulation F of the Board of Governors of
the Federal Reserve System requires that a committee of directors,
exclusive of any active officers of the bank, shall, at least once during each period of twelve months, make suitable audits of the
trust department or cause suitable audits of such department to be
made by auditors responsible only to the board.

Physical Safeguards

The physical protection of tangible personal property, such as household furniture, silverware, glassware, books, and works of art, requires the trust institution to furnish the kind of storage, whether in vaults or in warehouses, that a prudent man would furnish for that kind of property. The physical protection of intangible personal property, such as certificates of stock, bonds, and notes, requires the trust institution to furnish vault space with the protective devices and facilities that are in common use by trust institutions. The storage and securities vaults are marvels of protective equipment.

DISTINCTIVE FEATURES OF TRUST BUSINESS

It may be worthwhile simply to list some of the qualities or qualifications of trust institutions that enable them, in a superior way, to serve the needs of people in connection with estates, trusts, guardianships, and agencies. Among these attributes are the following: continuous existence, continuous capacity, financial responsibility, specialization, collective information, group judgment, adaptability, accessibility, and government supervision. It is thought that these attributes constitute the basic response of trust institutions to the needs of people for trust service and therefore should be presented and emphasized in trust advertising and trust representation.

Questions Based on Chapter XIV

1. What kinds of trust services are rendered by banks?
2. Distinguish between (a) an executor and an administrator; (b) a testator and a settlor; (c) a trustee and a guardian; (d) a living trust and a testamentary trust.
3. What agency services are performed by banks (a) for individuals? (b) for business organizations? (c) for institutions? (d) for units of government?
4. What are the four essential steps in the organization of a trust department?
5. How does a bank obtain its authority to engage in the trust business?
6. Mention four fundamental principles of trust institutions.

7. Describe some of the safeguards for trust property.
8. Briefly explain the advantages of selecting a trust department of a bank or a trust company to act as trustee.

Questions for Investigation

1. Does your bank have a trust department?
2. If so, by what authority or authorities is it supervised?
3. Who is in charge of the department?
4. What trust services are most frequently used by individual customers of your bank?
5. What trust services are most often used by business customers of your bank?

CHAPTER XV

FOREIGN FINANCIAL SERVICES

The Purposes of This Chapter:

1. To point out the basic differences between domestic and foreign operations of a bank.
2. To list the principal services provided by a foreign department.
3. To describe the instruments and documents customarily used by foreign departments.
4. To comment on foreign department activities in the smaller bank.

THE PRECEDING chapters deal with domestic banking. There are significant differences between domestic and foreign operations. In the broad sense, domestic financing is concerned with the production, the movement, and the distribution of goods within the United States. In an equally broad sense, foreign department operations are primarily concerned with the movement of goods between the United States and a foreign country. In a domestic shipment, the goods pass directly from the seller to the buyer with a minimum of documents. In a foreign shipment of goods, documents and obligations move from the seller to the seller's bank, from seller's bank in one country to buyer's bank in another, and from buyer's bank to buyer. In a domestic movement of goods, the financing is done between the buyer and his bank and between the seller and his bank. In a foreign movement of goods, financing is based on title to the goods moving between the banks in the two countries and from seller to buyer. In the sketch, Chart 10, the difference between the domestic and foreign movement and financing of goods is illustrated.

Services Rendered By the Foreign Department

The function of a foreign department is to carry out the banking transactions necessary for the smooth conduct of foreign trade and commerce. Some transactions, frequently encountered in

226

foreign department operations, are listed in the following outline.

1. Services to importers
   a. Opening commercial letters of credit to finance the importation of foreign goods and commodities

USUAL DOMESTIC EXCHANGE OF GOODS

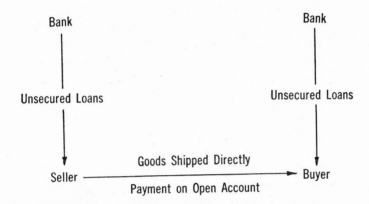

USUAL EXCHANGE OF GOODS IN FOREIGN TRADE

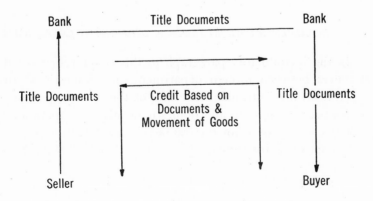

CHART 10. EXCHANGE OF GOODS IN DOMESTIC AND FOREIGN TRADE

    b. Selling foreign exchange necessary to pay for imported goods purchased in foreign currency

    c. Financing importers to enable them to carry imported goods between the time of payment and of their arrival in the United States and to provide subsequent storage, processing, sale, and collection of accounts receivable

2. Services to exporters

    a. Rendering reports on the credit standing of buyers in foreign countries

    b. Submitting reports on market conditions and import and exchange regulations abroad

    c. Collecting drafts drawn by American exporters on foreign importers

    d. Paying drafts drawn by American exporters under letters of credit of foreign or American banks and opened in their favor

    e. Advancing money against drafts for collection, or against letters of credit in favor of exporters

3. Services to travelers

    a. Selling foreign money, traveler's checks, and traveler's letters of credit

    b. Supplying letters of introduction to banks and other third parties abroad

(in addition, some banks conduct travel departments, in close association with their foreign departments, which look after travel matters of all kinds).

DOCUMENTS USED IN FOREIGN DEPARTMENT OPERATIONS

In the introductory paragraph to this chapter some of the differences between foreign department and domestic department operations are outlined. Since one of the most important differences between foreign and domestic department operations is the documents required for the transactions, some knowledge of these documents and instruments is essential. The following documents are those most frequently used.

1. The bill of exchange
2. The trust receipt
3. The warehouse receipt and delivery order

4. The bill of lading
5. The insurance policy or certificate
6. The letter of credit
7. The traveler's letter of credit and the traveler's check

The Bill of Exchange

A number of instruments which the domestic as well as the foreign banker meets in his daily work are bills of exchange, such as checks, drafts, and bankers' acceptances.

A typical bill of exchange, used in export collection work, is illustrated in Form 36.

First of Exchange

Second of Exchange

FORM 36. A TYPICAL BILL OF EXCHANGE

Bills of exchange may be payable at sight, at a specific number of days after sight, on a specific date, or a specific number of days after a given date. The time when a bill is payable is known as the tenor of a bill. In the process of sighting or accepting a bill, the drawee marks on the bill the word *Accepted,* the date, and signs it with the name of the firm and his authorized signature. The bill will sometimes be accepted and marked payable at a certain bank.

In foreign department work, bills of exchange are frequently prepared in duplicate or triplicate. Because the chief documents attached to bills of exchange, such as the bill of lading and the insurance policy or certificate, are generally prepared with several copies, it is usual to attach a bill of exchange to each complete set of documents. One copy is reserved in case the original goes astray in the mail.

The Trust Receipt

It is common practice for a foreign department to open a letter of credit covering the importation of a commodity and then, after taking possession of the shipping documents by payment of the accompanying draft, to release these documents on trust receipt to the customer. Thus the customer is enabled to make entry, to transport, to store (perhaps process), then to sell the commodity, to collect the account receivable, and to repay the bank. The credit line extended by a bank to an importer customarily includes a sum available for these trust receipt loans.

The trust receipt, which is also found in domestic transactions, enables the bank to retain title to the commodity (or the proceeds received from its sale) until certain requirements are met by the customer.

The Warehouse Receipt and Delivery Order

A warehouse receipt, issued by a warehouse, acknowledges possession of the goods or commodities shown and indicates the person for whose account the goods are held. The receipt may be either negotiable or non-negotiable in form. Deliveries against warehouse receipts are made either by presenting the properly indorsed negotiable receipt to the warehouse or, if the receipt is non-negotiable by a delivery order (letter authorizing delivery) signed by the person in whose name the warehouse receipt is issued. Banks generally find it easier to operate with a non-negotiable receipt, as it facilitates the handling of partial deliveries. Warehouse receipts are widely used as collateral in all types of commodity operations.

The Bill of Lading

Other than the bill of exchange, the document encountered most frequently in a foreign deparment is the bill of lading. The majority of letters of credit, which are issued, require a bill of lading in one form or another to be included among the documents. These bills of lading may be ocean bills of lading (the term is frequently abbreviated "bladings"), or rail, truck, or air bills of lading. Each of these has its special characteristics and a good knowledge of the bill of lading is a necessity for anyone working with documents in a foreign department. The ocean bill of lading is the type most frequently encountered. Its chief characteristics may be briefly summarized.

The *ocean bill of lading* (issued by the carrying steamship company or its agent) is also a receipt, a contract, and a title document. It is a receipt as it is only issued (or should only be issued) when the carrier has actual possession of the goods. It is a contract because the voluminous small print, rarely examined, states the obligation of the shipper and the carrier governing the transport of the goods in question. It is a title document because, dependent on the way it is made out, it either conveys a title, which can be assigned, or becomes a negotiable instrument, which passes by indorsement.

The Insurance Policy or Certificate

Another document generally found in sets of documents presented with bills of exchange, either for collection or under letters of credit, is the marine insurance policy or certificate. This policy protects the bank on advances it may make against goods shipped abroad, which are lost or destroyed en route.

The Letter of Credit

Commercial letters of credit are the most important instruments of a foreign department and may be classified as foreign or domestic. The only difference between the foreign and the domestic letter of credit is whether the transaction involves a foreign or a domestic shipment of goods. Only foreign transactions are discussed in this chapter, but in essence the considerations are the same in domestic transactions.

The use of the commercial letter of credit can best be explained by an example. Assume that an importer in Buenos Aires wishes to purchase pumps in this country. He gets in touch with the exporter in the United States, selects the type of pump he wishes to buy, and reaches an agreement with the exporter concerning the price and the terms of payment. If the exporter requires a letter of credit, the importer goes to his bank in Buenos Aires and arranges for the issuance of it in favor of the exporter.

Assuming that his bank follows customary American banking practice, the transaction would probably develop as follows: If the bank is satisfied with the credit standing of the importer, it asks him to complete an application for a letter of credit. In this document the importer asks the bank to open, by mail or by cable, a letter of credit in favor of the exporter for a stated maximum amount of money available by drafts drawn within a specified time, the drafts to be accompanied by specified documents pertaining to the shipment of the pumps, as agreed between the importer and the exporter. The bank also obtains from the importer an agreement, which sets forth the rights and obligations of the bank and the importer under the letter of credit. In some banks these two forms are combined into one.

When these formalities have been completed, the bank in Buenos Aires requests its correspondent bank in the United States, by letter or by cable, to open a letter of credit in favor of the exporter under the terms stipulated by the importer in his application for the letter of credit. Upon receipt of this letter or cable, the American bank notifies the exporter that the letter of credit has been opened in his favor and informs him of the documents that must accompany the draft at the time it is presented to the bank for cashing.

In due course the exporter makes the shipment and obtains negotiable bills of lading, a marine insurance policy or certificate, a certificate of origin, and such other documents as are required by the terms of the credit. The exporter then draws his draft on the

American bank designated in the credit and presents the draft to it together with the letter of credit and shipping documents. If the American bank finds that the draft and documents conform with the terms specified in the credit, it pays the draft and debits the account of the Argentine bank for a like amount. The bank then forwards the shipping documents to the Argentine bank. It may happen that at the time the American bank pays the relative draft, the Argentine bank does not have sufficient dollars in its account to cover such a payment and instead makes arrangements with the American bank to advance the necessary dollars. In this case, the Argentine bank would remit the dollars at a later date to the American bank to reimburse it for the relative payment. The American bank, of course, charges interest on the time such an advance is outstanding.

With a letter of credit the exporter has the assurance of the bank issuing the credit that, if the shipment is made according to the terms of the credit, he will receive payment for his merchandise. This advantage of the letter of credit is a valuable one to the exporter.

However, if a credit is issued only on the responsibility of a foreign bank, an exporter may feel that such assurance does not give him adequate protection. In such a case, the exporter may require a guaranty of payment of the letter of credit by an American bank. If such a guaranty is given, the letter of credit is known as a confirmed letter of credit. Alternatively, the American bank may be asked to issue its own irrevocable credit for account of the foreign bank, which has the same effect as confirmation.

The vast majority of letters of credit issued are irrevocable, that is, such credit cannot be amended or cancelled at any time without the consent of all parties concerned. Of course, such credits automatically expire at their date of expiration unless they are further extended by the issuing bank.

A revocable credit, however, is one that may be cancelled or modified at any time without notice even though shipment has been made and relative drafts have not been paid or negotiated.

A letter of credit should clearly state on its face whether it is irrevocable or revocable. When a letter of credit does not state that it is irrevocable it is presumed to be revocable. A commercial letter of credit covering imports is illustrated in Form 37.

THE INSTITUTE BANK
NEW YORK, N.Y., U.S.A.

John Streeter & Company

London, England

January 2, 1956

L/C No. 1813

Dear Sirs:

We hereby authorize you to draw on The Institute Bank, New York, N.Y., U.S.A., at ninety days after sight for any sum or sums not exceeding in total Fifty Thousand Dollars (U.S. $50,-000.00) for account of Benjamin Babcock & Company, New York, N.Y., for invoice cost of five thousand (5,000) tubs of butter to be shipped from London, England to New York, N.Y., C.I.F.

Your drafts must be accompanied by the following documents:

1. Invoices in duplicate
2. Consular invoice in duplicate
3. Insurance certificate in duplicate
4. Full set of Bills of Lading showing shipment consigned to the order of The Institute Bank, New York, N.Y., dated on or before April 1, 1956
5. Your letter stating advice of the drawing was sent direct to The Institute Bank, New York, N. Y.

The negotiating bank or banker must send one of each of the above documents direct to The Institute Bank, New York, and their certificate to this effect must accompany the draft together with the balance of the documents.

Each and every draft drawn under this credit must bear upon its face the clause "Drawn under Credit No. 1813 dated January 2, 1956 of The Institute Bank, New York, N.Y., U.S.A."

The amount of each draft negotiated and the date of negotiation must be indorsed on the reverse hereof by the negotiating bank.

Drafts must be drawn and negotiated on or before April 1, 1956.

We hereby agree with the drawers, indorsers, and bona fide holders of bills drawn and negotiated in compliance with the terms of this credit that said bills will be duly honored on presentation at The Institute Bank, New York, N. Y., U.S.A.

Respectfully yours,

The Institute Bank

by Richard Smith

Vice President

by John Franklin

Cashier

Form 37. Commercial letter of credit

234

The Traveler's Letter of Credit

The traveler's letter of credit, sometimes known as a circular letter of credit, requires that the traveler be paid amounts up to the sum indicated. It may be presented for payment to any of the foreign correspondents listed as paying agents of the issuing bank. Although traveler's letters of credit issued by an American bank are generally expressed in dollars, the currency of payment abroad is governed by local regulation as well as the wishes of the beneficiary (traveler). The purchaser of a traveler's letter of credit is given a formal letter of identification, over the issuing bank's authorized signature, introducing him to the paying banks and guaranteeing his signature as it appears on the letter of indentification. Sales of traveler's letters of credit are made either on a cash or credit basis, that is, guarantee of reimbursement for amounts drawn. To a considerable extent, traveler's letters of credit have been replaced by traveler's checks, due to the convenience of cashing the latter outside of banks.

Traveler's Checks

The traveler's check is a specialized form of negotiable instrument sold by banks and others, and is essentially the same as a cashier's check. It bears the signature of the person for whose use it is intended, affixed by him at the time of purchase. A space for a second signature of the holder is also provided, and indentification is accomplished by requiring the holder to affix his second signature in the presence of the person who is cashing the check.

Traveler's checks are the safest form of travel money. Because they bear a bank's guarantee of payment, they are readily cashed by banks, hotels, steamship agencies, department stores, and others to whom they may be presented by travelers. If a traveler's check is lost or stolen, the purchaser can notify the bank from which it was purchased to stop payment on the check. The purchaser can then obtain a refund within a reasonable time. One type of traveler's check is shown in Form 38.

Traveler's checks issued in this country are usually in denominations of $10, $20, $50, and $100 and they are negotiated in a foreign country at the prevailing rate of exchange for dollars in that market.

Similarly, traveler's checks issued in a foreign country are usually expressed in the currency of that country and, on being cashed in this country, are converted into dollars at the prevailing rate of exchange for that currency.

$10.00   Issued to $10.00

William J. Robinson................................19......

When countersigned below with this signature

INSTITUTE BANK
NEW YORK, N.Y., U.S.A.   No. 859478

through its correspondents will pay this check

To the order of...

Ten Dollars in United States Currency or its equivalent in the currency of the country where presented, conversion to be made at bankers' buying rate for Bankers' U.S. Dollar Checks on New York.

Countersignature   Institute Bank
                                             A. R. King
--   Cashier

FORM 38. TRAVELER'S CHECK

FOREIGN OPERATIONS OF THE SMALLER BANK

About one hundred institutions carry on practically all the foreign business which banks of the United States do directly with banks and customers abroad. Of these institutions a considerably smaller number concentrated in New York and other large cities transact a predominate part of that business. Many banks offer foreign services, but as a practical matter they request a larger city bank to complete the transactions for them.

This relative concentration of foreign department work among a few banks rests on a number of factors. Primarily, foreign banking is a specialized field and the advantage to the customer of such specialization is considerable, whether it be in letter of credit work, maintenance of a large number of direct foreign correspondents, ability to handle foreign languages, or up-to-date information on conditions abroad.

In addition, foreign banking, like foreign trade, is a two way street, and foreign operations are much more likely to be profitable if business is received from foreign banks as well as sent to them. Indeed, one of the more remunerative features of foreign banking arises from the extension of credit to banks and customers abroad. This extension of credit, however, entails taking a credit risk in a foreign country, which many banks are not prepared to do. Likewise, a domestic bank planning to enter foreign work on a significant scale must establish its own credit standing abroad in order that its letters of credit can be negotiated easily. The profit factors in foreign department operations are difficult to forecast. The routine operations of selling drafts, opening letters of credit, and handling collections involve considerable clerical detail, and it is questionable whether the commissions cover the cost. Foreign department operations primarily become profitable when they attract deposits, domestic and foreign, and when acceptance business and advances can be developed. However, it is not always easy to foresee when this type of business may be available.

Aside from the factors previously discussed, the most serious limitation on the foreign operations of the smaller banks is that of finding trained personnel. There is rarely enough foreign activity consistently available to enable a small bank to train its staff in handling foreign transactions directly with foreign correspondent banks. Then, too, it is difficult to spare the staff specialist from current foreign work long enough to enable him to spend the necessary training time outside his bank with a larger foreign department. Finally, there is little question but that running a one or two man foreign department can be a most difficult feat in banking, as each individual must be able to do everything.

However, despite these problems there has been since World War II a very considerable increase in foreign department activity on the part of banks outside the larger cities. Foreign trade of the United States has more than quadrupled, and smaller banks have become more aware of the foreign trade opportunities in their own communities and have been more willing to make the sacrifices in training personnel in order to participate in it. The local exporter or importer frequently prefers to transact his foreign business in his community, if adequate foreign services can be offered. Letters of credit and collections can be handled more expeditiously, and he can get his money sooner. Likewise, he has the flexibility which comes from dealing with a bank that knows his credit standing well.

The smaller bank may find it advantageous to use a domestic correspondent bank for foreign transactions, rather than establish its own connections abroad. The decision depends not only on the volume of its foreign business but also on the exact type of business in its own community. Likewise, it will depend to a considerable extent on the degree of foreign training of its own personnel.

Questions Based on Chapter XV

1. Describe the basic factors which differentiate foreign department transactions from domestic transactions.
2. List the primary services supplied by a foreign department.
3. What are traveler's checks? How do they safeguard the funds of purchasers?
4. In foreign department financing, what purpose is served by trust receipts?
5. Explain the use of a letter of credit in financing the importation of goods.
6. Why do smaller banks rely on their city correspondents to handle foreign transactions for their customers?

Questions for Investigation

1. Does your bank have a foreign department?
2. How would a request for the use of foreign department banking services be met in your bank?
3. Describe foreign exports and imports of the area served by your bank and the type of firm engaged in them.
4. What would be the advantages and the disadvantages of doing your customer's foreign business directly with foreign correspondents, as compared with handling it through the foreign department of a domestic correspondent?

CHAPTER XVI

SAFE DEPOSIT DEPARTMENT

The Purposes of This Chapter:

1. To explain why safe deposit service is a banking function.
2. To discuss the renting of safe deposit boxes and to mention the kinds of contracts used by banks.
3. To present the main features of access procedure.
4. To discuss the qualifications of safe deposit personnel.

IN ANCIENT times two of the major functions of banks were handled independently. Money was loaned by money lenders; the safekeeping of valuables and money was a separate service. Today, for the most part, the two functions are housed under one roof in a bank. Money is deposited in a bank either to earn interest or to be drawn down by check. The bank may loan the deposited funds to others. Securities and other valuables are left in a safe deposit box, unless the securities are held in a custody account or as collateral for a loan. All kinds of valuables are kept in safe deposit boxes, including securities, jewelry, bankbooks, business records, and other papers. Bulky articles, such as silverware, are kept in a storage vault.

Safe Deposit as a Service Department

If boxes are not made available to customers, they may take their banking business elsewhere. Renters bring to other departments of the bank such business as trust accounts, commercial accounts, foreign transactions, savings accounts, corporate accounts, and the like. Remarks by customers often can be followed to develop other business advantageous to the bank. Payment of box rent by a check drawn on another bank, or in cash, suggests an opportunity to sell your own bank's service. The amount of other bank business developed is often used to measure the profitability of the safe deposit department. Many safe deposit customers later become depositors.

239

The Identification of a New Box Renter

If a new box renter is making his first visit to the bank, courteous treatment will make a favorable impression on him. A bank may find, however, that it does not wish to accept all the business that it is offered. It is important to know with whom the bank is dealing. If the customer has a bank account, it is possible that the bank has already satisfied itself concerning his references and background. If not, it should verify his references and investigate his background. The customer will appreciate this care in the selection of the renters of safe deposit boxes.

If a customer does not have an account, he should be otherwise identified. Boxes are not rented to anyone using an assumed name, unless the renter has the right to use that name, such as a pen name or trade name. If the contract is filed under the assumed name, a cross reference should be made to the true name. It is not desirable to rent to criminals since such renters may cause trouble for the bank and concern to other customers. A customer should not be permitted to give his address in care of the bank as this practice complicates the matter of giving legal notice, especially if his rent should become unpaid.

Some banks refuse to rent to persons who are under the legal age established by state law. When a bank rents to a minor, it does not permit appointment of a deputy.

THE SELECTION OF THE BOX AND THE CONTRACT BY THE CUSTOMER

A customer is usually allowed to select at random the box he wishes to rent. A record should be maintained showing the numbers of unrented boxes in the various size and price groups. The type of key or lock used is usually explained to the customer. The fact that the keys issued to the customer have been under joint control is emphasized; in giving the keys to the customer it is well to separate them and to explain the desirability of keeping each key in a separate place.

When a customer is ready to sign a contract, the various types should be explained to him and he should be allowed to choose one of the types described.

The Individual Contract and the Customer's Deputy

A common contract or lease is the individual rental which contains a provision for the appointment of a deputy or deputies. If the customer appoints a deputy, a special form must be signed. If the deputy is not present, it may be advisable to permit the customer to take a form to be signed and returned. A record must be kept indicating that he has such a form. It is better practice to have both parties (the customer and the deputy) present, in order that the customer may identify the deputy and witness the signature of the deputy. Deputies need not be of legal age but must be mature.

The Co-lessee Contract

Some banks provide for rentals on a co-lessee contract which gives the right of access to the survivor of the lessees. If one lessee dies, the survivor has the right of access provided there is compliance with any local tax restrictions.

Another type of co-lessee contract permits access to either of the lessees during his lifetime, but after death of one, only to the survivor when accompanied by the accredited representative of the estate of the decedent, or by one or the other of them by their mutual consent. In this case also, there must be compliance with local tax restrictions, if any.

Under both types of contract the lessees, by signed agreement, may appoint deputies pursuant to the rules and regulations of the bank on forms provided by it.

Such contracts should not be described in a way that misleads customers into believing that the title to property may be transferred thereby. (Hence the word "co-lessee" is used instead of "joint tenants.") Any statement made to the customer about such a contract should be limited to an explanation of how access may be granted after death, without any mention of the transfer of title to the property in the box, if any.

Fiduciary Contract

If the customer is a fiduciary (such as a person representing an estate or trust, sometimes described as an executor, administrator, or trustee), the box should be leased on that basis with a clear indication of the fiduciary relationship. Proper papers should be filed to indicate the authority of the fiduciary. Some banks, by advice of counsel, believe that, unless a will or other instrument from which a fiduciary derives his authority clearly expresses the right to delegate what is known as discretionary power, or specifically states he may appoint someone for access to a safe deposit box, such fiduciary cannot appoint a deputy for safe deposit access. The decision concerning whether to accept such an appointment depends on the policy of the bank and the advice that it receives from its counsel.

When there are plural fiduciaries, they may make access arrangements to suit themselves, provided the arrangements are in accord with the bank's policy.

Every bank has occasion to deal with a fiduciary when a customer dies. For this reason the safeguards emphasized in these paragraphs should be kept in mind.

Corporation Contract

If the person is acting for a corporation, he should sign the lease on behalf of the corporation and a corporate resolution regarding access arrangements should be filed with the bank. If necessary, a certificate of election should also be filed. A corporate resolution concerning a bank account is not sufficient; the resolution should contain *specific* reference to a safe deposit box and no deviation from the terms of the corporate resolution should ever be permitted by the bank.

Unincorporated Associations

Arrangements for the rental of and access to the box of an unincorporated association are made substantially in the same manner as those for rental and access to the box of a corporation.

Partnership Contract

If a box is rented to a partnership, the contract by its phraseology should indicate this fact. Partners sometimes sign only the firm name, but some banks believe it is advisable also to have a record of the *individual* signatures of the partners. The contract should indicate clearly which partners are general and which are special, since the latter have limited powers. Signed instructions for access may grant the right of access to a nonpartner, such as a deputy.

Miscellaneous Contracts and Supplements

There are certain special types of rentals, such as rentals to escrowees and to court officers appointed by special court order. Such business should be directed to a safekeeping or custody arrangement away from the safe deposit vault.

The contracts or supplemental forms provide for address (both residence and business) for references, for specimen signatures, and in some banks for physical descriptions of persons authorized. Sometimes the maiden name of the mother of the person authorized is recorded since this information is not likely to be known by an imposter applying for access whose identity is challenged. Some banks obtain finger prints. Passwords selected by customers are sometimes used. Forms should not be issued indiscriminately. If forms are released to be taken off the premises, the name of the person to whom and the purpose for which the form is issued should be recorded.

A form for power of attorney is sometimes used by an individual customer to name someone to go to the box for an unspecified purpose. Since the customer cannot be physically present to sign a deputy form, the bank's form may be used for this purpose. Avoid acceptance of general powers of attorney. Blank powers should not be released except to, or on the instructions of, customers themselves.

Some banks combine all types of contracts on one form, whereas others have separate forms. Contracts are confidential arrangements between the bank and the customer. Be sure the customer is aware of the rules and regulations to which he agrees. A receipt for the payment of the rental, signed by the customer, may have the rules printed on the reverse side.

THE HANDLING OF KEYS AND LOCKS

A careful system to protect the keys and the locks is important both for the bank and the customer. The care of keys is something about which a customer is especially concerned since his key is the symbol of safety for his valuables. A carefully operated procedure for handling keys benefits both the employees and the customers since it precludes a charge that any employee at any time had sole control of the key to a customer's box. All keys for unrented boxes and locks, therefore, should be under joint control. There are several types of key locks designed for safe deposit boxes.

The Chase Manhattan Bank, New York

SAFE DEPOSIT VAULT

Fixed Tumbler Lock

The fixed tumbler lock is commonly used. As the term implies, the tumblers are fixed to a customer's key. It is generally considered that the best control over unrented boxes with this type of lock is either to keep the keys in envelopes corresponding with the box or lock numbers or to hang them in a slotted tray specially designed for that purpose. New tumblers can be fitted to the locks if it is desired to adjust them to a key with different cuts. Adjusting the tumblers of a lock should be done only by a lock manufacturer specializing in this type of lock.

Changeable Key Lock

The changeable key lock differs from the ordinary key lock because it has variable elements to make the different key changes. In this type of lock the tumblers are changed by using a special "changing" key instead of taking the lock apart. The keys are kept usually in sealed envelopes. When the customer selects an envelope at random, breaks the seal and removes the keys, he is the first person to see or touch the keys since the envelopes were sealed. The lock is set to the keys with the assurance that there are no other keys which operate it. Whenever a change is desired, the lock can be reset to new keys. A change can be made only when the door is open and the bolt is in the locked position. It is necessary to insert the customer's key whenever such a change is desired.

Combination Locks

There are also combination locks which should be set by the customers themselves under the direction of someone familiar with the operation. The bank should not be aware of the numbers used. Whenever a combination safe is being opened, the vault employee should not stand close enough to see the combination operated. Blinders may be installed on the locks to prevent the numbers from being seen by anyone but the operator. Locks with collars on combinations are advisable to prevent the operation of the lock until proper persons authorized for access are present.

Care of Keys and Locks in Transit

It is often necessary to send keys or locks or both to an accredited safe or lock company. Shipments of new locks also are received periodically. The new locks should be in the custody of at least two responsible employees at all times. Locks affixed to doors of *unrented* boxes should be under joint control, so that no one employee can open them. The requirement for joint control applies to *all* types of locks. Spare locks should be similarly controlled. It is important that a properly signed record be kept of the dispatch or receipt of all keys and locks to strengthen the joint control.

Keys to Rented Boxes

A bank should never willingly come into possession of keys to rented boxes. It should not accept customers' keys for safekeeping, since by so doing it then has full control of access. Instances of such custody may be criticized by bank examiners.

Keys should not be left in the safe door when a customer goes to a coupon room. The keys should always be under his observation. The safe door should be locked *shut* when the customer goes to a booth. It is especially important to have the door locked if it is equipped with a combination lock. This practice precludes a charge that a bank employee dishonestly made a duplicate key or tampered with the lock on the door.

The Return of Keys by Mail or Messenger

Sometimes a customer sends his keys to the bank by mail or by messenger with a written request that the lease be canceled since the box is empty. The box may then be opened and examined in the presence of employees and officers (at least two). If the box is found to be empty, an acknowledgment to that effect is sent to the customer.

If the box has contents, the bank should refrain from keeping the keys. The customer should be asked to come in personally to pick up the keys or have his deputy do so.

There may be other variations in the way customers cancel leases by mail; each cancellation must be carefully handled in accordance with the bank's policy.

Keys Found on Premises

If a key is found on the premises, it is referred to an officer who determines what should be done with it to minimize the responsibility of the bank. In any event, when a customer claims a lost key, the lock on his box must be changed, and he must acknowledge that the contents, if any, are intact.

New Rentals, Exchanges, and Surrenders

When boxes are rented, it is a wise practice to advise customers to keep the keys separate. The contract should provide for the customer's signature acknowledging receipt of *two* keys. Contract forms also may provide for a record of the initials or signatures of the two employees who delivered the keys from joint control in the presence of the customer; similarly, these employees should sign for keys returned to joint control when a safe deposit box is surrendered.

Lost Keys

If one key is lost, the customer must be required to return the duplicate and receive two new keys for a new lock or box. If both keys are lost, the services of a mechanic must be obtained from an accredited safe and lock company since the lock must be forced at the expense of the customer. Without written instructions from the customer, it is preferable not to force a lock for the deputy.

Lock Changes

The lock of a surrendered or exchanged safe should be changed before rerental. Both nest and tin should be examined in the presence of the customer when he surrenders his box, and the signed record may include this point.

Preparatory and Grille Gate Keys

Preparatory keys are referred to as such, but obviously, never as master keys. Such a key must be used before a customer can open his box with his own key. Vault clerks should retain control of the preparatory keys and never permit customers to use them.

A careful procedure should be followed during the relief of the regular attendant to make certain that only authorized substitutes or officers have possession of keys. If the bank has adopted a policy of permitting employees in control of preparatory keys to rent boxes of their own in the vault, such employees preferably should be given access by other employees, perhaps after hours. A customer may receive a wrong impression when he observes a vault clerk opening his own box.

THE RIGHT OF ACCESS

The methods used by banks in granting access to safe deposit boxes differ with the physical arrangements of the facilities. Most banks require the visitor to sign an access slip, even though the visitor is well known to the vault clerk. The signature should conform to the specimen signature on file.

A basic principle of vault operation is that no access shall be granted unless the person's right of access has been verified by the vault attendant and unless the person has been properly identified. A key to a safe deposit box is not proof of the right of access. If documents are exhibited as evidence of the right to access, those documents must be valid and must be left with the bank for its files. The right of access should be verified by reference to the signature card regardless of how well the bank employee knows the person. On receipt of a notice that access authority, for instance of a deputy, has been canceled, the persons charged with the operation of the vault should immediately review the records and should change them promptly. When the vault attendant refers to the records to verify the customer's right of access, he should make certain that the customer cannot see any of the names in the files. Remember, however, verification of the right of access is of paramount importance, even when the visitor is recognized.

Forms for Record of Access

Many banks keep a record of access by the use of a numbered slip. The slip records such information as the following:

1. the visitors's signature or name, if he cannot sign except by mark,
2. the time he went into and the time he came out of the vault,
3. the date of his visit,
4. the initials of the employee who identified him and who verified his authority to access,
5. the number of the booth he occupied,
6. the initials of the employees who escorted him to and from the booth, if used, and who examined it, identifying it by number,
7. the number of persons accompanying the visitor with his consent,
8. the initials of the employees who opened his box and locked it or saw it locked by the visitor, and
9. the initials of the employee who examined the floor of the vault if the visitor did not use a booth.

Obviously the slip should also include a record of the box number and the name under which it was rented. If the visitor is not recognized, his signature need not be the sole means of identifying him; he can be further identified from his physical description noted in the records or from the use of a password.

The First National City Bank of New York

Safe Deposit Procedure

The date and number of the slip may be posted to a cumulative visitation record card that is filed by box number, or some equivalent record may be kept. The slip is filed by control number.

The Handling of the Box and the Key

The customer must enter the vault to open his box, and while the box is open, he must keep it in his full view. He should not

be left alone in the vault. It is a good practice for the vault clerk
to ask the customer if he wishes to insert the key himself and
handle his own tin box. Many customers do not wish to do so,
especially if their boxes are located in a high tier. After the tin
box is removed, the customer is escorted to a coupon room. If the
compartment is locked, the key should be tried in the customer's
presence. When the tin box is carried by an employee of the vault,
it should be kept in full view of the customer.

The customer should not be permitted to leave the coupon room
without taking his tin box with him. It is better for a customer to
go to a coupon room to enjoy his privacy and to avoid dangerous
congestion in the vault. The staff should avoid assisting the customer in cutting coupons or in otherwise handling or viewing
contents. If the lessee removes the tin box from the premises, a
record of that fact must be kept.

COLLECTION OF RENTALS

In some renting systems, all rentals mature on one day in the year
and new rentals are collected on an adjusted basis. Under another
system, the rentals mature on the first day of a month or on some
other selected common date. Still another system may provide for
maturities on the anniversaries of rentals. Bills for maturing rentals are usually mailed at a prescribed period in advance of maturity. With the consent of the customer, arrangements can be made
to charge his bank account. All charges and payments are usually
recorded in a ledger. When payments are made, a record of the
form of payment should be kept, that is, whether by cash or check,
and if paid by check, the name of the bank on which the check
was drawn.

RECORD KEEPING

All records should be kept neatly. They may be required by a
court if the bank becomes involved in a legal dispute. A bad impression may be created if records are in poor condition.

In the absence of any legal requirements, many banks follow
the practice of destroying all records of surrendered boxes after
ten years from the date of surrender.

Death

The death of a customer normally precludes access by anyone except by court order or by the accredited representatives of his estate. (See Fiduciary Contract for restrictions.) In some states the box may be opened in accordance with statutory procedure prior to the appointment of the accredited representative of the estate. The purposes for which the box may be opened are: the search for a will to be delivered by the bank to the court, the immediate removal of any cemetery deed, and the delivery of life insurance policies to named beneficiaries. Before opening the safe, the consent of state tax authorities may also be required. A signed record is kept.

In other states, banks may allow the next of kin, or others, to search for a will, cemetery deed, or other essential document. Whatever the practice is, it should be carefully observed with full realization of the risks involved. Complete records of access should be maintained.

After his appointment, the accredited representative of the estate of a decedent is entitled to access depending upon the nature of the appointment, evidence of which must be filed with the bank. Such evidence should be carefully reviewed. Tax restrictions, if any, must be observed.

If a co-lessee dies, it may be necessary to require the presence of the survivor before access is permitted to the accredited representative of the estate of the decedent, or it may be necessary to require the presence of one or the other. Contracts in effect and statutes applicable, if any, must be reviewed. Tax restrictions, if any, must be observed.

In some states the death of a person, other than an individual or co-lessee, does not serve to interfere with access by those who are or may become authorized to have access. Each case must be referred to an officer.

The death of an individual acting in a fiduciary capacity usually precludes access to the box except to his accredited successor or by other proper court procedure. If access is allowed to the successor fiduciary, it is good practice to request the presence or consent of the accredited representative of the estate of the deceased fiduciary. Under some state laws and practices, if one of plural fiduciaries

should die, the survivors have the right of access without inter-
ruption, but such contracts and the law regulating them should be
referred to an officer in all such cases.

It is important that immediately upon notice of the death or the
incompetency, everyone charged with the operation of the vault
be advised and the records be changed. The deputy appointment
contract and forms should be reviewed to see if the situation is
covered.

Participation in inventories of box contents should be avoided
unless it is necessary to make certain that nothing is removed other
than a will, cemetery deed, or the like. When complete inventories
must be made or certified, a signed record should be kept. All
requests for such service should be referred to an officer for decision on policy.

Any applicable tax requirement must also be considered.

Incompetency

In the event a customer is legally adjudicated an incompetent,
access may be permitted by the fiduciary appointed by the court
to handle the incompetent's property. No inheritance tax restrictions apply unless the incompetent subsequently dies. Access after
death is similar to that granted to a box of a deceased individual;
however, consideration must be given to the interest and status of
the fiduciary who had custody of the incompetent's property prior
to the latter's decease.

Selection of Personnel

If the volume of business is sufficient to require full-time personnel, the person so selected should be efficient, careful, and capable
of exercising mature judgment. He should be well trained and
should realize the responsibility of his position. He should be able
to recognize situations in which a snap judgment cannot be made
and in which it is advisable to confer with officers and possibly
counsel. He should not allow himself to make a quick decision on
a questionable request for access. He should realize that he need
not "refuse" access, but he can always "defer" granting a request
for access in order to be allowed a reasonable time for consultation. It is advisable to refrain from identifying him as custodian,
since the word may connote custody of property or bailment.

Some banks may not have a volume of accesses or a sufficient number of boxes to warrant the employment of a full-time clerk to supervise the vault. When the responsibility is divided, all officers and clerks charged with vault operations should meet the requirements listed.

The Need for Good Judgment

No chapter of this size can adequately cover the many phases of the operation and control of a safe deposit vault. Even a manual must leave much to the sound reasoning of the officers of the bank who are paid to exercise good judgment.

If a claim is ever made against your bank, observance of some of the rules suggested in this chapter *may* assist you in proving that you have exercised "reasonable care" or better. Kinds of vault operations which do not accord with the requirements mentioned in this chapter, and the many other operations not included, may still be good practice, but consideration should be given to the psychological effect of those practices on an uninformed jury.

Questions Based on Chapter XVI

1. Other than from rentals, does the operation of a safe deposit vault improve the income of a bank?
2. What factors should a bank consider in renting boxes to new customers?
3. What are the main differences between an individual rental contract and a co-lessee contract?
4. Name several types of locks designed for use on safe deposit boxes. Describe the principal features of each kind of lock.
5. What precautions are taken by the lessor to safeguard the safe deposit keys and locks (a) of unrented boxes? (b) of rented boxes?
6. What practice do banks follow in regard to lost keys?
7. What is the procedure in opening a box when the renter himself desires access?

Question for Investigation

Review the inheritance tax laws and regulations of your state and discuss their applicability, if any, to safe deposit operations.

CHAPTER XVII

GENERAL BANK ACCOUNTING

The Purposes of This Chapter:

1. To state the scope, needs, and objectives of bank accounting.
2. To explain briefly the principles of accounting for assets and liabilities and the operations of the general books.
3. To discuss briefly the methods of accounting for income and expense.
4. To point out the purposes and the methods of cost accounting.
5. To outline the uses of the statement of condition.
6. To mention the items usually appearing on the statement of condition.

BECAUSE every transaction in a bank requires some kind of record, it can be said that accounting enters into every phase of banking; every person in a bank engages in some form of accounting. Some employees give all their time to accounting, and others very little, but everyone contributes to the mass of bank records. It is highly important, therefore, that every employee understand the part he plays in maintaining proper and accurate bank information.

THE SCOPE OF BANK ACCOUNTING

Bank accounting covers two general fields: (1) accounting for the bank's own assets and liabilities and its own income and expense and (2) accounting for the customers' assets temporarily held by the bank. For instance, the bank may hold security for loans or it may collect the proceeds of bond coupons for customers. In this chapter we discuss primarily the first of these two fields.

The Need for Bank Accounting

The need for bank accounting is quite apparent when consideration is given to the volume of activity which takes place daily in every bank and to the relationship of the bank to its depositors, borrowers, stockholders, the public, and supervisory authorities.

Banking laws, both national and state, require that banks submit sworn statements of assets and liabilities upon notice from supervisory authority. The accounting processes of every bank must be adequate, therefore, to provide an accurate and complete statement of what a bank owns and owes every day. The bank's management, its board of directors, and its stockholders must be appraised of the bank's financial condition and of the results of its operations in terms of profit or loss. Depositors also are interested because the financial condition of the bank affects the safety of their deposits.

Bank bookkeeping provides a method of accounting for all items and transactions while they are being processed or handled. In the handling of a check, for example, the records must be such that the check can be traced from the time it is deposited or cashed to the time it is paid or returned to the customer. Since items are often handled by more than one person, records are also useful as a means of placing responsibility for work performed or for errors committed.

Since bank records are often required long after a transaction is completed, they must be available in a relatively permanent form. Often bank records must be produced upon the request of customers or in legal disputes. Permanent records afford the bank protection as evidence of the fact that past transactions have been correctly handled.

Bank management must know what the current financial condition of the bank is, and it should also know whether its policies have resulted in profits. Bank management must also have information which enables it to analyze its operations for the purposes of setting future policies and of taking corrective operational steps when they are needed.

The Objectives of Bank Accounting

The objectives of bank accounting may be summarized as follows:

1. The preparation of a statement showing the bank's financial condition as of a particular day (Statement of Condition or Balance Sheet)

2. The preparation of a statement showing the income and expense for a certain period of time (Income Statement, Statement of Income and Expense, or Profit and Loss Statement)

3. The tracing of items step by step through their processing

4. The furnishing of information sufficiently detailed to permit management to determine which operations are profitable (cost accounting) and to establish future policies concerning income and expense (budgetary control, that is, profit planning).

The use of accounting in the preparation of the daily statement of condition is mentioned later in this chapter.

The means by which items in the process of collection are identified and recorded in receiving teller work and in the central proof, transit, clearings, and bookkeeping operations are discussed in the earlier chapters of this text. The establishment of a record of past transactions is well exemplified by the customers' ledger or by microfilms of it.

Today the use and knowledge of bank costs are of great importance in determining the expenses of various departments, functions, or activities for the purpose of setting proper prices for services, of increasing the efficiency of operations, or of deciding where to place greater stress to increase profits. A knowledge of bank costs is helpful in planning for a better net income and in enabling the bank to compare its performance with its anticipated goal, both in expense and income. Bank cost accounting is explained in more detail later in this chapter.

KINDS OF RECORDS

Two general kinds of records commonly appear in bank accounting. The first is the temporary record. Adding machine lists and batch proofs are examples. Although these records are convenient and save time, they are rendered obsolete by more permanent records produced subsequently as the work flows through the bank. Many temporary records are not needed after the day's work is completed and are discarded at once or kept a very short time. In the majority of banks, however, summaries of temporary records in the form of final proof sheets are retained for a time even though the supporting records are destroyed.

Other types of temporary records may be used for a few days or weeks and then replaced by more permanent records. Many temporary records are simply copies or duplicates of other records which are preserved indefinitely. Duplicates of transit letters are used until the items listed in them are disposed of, either by payment and credit or by nonpayment and return. These temporary records are filed for a short time in case reference to them may be helpful, and then they are destroyed.

The second kind of accounting record is the permanent record, such as the ledgers and, in some cases, the journals. File copies of collections, loan and discount journals and ledgers, and the general books (journals, ledgers, and subsidiary detail records) are examples of the usual permanent records. These records are preserved for a certain number of years, depending on bank policies or legal requirements. Many banks have destruction schedules to show the minimum time for the retention and preservation of specific records. These schedules protect the bank and, at the same time, permit it to discard obsolete and unnecessary records and to eliminate the danger of discarding essential records prematurely.

Since most bank records are in the conventional form of typed, handwritten, or machine-posted paper tapes or sheets that require a large amount of storage space, the use of microfilming devices is increasing. There has also been an increase in the use of punch card accounting; certain data is punched in specially designed cards which may be transferred, through the use of special tabulating machines, to printed form. More recent and still not widely used by banks are electronic accounting machines.

Double Entry Bookkeeping

It is impossible in this course to give a complete explanation of accounting, but it is necessary for the student to understand the basic principles.

The property owned or held by a bank, consisting principally of cash, cash items in process of collection, loans, investments, and the bank building, are the bank's *assets*. The amounts owed to creditors, primarily depositors, are the bank's *liabilities;* and the amount owned by the bank's stockholders is called its *capital* or *net worth*. The bank's assets are subject to the claims of its creditors; the remainder belongs to the stockholders. Therefore, the assets equal the liabilities and net worth. This fact can be expressed by the equation:

$$\text{Assets} = \text{Liabilities} + \text{Net Worth}$$

The principle of this equation is used in the double entry system of bookkeeping. In this system, every transaction must be recorded in such a manner that the total assets equal total liabilities (plus net worth), that is, the assets and liabilities are in balance. For example, if a deposit of $100 is made, the asset "cash" is increased by $100 and liabilities to depositors are increased by an equal amount. One or more asset accounts may be increased at the same time and in the same amount as other asset accounts are decreased. Similarly, one or more liability accounts may be increased at the same time and in the same amount as other liability accounts are decreased. Assets may increase or decrease at the same time and in the same amount as liabilities. The changes taking place in any account are referred to in terms of debits or credits. Debits increase asset accounts and decrease liability accounts; credits increase liability accounts and decrease asset accounts. Observe that in double entry bookkeeping every debit must have an equal or corresponding credit. We may apply this principle to the example given. The cash is increased by a debit of $100 and the liability to depositors is increased by a credit of an equal amount.

The use of the double entry system in the general books is illustrated by the example. The system also provides us with the assurance that the transaction is accurately handled at each stage of its processing.

Consider the operations required in handling deposits which include checks on us, clearings checks, and transit checks. The proof clerk totals separately all checks on the paying bank (checks on us), all clearings checks, and all transit checks. The total amount of checks on us charged against the bank's customers by the bookkeepers must equal the total of checks on us handled by the proof clerk. The checks going from the proof clerk to the clearings clerk affect two records. One is the total of the clearings checks handled by the proof clerk, and the other is the total of the checks sent by the clearings clerk to the clearing house. Similarly, the total amount of the checks sent by the transit clerk to various banks must agree with the amount of transit checks handled by the proof clerk. If the totals of the proof clerk agree with the totals from bookkeeping, clearings, and transits, it is evident that they have been accurately handled.

In the meantime, the deposit slips on which the checks were listed have gone to the bookkeepers for credit to the customers' accounts that are affected. The amount of credits received by the bookkeepers must agree with the total of deposits handled by the proof clerk.

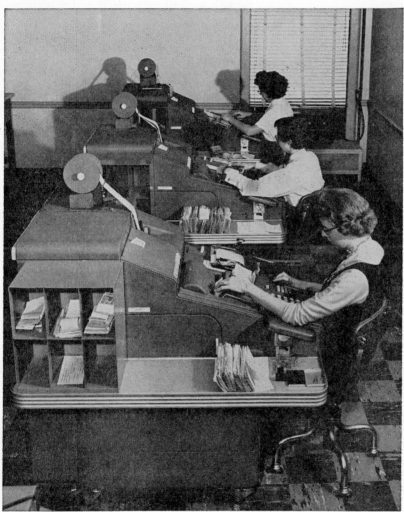

The First National City Bank of New York

ACCOUNTING MACHINES

The accounting procedure for these transactions affects four accounts on the general books, two asset and two liability accounts, as follows: (1) for the checks deposited: an increase (debit) to the asset account, Exchanges for Clearing House, for the amount of clearing house checks; an increase (debit) in the asset account, Due from Banks or Transit Account, for the amount of the transit checks; a decrease (debit) in the liability account, Deposits, for the amount of checks on us; and (2) for the deposits: an increase (credit) in the liability account, Deposits.

The flow of accounting figures through the bank until the transactions are recorded in the general books is presented graphically in Chart 11.

Classification of Records

Since a large number of transactions are performed during each day, an unreasonable amount of work would be involved if the details of each day's transactions were presented in the general ledger. The information is sufficient if the general ledger reflects the effect of groups of similar transactions. It is, therefore, more convenient and equally satisfactory to maintain a separate classification for each type of asset, liability, capital, income, and expense, and to show on the general ledger only the total daily increases and decreases for each of these classifications. The record kept for each classification is called a *general ledger account* and a group of such accounts is called a general ledger. The term account is used in many ways. For example, in the general ledger a single account may represent all of the loans and discounts, or all of the savings deposits, and so forth; in the individual bookkeeping ledger it may refer to the checking account of a given depositor; or in the loan and discount ledger it may refer to the account of a given borrower.

The general ledger accounts furnish summarized and classified information, not details. Because of the difficulty in connecting and tracing errors and because of the mass of detail coming from many sources, it is necessary to make a preliminary record of detailed transactions as they occur. Such a record is called the *journal*.

Various kinds of journals and ledgers are used in the bank, depending upon the need for records of a more or less permanent nature. Ordinarily entries are actually made first in the journal and then in the ledger, but multiple forms can provide both records in the same operation.

Bank accounting is a constant process of consolidation of transactions into group totals. The ultimate objective of these consol-

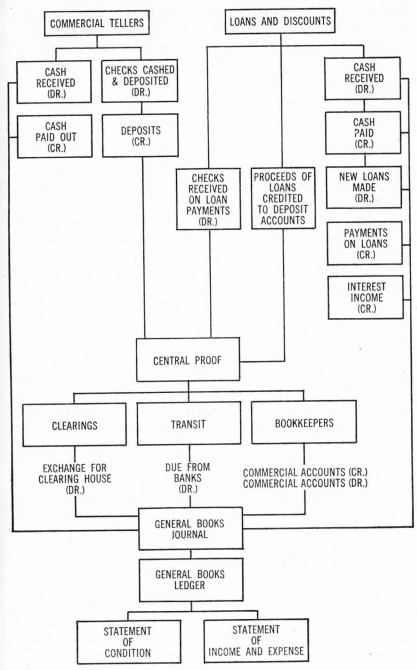

CHART 11. FLOW OF ACCOUNTING FIGURES TO THE GENERAL BOOKS

idations is to summarize the day's work (1) to reflect the effects of the day's transactions on the bank's assets, liabilities, and capital accounts and (2) from the new totals in the ledger accounts, to construct a current statement of condition. In many banks, daily statements of income and expense are also made.

GENERAL BOOKS

The summaries of the various asset, liability, capital, income, and expense accounts are carried in the bank's general ledger which, in banking, is referred to as the general books. The details of the accounts carried in the general books are shown in supporting subsidiary records consisting of journals, summaries, and subsidiary ledgers. The general books are characterized by relatively few accounts and by permanency of the records.

A small bank can start business with the general ledger as the only accounting record, aside from the daily journal. As the number of its depositors increases, it establishes a subsidiary ledger for deposit accounts to show the account of each depositor, keeping only a control account or total balance of all deposit accounts on the general books. Likewise, an increase in the number of loans may necessitate a separate subsidiary record for loans, with only a control account on the general books. This ledger becomes the loan and discount ledger. Similarly, a separate security ledger may be necessary to show the details of the bank's securities investments.

Although machine bookkeeping is widely used to post on loose leaf sheets the general ledger accounts, some banks still use permanently bound journals and ledgers posted in pen and ink.

The accounting entries affecting the various accounts on the general books are first consolidated in the general books' journal and then posted in summarized form to the proper general ledger accounts. The amount of activity in different general ledger accounts varies considerably. The balances of many accounts, such as Cash and Due from Banks, Loans and Discounts, and Deposits, change daily. Other accounts, such as Capital Stock and Surplus, are relatively inactive and change only infrequently. General accounting practices and the accounts carried on the general books are considered in some detail later in this chapter.

In a small bank, a combination journal and ledger may be

adequate. In larger banks the journal and ledger may be divided into sections, with details shown in subsidiary journals and ledgers. The details for individual deposits, for example, may be journalized and posted in the deposit ledger and only a total debit and a total credit posted to the general ledger account, Individual Deposits. In some larger banks, the accounting for income and expense accounts is assigned to a separate person or division and only the net change is reflected in a control account, Undivided Profits, on the general books.

Duties of the General Bookkeeper

The principal duty of the general bookkeeper is the maintenance of complete, accurate, and current records of transactions on the general ledger in order to properly disclose the financial condition of the bank. Therefore, the general bookkeeper must maintain a journal summarizing and classifying both the accounting information directly assigned to him and the information coming to him from throughout the bank. To this duty is added the maintenance of adequate detail and accuracy in subsidiary records.

When the general bookkeeper has subsidiary ledgers relating to certain deposit accounts, he is responsible for paying the checks drawn against the accounts in the subsidiary ledger. For example, when a subsidiary ledger for certified and cashier's checks is maintained in connection with the general books, the general bookkeeper must *pay* these checks. If the accounts of other banks are kept on the general books, instead of on the ledgers of the bookkeepers, the general bookkeeper must also pay checks on these accounts.

The general bookkeeper must prepare the daily statement of condition and the statement of income and expense. He must furnish all other information and reports requested by the bank officers and directors, and he must submit reports to various supervisory authorities. In some larger banks a separate reports division is responsible for the preparation of statements, but the necessary information still must be provided by the general books.

Income and Expense Accounting

No discussion of bank accounting would be complete without some discussion of accounting for the income and expense of the bank. The total of the capital accounts on the bank's ledger represents the stockholders' interest, or net worth. This net worth normally either increases each year through net profits or decreases through net losses or through dividends paid. It is not sufficient to show the net increase or decrease in net worth because management, stockholders, supervisory authorities, and income tax officials also must know the source of the income and the cause of the expenses. It is necessary, therefore, to set up other accounts on the general ledger to show how capital (net worth) is affected by each type of income and each type of expense.

Some of the more important items of income for a bank are interest on loans and securities, service charges on deposit accounts, exchange charges, and income from safe deposit operations. Some of the more important items of expense are salaries, interest on time deposits, depreciation on buildings and equipment, and taxes. If income for the year exceeds expense, the bank has a net profit.

Banks may use either of two different methods of accounting for income and expense: (1) the cash basis or (2) the accrual basis. Under the cash basis, which is used by many smaller banks, income is entered on the bank's books only when it is received, and expenses are entered only when they are paid. This method sometimes results in a distortion of net profits for a year in which large amounts of cash income have been received or large expenses paid, even though the income may actually have been earned in a different year or though the expenses paid were of benefit in a different year.

To avoid this distortion in net profits, many banks use the accrual basis of accounting for income and expense. Under this method, income is entered on the bank's books when it is earned, even if the cash is not received, and expenses are entered when the expense is incurred, even if the cash is not paid. For example, although interest on a ninety-day loan is paid only at maturity, one day's interest is earned each day that the loan is on the bank's books. The bank on the accrual basis might record an additional day's interest each day or an additional month's interest each month. The interest that is building up each day is said to accrue or to become an accrual. Similarly, appropriate amounts for taxes, which the bank anticipates it must pay sometime in the future, periodically are accumulated as expense until paid.

Accruals also cause the creation of certain asset and liability accounts. The accounting procedure for an accrual of interest on loans, for example, shows: (1) an increase (debit) in the asset account, Accrued Interest Receivable, and (2) an increase (credit) in the income account, Interest on Loans. When the cash is received for the interest due on the loan, the asset account, Cash, is debited and the asset account, Accrued Interest Receivable, is credited, thus eliminating the interest receivable on that loan.

The accounting procedure for the accrual of interest on a discounted loan would result in (1) a decrease (debit) in the liability account, Unearned Discount, and (2) an increase (credit) in the income account, Interest on Loans. At the maturity of the loan the Unearned Discount on that loan is eliminated and the total amount of discount is taken into income.

Similarly, the accrual for interest payable on savings deposits shows: (1) an increase (debit) in the expense account, Interest Expense, and (2) an increase (credit) in the liability account, Interest Payable. When interest payable is actually transferred to the various savings accounts, Interest Payable account is eliminated (debit) and Savings Deposits increased (credit).

COST ACCOUNTING

It was stated previously that bank management and stockholders must know the sources of the bank's income and the different kinds of expenses incurred. These figures are provided through ordinary bank accounting. Cost accounting goes further; it relates the items of income and of expense to the specific work performed and the particular services rendered by the bank.

It is useful to management to know the income and expense of each of the major bank services or functions, those that use or invest the bank's funds such as the loaning function or the securities investment function and those that provide funds to the bank, such as the commercial deposit service or the savings deposit service. It is also helpful for management to know how profitable or unprofitable the various nondeposit services are, such as the safe deposit service.

In setting prices charged for various bank services, management wishes to know the actual cost of handling a particular kind of transaction or item. A computation which uses arbitrary item charges and arbitrary earnings rates on average balances may determine how much a service charge should be on a given checking account, but the true profit or loss on the account can only be determined by using actual item costs and actual earnings rates. For other services, as well, item costs are of great value in making adequate, but not excessive, charges for services.

Supervisors may find it helpful to compare the expenses incurred and the amount of activity or work handled by their staffs for successive periods.

Not only is a bank concerned with its past performance, but it is interested in its future. Profit planning is made easier for management when the bank has cost accounting figures available.

Cost Accounting Procedure

Cost accounting procedures vary widely among banks, depending upon the amount of information desired. It is possible, however, to follow a procedure or pattern that enables a bank to assemble less information initially and then to expand its cost accounting procedures in various stages of development as further information is desired.

In accordance with the need for cost accounting figures and the willingness of the bank to make the effort to acquire them, the bank may undertake to develop them in such stages as the following:

1. Accumulation of the number of items of various kinds that are handled in each department or operation. A knowledge of the number of items handled is helpful in planning the bank's work.

2. Distribution of expenses to each department or operation. A comparison of the expenses of a department or operation for several periods is very helpful in expense control.

3. Determination of the total income and expense attributable to each function, that is, to each general category of bank service. Gathering up the income and expenses applicable to any general bank service or function permits a comparison with previous periods to be made and, in the case of such a function as the loaning function, permits the earning rate on loans to be expressed as both gross and net after expenses.

4. Determination of item costs or other unit costs by relating

items or units processed with their processing expense. Cost of items, which includes the cost incurred by the entire bank for any given service, is a reliable aid in reviewing charges for service and in comparing the efficiency of handling such service in different periods.

STATEMENT OF CONDITION

The statement of condition is a summary of the assets and liabilities of the bank. It is used as a source of information for the bank officers and directors in connection with the work of the bank. In addition, it is a vehicle for supervisory control since both state and federal banking laws require the periodical submission of statements of condition to supervisory authorities for their information and the publication of these "official" statements for the information of the public.

Use of Statement of Condition by Officers and Directors

The statement of condition is prepared daily in connection with the work of the bank, for the information it contains governs decisions by the directors, officers, and other supervisory employees. The amount of detail shown depends upon the purpose for which the statement is to be used.

A condensed statement comparing the assets and liabilities with those on other dates normally is sufficient for the bank directors and executive officers responsible for general bank policies.

The statement of condition when used in conjunction with other reports (reports on new and closed accounts, loans made and paid, lists of securities with appreciation or depreciation in values, and the like) portrays completely the current position of the bank.

It is common practice for banks to use the condensed statement of condition for advertising purposes, often at the time reports must be submitted to supervisory authorities. The statements are usually published not only in newspapers but also in folder form for distribution to customers and prospective customers. In addition to the statement of condition, the published folders often include other information. The names and business connections of bank directors are frequently included, to emphasize the caliber of the men responsible for the bank's management. The major services of the bank—such as loaning, commercial deposit, savings deposit, and trust service—are often featured with a brief statement about each.

Use of Statement of Condition for Supervisory Control

Requests for submission of statements of condition by supervisory authorities are referred to as "calls" or "statement calls." The Comptroller of the Currency is required by law to make at least three calls a year on national banks. State laws and regulations vary, some stipulating the number of calls and others leaving that to the discretion of a state official, usually the state commissioner or superintendent of banking. Calls are made without previous notice and at varying intervals, in order to prevent shifting of assets by a bank in contemplation of a call.

Upon receiving a call, a bank must submit its statement to the proper authority within a limited period, generally not exceeding ten days. The statement must be submitted on prescribed forms furnished by the supervisory authorities and must be sworn to as correct by officers and directors of the bank before a notary public. In addition to submitting the statement, the bank usually must publish the report in a newspaper of general circulation in its vicinity, for the purpose of informing the public. A copy of this official publication, certified to by the publisher, is sent to the supervisory authority as proof of compliance with the law.

Preparation of the Statement

The daily statement is prepared from the general books. As the figures reflecting the various bank operations are reported to the general books, they are first entered in the journal and are then posted to the ledger under the proper classifications. From the ledger, they are further consolidated and set up on the statement of condition. Although most statements are usually consolidated in some way, the general books and subsidiary records must furnish any necessary details that may be required.

To illustrate this operation, consider the statement item Cash and Due from Banks, shown in Form 39. The head paying teller's balance is reported under two designations, vault cash and tellers' cash funds. These designations may appear on the general books. The total of items in the process of collection (the float) also appears on the general books. The names of the banks in which balances are kept and the amounts of these balances are carried on the general books; or if a Due from Banks ledger is used, only the total debit balance is carried on the general books. For Federal Reserve member banks, the balances at the Federal Reserve bank are noted in a separate account. These Federal Reserve balances are carried in two sections, reserve account and deferred (or collection) account. The total of checks held for clearings the following business day is carried in its own account. Yet in the statement of condition all these general book accounts may be totaled in the single item Cash and Due from Banks.

The demand deposit balances are consolidated into one total. The totals of various types of loans are added to give one or more figures in the statement of condition. The securities owned by the bank are consolidated in at least two totals, one for United States government obligations and one for other securities.

The result of these and other consolidations is a brief but sufficiently detailed picture of the condition of the bank, with its assets and liabilities segregated into major classifications.

The Assets or Resources of the Bank

Note that in the specimen statement of condition, Form 39, the form shows the balancing of the equation,

$$\text{Assets} = \text{Liabilities} + \text{Net Worth}$$

(Capital, Surplus, and Undivided Profits). The term resources is often used instead of assets. Assets usually consist of cash, balances due from other banks, investments in securities, loans and discounts, bank premises, and other property owned.

Cash and Due from Banks

Cash and Due from Banks is usually the first item appearing on the assets side of the statement. It may be a single item, as already noted, or it may be divided into three or more items—for example, Cash on Hand, Due from Banks and Bankers, and Due from Federal Reserve bank.

When so divided, Cash on Hand represents the cash in the vault and held by tellers. Due from Banks and Bankers represents the balances maintained with correspondent banks for transit, collection, and other purposes; it also includes transit items in

INSTITUTE NATIONAL BANK
Institute, Pa.
June 30, 1956

ASSETS

Cash and Due from Banks	$ 3,233,213.15
United States Government Obligations, Direct and Fully Guaranteed	4,295,087.13
Municipal Bonds	1,412,715.51
Other Bonds	202,013.01
Loans and Discounts	2,250,047.74
Federal Reserve Bank Stock	21,300.00
Customers' Liability on Acceptances	9,890.84
Banking House	40,241.11
Furniture and Fixtures	10,100.10
Other Real Estate	140.60
Other Assets	2,827.13
Total Assets	$11,477,576.32

LIABILITIES

Demand Deposits	$ 9,255,154.38
Time Deposits	980,143.92
United States Government Deposits	426,391.82
Certified Checks, Cashier's Checks, and Bank Drafts	10,671.98
Total Deposits	$10,672,362.10
Reserves for Taxes, Interest, and Other Expense	26,641.91
Unearned Discount	21,663.44
Liability on Acceptances	9,890.84
Other Liabilities	1,620.20
Total Liabilities	$10,732,178.49
Capital Stock	500,000.00
Surplus	210,000.00
Undivided Profits	35,397.83
Total Liabilities and Capital	$11,477,576.32

Member—Federal Deposit Insurance Corporation

FORM 39. STATEMENT OF CONDITION

the process of collection through the Federal Reserve banks and clearing items on hand for exchange the following business day. Due from Federal Reserve Bank includes legal and excess reserves held by the Federal Reserve bank of the member bank's own district.

Investments

After the items Cash on Hand, Due from Banks and Bankers, and Due from Federal Reserve Bank, the totals of the investments in government, municipal, and other bonds are listed.

It is common practice to show United States Government Obligations as a separate total on the statement of condition. This item includes government bonds, treasury bills, treasury certificates, and any other bonds fully guaranteed (as to both principal and interest) by the United States Government. Banks invest in Government Bonds for the purpose of obtaining the highest grade and most readily marketable investments. Member banks may use these bonds as security for loans at the Federal Reserve banks.

A separate classification is often made for Municipal Bonds, which are the bonds and warrants of states, cities, sanitary districts, school districts, and other governmental subdivisions.

The bonds of railroads, public utilities, and industrial concerns are generally carried in one total, listed as Other Bonds.

Because there are laws requiring the pledge of securities as additional protection for the deposits of governmental bodies, it is customary to show the amount of deposits which are secured by assets and, in some cases, the record of assets pledged. When the latter procedure is followed, the bonds so pledged are listed as "pledged to secure public funds."

Loans and Discounts

Normally, one of the largest items on the statement of a commercial bank is Loans and Discounts. This item also represents one of the largest earning assets. Instead of the single item, Loans and Discounts, the various kinds of loans are sometimes detailed.

Federal Reserve Bank Stock

Every member bank must own stock in the Federal Reserve bank of its district, and sometimes this stock is carried as a separate item in the statement.

Mortgage Loans

Loans secured by first liens on real property are made by many commercial banks. Federal and some state laws restrict the total amount of real estate loans that may be made by the banks under their jurisdictions. For example, the Federal law prohibits a national bank from making real estate loans totaling more than the paid-in and unimpaired capital stock and surplus of the bank or totaling more than sixty per cent of the amount of the bank's time and savings deposits, whichever is the greater.

The amount of real estate loans that can be made, however, is still a sizable proportion of the bank's assets. Banks in recent years have been giving a much greater service to the public through the making of real estate loans.

Banking House

Often a bank owns its business premises and carries them at a conservative valuation on the statement of condition. Although adequate premises are necessary for the conduct of the bank's business, the amount invested in the building should be moderate in proportion to the capital and surplus. As a matter of policy, banks (at least annually) reduce the book value of the premises by depreciation charges made against current earnings. It is not uncommon for a bank to so reduce the book value of land and bank building over a period of years that the land alone is worth more than the book value of both the land and the building together.

If the item Banking House (or some similar title) does not appear on the statement, the inference is that the banking premises are leased. Frequently, the building is owned by a subsidiary corporation which the bank owns through stock ownership. The bank then carries only the value of such stock on its books. Many banks prefer to lease quarters during the early years of their existence, deferring the building of their own quarters until they are more certain of their space requirements.

Furniture and Fixtures

If the banking house is owned by the bank, furniture and fixtures are often included in the general account Banking Premises and Equipment. If the bank does not own the building, these items are ordinarily carried on the statement as Furniture and Fixtures, the account including the investment in vaults, cages, machines, and furniture necessary for the bank's business.

Some banks carry the equipment on their books at a figure that is lower than its original cost less ordinary depreciation or even at some nominal value. When new equipment is purchased, depreciation is so determined that the cost, on a conservative basis, will be spread over the estimated life of the equipment. In each accounting period, the carrying value is reduced directly or by means of a depreciation reserve.

Other Real Estate

Real estate other than that in use by the bank for the conduct of its business is included in the item Other Real Estate. Most of this real estate was pledged as security for loans or other advances that proved to be unsatisfactory, and therefore, the real estate was taken over by the bank. Every endeavor is made to dispose of such real estate within a short time, and during the time it is owned by the bank it is often valued below the amount expected to be realized by subsequent sale. State and national laws and regulations require that other real estate be sold as soon as reasonably possible and that periodic charge-offs be made if the property is held beyond the legal limits.

Other Assets

The classification Other Assets includes all assets that do not properly belong in any of the other classifications, and usually the total is relatively small. It may include such assets as safe deposit company stock owned by the bank, property acquired in the settlement of claims, miscellaneous accounts receivable, and so forth. The assets included in this item vary widely among banks.

Liabilities

The second set of figures in the specimen statement of condition, Form 39, is headed *Liabilities*. The liabilities represent the bank's obligations to depositors and others and the bank's net worth to its stockholders. The largest of the liability items, which is the first to be considered, is the amount due to depositors. Following this item are the liabilities to others, which are not large in proportion to total liabilities. Both deposit liabilities and liabilities to others must be completely satisfied before the bank's net worth to stockholders is established.

Deposits

The largest item of a commercial bank's obligation to depositors is usually its demand deposit liability. The second item in size is generally the item of time, or savings, deposits. These items may simply be listed on the statement as Demand Deposits and Time Deposits, or they may be further detailed in accordance with the types of time and demand deposits.

Banks regard their deposit growth primarily in terms of private funds and often show these funds on the statement of condition under the heading Demand Deposits of Individuals and Corporation, and then they make a separate listing for the Public Funds that they hold.

In recent years United States Government deposits have increased to such an extent that in many banks they require a separate listing. Time Deposits may be segregated into Savings Deposits and Other Time Deposits.

Due to Banks and Bankers

Transit and collection items are cleared and many other transactions are completed by means of arrangements between commercial banks. To expedite these transactions, banks find it desirable to carry balances with each other. Metropolitan banks, for example, have as customers many banks located in adjacent territories and in every part of the United States.

If the number of accounts of other banks is not large, the bank usually carries these accounts on the general books, and consolidates the balances in the statement item Other Deposits. If the number of accounts containing deposits of other banks is large, these accounts are carried on the deposit ledgers with the total set up on the statement as Due to Banks and Bankers.

Certified Checks, Cashier's Checks, and Bank Drafts

When the bank certifies a check, it assumes the obligation of paying the amount to a holder in due course. This obligation is often shown in the statement with similar obligations arising from cashier's checks and drafts issued by the bank. A common title used for these items on the statement of condition is Cashier's or Treasurer's Checks, Drafts, and Certified Checks Outstanding.

Reserves for Expenses

It is customary for banks to set up liability accounts for expenses incurred but payable later. Such funds are called expense reserves. By means of expense reserves, provision is made for taxes (both local and national), interest on time accounts, examination expenses, and other obligations. These reserves represent the actual or estimated unpaid expenses as of any given date, and they result from the entries mentioned previously in the discussion on accrual accounting. The reserves may be the full amount of expense or may be only a partial accrual of expenses, with the full amount not being due until sometime in the future. For example, the Reserve for Income Taxes on June 30 shows the amount of taxes on income only for the first six months of the year, but the full tax is not established until the full year is completed. The funds thus set aside may be shown separately on the statement as Reserve for Taxes, Reserve for Interest, and so forth, or they may be consolidated in a single item.

In addition to specific expense reserves, banks usually set aside funds for meeting contingencies which cannot be estimated accurately but which may occur, such as losses on loans and investments. These are general or contingent reserves and in most banks they are usually carried in the capital section of the statement of condition.

Reserves for taxes and interest are liabilities which have accrued, although they may not be payable at the time of accrual. They are included in the liabilities because they represent funds set aside to meet specific purposes; these funds will be paid out eventually. General or contingent reserves are not set up to meet known liabilities but to cover unforeseen losses or reductions in assets, which at some future time may prove to have been overvalued in the beginning.

Capital

The third section of the specimen statement of condition is the capital section which shows the liability of the bank to its stockholders. Capital is made up of four types of accounts, Capital Stock, Surplus, Undivided Profits, and Reserves. Each of these accounts is discussed separately.

Capital Stock

Until the passage of the Emergency Banking Act of 1933 (March 9, 1933), banks had only one class of stock, and the capital account carried on the statement represented the ownership of the stockholders in the bank. This amount, of course, was subordinate to the bank's obligations to depositors and others.

If Capital Stock is the only account shown on the Statement of Condition, it indicates that only common stock is outstanding. If the bank has also issued preferred stock, the Statement of Condition indicates both the amount of the common stock and the amount of preferred stock. The owners of preferred stock usually are paid a fixed rate of dividend, which is paid before common stockholders receive dividends.

Surplus

The surplus account represents funds derived from two sources: (1) contributions by stockholders when the bank was organized (plus subsequent contributions by stockholders) and (2) the accumulated earnings transferred from undivided profits. Funds in the surplus account are regarded as permanently invested in the business, subject only to extraordinary charges. Thus surplus provides an additional protection to both depositors and stockholders, since it can be used to meet unusual losses without impairing the capital stock.

It is mandatory for national banks to set aside at least one-tenth of their earnings each six months until the surplus account equals capital. A similar requirement is provided by most state laws.

Undivided Profits

The item Undivided Profits represents the remaining accumulated net earnings of the bank after dividends to stockholders and transfers to Capital, Surplus, or Reserves.

When the Undivided Profits account becomes large in proportion to Capital and Surplus, the bank may transfer a part of Undivided Profits to Surplus or to Capital Stock. Frequently the Surplus account, in turn, becomes large in proportion to Capital Stock, and a part of Surplus may be transferred to Capital Stock. Transfers from Undivided Profits or Surplus to Capital Stock are accomplished through stock dividends, by which new stock instead of cash is issued to stockholders.

Reserves for Bad Debts

Beginning with the year 1947 the Internal Revenue Service permitted banks to set up a Reserve for Loan Losses and allowed the banks to deduct in their income tax returns the amount put into the reserve as though it were a realized expense or loss. The amount that can be put into the reserve, however, is limited by definite rules promulgated by the Internal Revenue Service. Since this regulation was promulgated, most banks have found it advantageous to set up such reserves on their books. In preparing their condensed statement of condition, some banks deduct this reserve from loans and discounts, and others show this reserve separately under liabilities.

Other Liabilities

Like Other Assets, the item Other Liabilities represents liabilities that cannot be properly included in any of the other classifications. Usually the amount of this item is small in comparison with total liabilities.

Other Statement Items

Certain other items frequently appear on statements of condition. Some of these items appear in asset accounts and others appear in liability accounts.

1. Interest Earned but Not Collected, an asset, represents interest accrued on investments and loans, that is, interest that has been earned but either is not yet due or has not yet been collected. Interest on demand notes, for example, is usually collected once a month; hence during the month some part of the interest is earned but not collected. Time notes frequently provide for the payment of interest monthly or at maturity; in the meantime interest is earned but not yet due.

2. Customers' Liability on Acceptances, an asset, represents the amount due to the bank from customers because of the liability assumed by the bank in accepting drafts.

3. Unearned Discount, a liability, represents interest included in the face value of the notes at the time loans were made. The

Unearned Discount account is adjusted at regular intervals to show the amount still to be earned.

4. Liability on Acceptances (or Acceptances Executed for Customers), a liability, represents obligations incurred by the bank in accepting drafts drawn under letter of credit arrangements (explained in Chapter XV).

5. Bills Payable (or Rediscounts), a liability, represents the amount borrowed by the bank from the Federal Reserve Bank of its district or from a correspondent bank.

Statement Form

The form in which the statement of condition is prepared varies in accordance with the purpose for which it is prepared. The statement of condition required by the supervisory authorities must be prepared on forms furnished by the authorities. Statements of condition prepared for other purposes differ primarily in the amount of detail shown. Often the same bank may prepare both detailed and condensed statements to serve different purposes. For folders or booklets furnished to the public, the statement may be prepared in an even different form. Whatever the purpose of the statement, it should reflect conservatively and accurately the condition of the bank as of the date shown on the statement.

Questions Based on Chapter XVII

1. Why is bank accounting necessary?
2. What are the objectives of bank accounting?
3. What two kinds of records commonly are found in bank accounting? Illustrate.
4. In what equation is the principle of double entry bookkeeping expressed?
5. What are the purposes of double entry bookkeeping?
6. What is the general ledger? Journal? Subsidiary ledger?
7. State the position of the general books with regard to bank accounting.
8. List the duties of the general bookkeeper.
9. Name and explain two methods used for income and expense accounting.
10. What additional information does cost accounting furnish?

11. What determines the cost accounting procedure used by a bank?
12. Mention the two main sections of the Statement of Condition. What does each section show?
13. For whom is the Statement of Condition prepared?
14. Are there different kinds of reserve accounts? Illustrate.
15. What is a "statement call?"
16. What is meant by the item Undivided Profits?
17. On the Statement of Condition what does the item Due to Banks and Bankers represent?
18. On the Statement of Condition what does the item Cash include?
19. What different types of deposit items are there?
20. In what order are assets usually listed in the Statement of Condition?
21. What does the Surplus account represent?
22. The Statement of Condition of the Institute State Bank on June 30, 1956 contained the items and amounts which follow. From this information construct the Statement of Condition, supplying the correct amount for Undivided Profits.

Cash and Due from Banks	$ 353,629.36
United States Government Obligations	727,729.33
Time Deposits	400,615.38
Interest Earned but Not Collected	27,624.13
Reserve for Taxes	10,618.49
Reserve for Interest	5,132.23
Time Loans	418,714.27
Demand Loans	19,614.29
Unearned Discount	2,626.13
Federal Reserve Bank Stock	3,000.00
Capital Stock	50,000.00
Surplus	50,000.00
Other Assets	3,600.00
Banking House	31,000.00
Reserve for Securities	15,000.00
Demand Deposits	1,124,352.28
Other Bonds	96,253.00
Furniture & Fixtures	10,689.22
Reserve for Bad Debts	7,629.47
Undivided Profits	?

Questions for Investigation

1. List the various subsidiary ledgers used in your bank.
2. What accounts on the general books are affected by the results of the work of your department?

3. For what purposes is cost accounting used in your bank? Who furnishes the cost accounting information?
4. What method of income and expense accounting is used in your bank?
5. How often is the Statement of Condition prepared in your bank. By whom are copies of it received?
6. What supervisory authority issues the statement call for your bank?
7. What reserve accounts are shown in your bank's statement?
8. How many different forms of Statement of Condition are prepared in your bank during the year?
9. Other than the statement itself, what information is contained in the statement folder of your bank?

CHAPTER XVIII

ACCOUNT ANALYSIS AND SERVICE CHARGES

The Purposes of This Chapter:

1. To explain the meaning of the terms account analysis and service charge.
2. To provide information regarding the transactions usually considered in analyzing checking accounts.
3. To discuss the costs of handling checking account balances, and the earnings derived from the investment of these balances.
4. To illustrate and explain some of the more widely used methods of analyzing regular and special checking accounts and savings accounts.
5. To mention the services generally included in miscellaneous service charge programs.

IN PREVIOUS chapters, we discuss how banking differs from other types of business. Practically all the activities discussed in this text are unique to banking; other businesses do not engage in them. Banking, however, is similar to other businesses in some respects. In this chapter we discuss some of these similarities, the most important of which probably is the sales factor. Banks, like other enterprises, have to sell their wares; banks sell service. Of all the services that banks render, the most familiar is the paying and the collecting of checks. Each service that the bank renders is provided at considerable cost and, therefore, the bank must know the cost of each operation.

When the grocer establishes a selling price for a pound of potatoes, he considers what the potatoes cost him, as well as such factors as his overhead and his profit. Likewise, in selling services, a bank must take a similar approach in determining the price to be placed on each service. It must know not only its own costs and earnings but also average costs and earnings of other banks.

Early Development of Service Charges

For many years banks were not interested in obtaining detailed information regarding their costs and their earnings because they were making good profits. In fact, banks not only believed it was unneccessary to establish charges for the services that they rendered to checking account customers, but they also thought it good practice to pay interest on the balances maintained in checking accounts. A few bankers recognized that this policy was unsound. They were pioneers in setting service charges. They reasoned that banking is similar to other businesses, and therefore, it is entitled to be paid a fair price for services performed. During the 1920's many banks recognized the usefulness of service charges as an additional source of income. They found that this new income was needed, not to increase their profits, but rather to offset their losses; losses suffered because they serviced, without charge, checking accounts that did not carry balances large enough to provide earnings sufficient to cover the expenses involved for the bank in servicing them.

In recognizing the need for adequate service charges, banks also realized that they needed more complete information about banking costs. Furthermore, the best answer to the customer's question, "Why do you make a service charge?" was found to be a statement of the cost of the items included in the service charge. Bank employees, from the janitor to the president, are often asked about the bank's service charge plan. When you are asked this question you have an excellent opportunity to sell your bank's services. To make full use of your opportunity you must be fully acquainted with and convinced of the fairness of the service charge plan, and you must understand the basis of service charges and account analysis.

Account analysis and service charge are two of the most widely used in terms in banking. Although they differ considerably in meaning, too often these terms are used carelessly with little or no distinction being made between them.

Account analysis is a method of determining the profit made, or loss sustained, in servicing demand deposits, that is, checking accounts. Account analysis is based on a consideration not only of the expenses incurred in servicing the account but also of the earnings derived from the investable portion of the depositor's balance. The difference between the earnings on the account balance and the expense of servicing the account represents the profit or loss on that account.

The term service charge refers to the rates established for various services performed. Although checking accounts produce the major portion of the income derived from service charges, these charges are also applied to practically all services which the banks render to their customers.

There are many different methods of analysis in use and many different rates are charged for services, but the fundamental objective is always to obtain adequate compensation from the customer to offset the losses incurred in the handling of his banking transactions.

The Analysis of the Checking Account

To obtain a basic knowledge of account analysis, it is necessary to consider those items which are generally included in most analysis plans. Most plans include such cost factors as maintenance of the account, deposit tickets, checks on us, transit items, clearings, and the earnings credit, that is, the earnings factor.

The cost figures shown under each of the following headings were derived from a current survey covering a representative group of banks.

COST FACTORS

The factors considered in most analysis plans are maintenance, deposit tickets, checks on us, transit items, and clearings items. Many banks include charges for other miscellaneous services, some of which are discussed subsequently.

Maintenance

There is a basic cost in the handling of every account, irrespective of its size or activity. This cost includes rendering statements, balancing ledgers, furnishing balances, and so forth. These costs have little or no relation to the number of transactions handled. Charges for maintenance over a period of years have been favorably accepted by customers.

The maintenance costs of a bank have been likened to those of a public utility company. Plant and equipment, investment and tax obligations exist regardless of individual service activity. There must be an office and an adequate staff of well-trained personnel to meet the demands of the customers, in other words, a readiness to serve at all times.

Costs for maintenance (per month)
High $2.108
Median .... .615
Low .... .380

Deposit Tickets

The deposit ticket is one of the most costly of items. Although some deposits are received through the mail and in night depositories, almost all come into the bank through the teller's cage. Over-the-counter operations increase costs considerably because of the higher salaries, the rent, and the standby time of tellers.

The handling of a deposit ticket generally requires the following steps to be taken.

1. The teller accepts the deposit and enters the amount in the passbook, or he validates a duplicate deposit ticket.

2. If the bank requires that calculations be made for float, this information is recorded.

3. The proof clerk proves, sorts, and distributes the deposit tickets to the bookkeeper.

4. The bookkeeper sorts alphabetically, posts to the customer's account, and files the deposit tickets.

Some bankers make no charge for deposits in their service charge schedules; others make no charge for deposit tickets as such but include this factor in their charges for such other services as checks paid or items deposited.

Bank depositors now are accepting charges for deposit tickets more readily, since customer relations programs explain that the depositor is being charged not for "depositing his money" but rather for the cost involved in handling the deposit.

Costs for Deposit Tickets
High ....$ .283
Median ...... .155
Low .... .105

Checks on Us

The establishment of a rate for checks on us is found in nearly all types of service charge plans.

For analysis purposes the usual practice is to establish only one rate for paying checks on us, regardless of the source from which the check is received. Actual costs, however, vary in accordance with the manner in which these checks enter the bank. There are six ways that banks generally receive checks on us.

1. Cashed over-the-counter
2. Deposited over-the-counter
3. Deposited through the mail
4. Deposited in night depository
5. Received in transit letters
6. Received in local clearings.

The checks on us cashed over-the-counter are the most costly of all; normally they cost two to three times more than those received in other ways.

Customarily no charge is made against the *depositor* for checks on us included in a deposit; instead, all costs for handling these checks are charged to the individual issuing them rather than to the person cashing or depositing them. This method is believed to be entirely fair to the bank customer.

Costs for Checks on us Paid (Average)

High	$ .088
Median	.050
Low	.033

Transit Items

Transit items are those checks that are received by a bank, usually in deposits, drawn on out-of-town banks. They are also referred to as remittance items, or out-of-town checks. Next to checks on us, transit items represent the largest volume of all those items considered for analysis purposes. The bank of deposit does not obtain credit for these items immediately. Therefore, the bank has a good reason for not allowing customers to draw on such funds until collection has been effected.

Float is the term applied to the funds represented by checks that are in the process of collection.

Costs for Transit Items

High	$ .053
Median	.021
Low	.011

Clearings Items

Clearings items refers to checks received by a bank that are drawn on another bank in the same town, city, or area, and can be presented to the paying bank either directly or through a clearing house. The checks are handled the smallest number of times and, of all the items included in the analysis, they cost the least.

Costs for Clearings

High   ....$ .047

Median 017

Low 005

EARNINGS CREDIT

The earnings credit is the net allowance given to checking account depositors for balances maintained by them. It is intended as an offset against certain service charges. The earnings credit allowance is based on the income received from the investment of available demand deposits minus the cost of investing and protecting the funds. This allowance is computed in various ways. Three widely used methods are:

1. So many cents for each unit of balance (for instance, ten cents for each $100 of minimum or average balance).

2. A percentage rate (for instance, 1.2% of minimum or average balance).

3. So many "free" checks per unit of balance (for instance, five free checks for each $100 of minimum or average balance).

There are many methods used to determine this allowance, the two most popular being the average balance method and the minimum balance method.

Average Balance Method

The average balance method is used generally in connection with complete analysis plans, as explained later in this chapter. In determining the earnings credit through the use of the average balance method, the following six steps are usually required.

1. Averaging daily ledger balances for the month,

2. Averaging daily float,

3. Subtracting float from average balance to determine average net collected balance,

4. Figuring reserves carried,

5. Subtracting reserves to arrive at loanable balance,

6. Applying earnings rate to investable balance to determine earnings credit.

In a typical analysis plan, one method of calculating the earnings credit, based on average balance, may be illustrated as follows:

Step A. Average daily ledger balance for month....$2500.00
Step B. Less average daily float 500.00
Step C. Average net collected balance 2000.00
Step D. Less reserves 25% of $2000 .... 500.00
Step E. Average investable balance $1500.00
Step F. Earnings credit at rate of 1.2% of $1500....$ 1.50

The step-by-step procedure is quite simple. The figure for Step A is determined by averaging the daily balances for the month. Step B provides for the deduction of float or what is sometimes called uncollected balance. The average daily float for the month (Step B) is deducted from the average daily ledger balance (Step A) to provide the average net collected balance (Step C).

Banks are required by law to maintain certain reserves in the form of deposited balances proportionate to their respective types of deposits. In actual practice, banks find it necessary to carry an additional margin of cash and other reserves to take care of daily fluctuations in receipts and withdrawals. Such reserves cannot be used for investment or loan purposes and provide no income to the bank. In computing the earnings value of checking account balances, therefore, a deduction is made from the collected balances of the bank's respective accounts to provide for reserves that the bank has found from actual practice and experience are necessary. For instance, a country bank, which is legally required to carry reserves of fourteen per cent against its demand deposits, could find from actual experience and practice that it must carry total reserves of twenty-five per cent. If such were the case, then twenty-five per cent should be deducted from the collected balance of each account to determine the amount available to the bank for loan and investment purposes. Thus, in the illustration, the twenty-five per cent is deducted for reserves (Step D), leaving an investable balance of $1500 (Step E).

When the earnings credit of 1.2% (shown in this illustration) is applied to the investable balance, the bank obtains earnings of $1.50 for the month on the balance carried by that customer. If the 1.2% earnings credit is applied to the $1500 loanable balance, the calculation would be as follows:

$$\$1500 \times 1.2\% = \$18.00$$

Since eighteen dollars represents the earnings for the entire year, this amount must be converted to a monthly basis:

$$\$18 \div 12 = \$1.50$$

The short cut method for determining monthly earnings on the basis of a 1.2% rate is to "point off" the amount by three digits. For instance, using the figure of $1500 in the above illustration, the decimal would be placed as follows: $1.500 or $1.50. Therefore, the 1.2% rate actually results in an allowance of ten cents per month per $100 of investable balance.

Minimum Balance Method

Minimum balances are being used increasingly for the purpose of establishing earnings credit in smaller and medium-sized banks. These banks report that their experience is highly satisfactory from the viewpoint both of the depositor and of the bank.

The average balance method of determining the earnings credit allowance is accurate for accounts with substantial balances, particularly when the balances fluctuate considerably. For the majority of accounts, however, the use of the minimum balance procedure is more popular, principally because the analysis time is reduced. Some banks report the reduction to be about 50%. The minimum balance for the month can be found quickly on the ledger sheet, and no deductions are necessary for float or for reserves.

Surveys indicate that in the aggregate, minimum balances are approximately twenty-five per cent less than average balances. The twenty-five per cent difference may be considered a close approximation to the deductions for float and for reserves when average balances are used. A recent survey among banks with assets under seven and one half million dollars revealed that out of the 2,409 banks using analysis methods, 1,937, that is 80%, were making earnings credit allowances on the basis of minimum balances.

METHODS OF ANALYZING ACCOUNTS

We have been considering the factors generally used in modern service charge plans. The next step is the selection of the method of account analysis best suited to the bank's particular needs. Keep in mind that the basic requirement is fair treatment for both the customer and the bank; the next important factor is simplicity and efficiency of operation, that is, the service charge plan should be easy to explain, simple to understand, and inexpensive to operate.

Furthermore, the plan should lend itself to the objective of uniformity of method among banks, that is, the banks would gradually adopt one basic method of analysis. Because customers must be convinced of the need for and fairness of service charges, it is important that a minimum number of analysis plans be in use. For instance, when a customer who moves to another town, transfers his checking account, obviously both the customer and the new bank are benefited if the new bank is using an analysis plan similar to the former bank's plan. Although a uniform method of imposing service charges is very desirable, there are good reason why rates vary between banks, chiefly because of differences in costs, in competition, and in other factors.

Basic Types of Service Charge Plans

During the past twenty years much progress has been made in the techniques of account analysis. Currently, the charges for bank services are more equitable than at any time in the past, however, there is still much room for improvement in methods of analysis and application. The results of a recent survey of the service charge plans and of the rates used by 5,287 banks under seven and one half million dollars emphasized the need for further improvement. The following types of analysis plans were found to be in use:

	No. of Banks
Flat—	
(Uniform charge made on accounts with balances below certain minimums or on all accounts, activity not considered)	505

No. of
Banks

Measured—

(Allowance of "free" checks for units of balance maintained or for basic charge made when balances fall below
specified minimums) 616

Analysis

(Charge on basis of earnings and expenses per account)

TYPES OF ANALYSIS PLANS:

Simplified analysis 2,340
Complete analysis 69
                                        2,409

Combination Plans 899
Item Rate Plans—Charge on basis of activity only.......... 230
Miscellaneous Plans—

(Either combination of more than two basic methods, or
plans that do not lend themselves to classification on any
of the above bases. Included in this group are approximately 250 reports that could not be accurately classified
because they were incomplete.) 305

No service charge plans 323

TOTAL 5,287

Special Checking Accounts 1,166

(In addition to the various plans used, a majority of the
reporting banks applied complete analysis to those relatively
few accounts that they considered unusual, regardless of
their basic plans.)

It may be seen readily that most plans (used by these 5,287
banks) can be grouped in three basic types, the Flat, the Measured,
and the Analysis. The analysis types can be further classified into
two groups, the complete and the simplified. An explanation of
these plans is given to indicate their main differences and to indicate some of their strong and their weak points.

1. The flat charge plan. The first plan generally used by commercial banks consisted mainly of a flat fee of, for example, 50¢
or $1 per month if an average balance in the account fell below
$50 or $100 during the month. This fee was a penalty against

small accounts rather than a reimbursement to the bank for the expense incurred in handling excessive activity in individual accounts. For the latter purpose it was wholly inadequate. Gradually, activity was recognized as an essential element that must be considered along with the size of the balance. With much assistance and encouragement from the American Bankers Association and many state associations, banks gradually adopted various types of measured service charge plans.

2. The measured (metered) charge. Early measured charge plans were a considerable improvement over flat types. The outstanding characteristic of these plans was a charge for checks paid over and above those allowed "free" on the basis of average ledger balance. There was, and still is, a tendency to allow entirely too much activity. The measured plans, generally used, allow the customer either five or ten checks for each $100 of average balance maintained. Based on current cost and earnings data, it is not unusual to find that in some cases the actual earnings credit allowed the customer on the basis of this plan is in excess of 10%, a rate far in excess of the bank's actual earnings on the account. The earnings allowance on the balance, expressed in terms of "free" checks, is typically excessive and constitutes a serious leak in earnings. Another weakness of most measured plans is that they lack a charge for deposit activity. It is important that the bank receive a fair rate of return on all ledger entries, credits as well as debits and also on certain deposited items, which are numerous and varied. This problem is taken care of to a limited extent in some improved measured plans.

3. Analysis plans. Surveys by the American Bankers Association and by state associations reveal that increasing numbers of banks are adopting improved types of service charge plans.

a. Complete Analysis. Although large city banks have made use of complete analysis plans for years, this type of plan has never been popular with the country banks. The complete analysis plan achieves the greatest equity between the depositors and the bank, and it is preferred by the larger banks. However, because the detail involved in complete analysis is both complicated and intricate, the plan has not been used widely by country banks. When a complete analysis plan is used on all accounts, these banks consider that the expense incurred is entirely out of proportion to the resulting benefits to the bank. In all banks the service charge on a small percentage of accounts should be determined by the complete analysis method. These accounts are those very active ones in which many items are cleared each month or in which the balances fluctuate widely. Although complete analysis plans vary somewhat between banks, Table 1 shows a typical plan as applied to a hypothetical account. The rates used are only for illustrative purposes.

TABLE 1. COMPLETE ANALYSIS OF AN ACCOUNT

(1)	Average daily ledger balance for month	$2500.00
(2)	Less: Average daily float	500.00
(3)	Average net collected balance	2000.00
(4)	Less: Reserve 25% of $2000 (3)	500.00
(5)	Investable balance	$1500.00
(6)	Earnings credit at rate of 1.2% of $1500 (5)	$ 1.50
(7)	Maintenance factor	$ .50
(8)	Deposits 7 @ 10¢ each	.70
(9)	Checks paid 25 @ 6¢ each	1.50
(10)	Clearings 10 @ 2¢ each	.20
(11)	Transit items 60 @ 3¢ each	1.80
(12)	Cash handled 30 minutes @ 4¢ per minute of handling time	1.20
(13)	Checks paid that create or increase an overdraft	—
(14)	Checks returned (drawn or deposited by customer) because of insufficient or no funds or other reasons 2 @ 50¢ each	1.00
(15)	Other related services	—
(16)	TOTAL VALUE OF SERVICES RENDERED— Total of lines (7) through (15)	$ 6.90
(17)	Less: EARNINGS CREDIT—from line (6)	1.50
(18)	NET SERVICE CHARGE	$ 5.40

Most of the information necessary to complete this type analysis appears on the customer's ledger sheet, including the daily listings of each deposit and check drawn, old and new balances, float information, and activity data covering the other items. b. Simplified Analysis. Based on recent surveys, simplified analysis is the most widely used of all plans. About three-fourths of the banks in the United States have total assets of less than $10 million each, and it is principally among the banks in this group that the plan has gained wide usage.

Although there are numerous variations of simplified analysis, the plan most generally used provides for an earnings allowance based on (1) the minimum monthly balance, (2) a maintenance factor, and (3) a uniform item rate for ledger entries, including checks paid, deposits made, and transit items in the deposits.

The step-by-step procedure involved in the calculation of service charges through the use of the simplified method of analysis is presented in Table 2. The rates are only for illustrative purposes.

TABLE 2. CALCULATIONS IN SIMPLIFIED ANALYSIS OF AN ACCOUNT

(1) Maintenance cost per month	$ .50
(2) Ledger entries 12 @ 5¢ each (Includes checks paid and deposits made)	.60
(3) Out-of-town checks deposited 2 @ 5¢ each	.10
(4) Other charges	—
(5) TOTAL cost of service performed	$1.20
(6) Less: Earnings allowance on minimum monthly balance—$300 @ 10¢ per $100	.30
(7) TOTAL CHARGE FOR SERVICE PERFORMED	$ .90

Simplified analysis lends itself to the use of a time saving table which covers the great majority of accounts. The table should include all the factors—the maintenance factor, item rate, and earnings credit—for varying numbers of items in the minimum balance groups of $100 or less, from $100 up to $200, and then increasing by $100 units. A workable chart could include as many as sixty items (transit items, checks paid, and deposits made) and minimum balances up to $3,000. Table 3 illustrates the service charge rates in actual use by a bank.

The figures shown in Table 3 are only for illustrative purposes. When using a table of this type, it is necessary only to count the transit items, the checks paid, and the deposits made, no other calculations are required. The net service charge can then be found simply by applying the total item count to the appropriate minimum balance column.

Special Checking Accounts

In addition to regular checking accounts, which are subject to analysis plans such as those previously described, a great many

TABLE 3. SERVICE CHARGE CHART

NOTE: *This chart is shown for illustrative purposes only. It is a reproduction of a portion of one which is in actual use by a bank. The figures thereon will not be applicable to all banks because of the variance of actual costs and earnings of banks.*

MAINTENANCE FACTOR .... 50¢

ITEM RATE, including Ledger Entries (Checks and Deposits) and Transit Items..... 5¢

EARNING ALLOWANCE per $100 of Minimum Balance in Even Hundreds.......... 10¢

MINIMUM BALANCE		Over $ 0 Under 100	$100 200	$200 300	$300 400	$400 500	$500 600	$600 700	$700 800
EARNING ALLOWANCE		.00	.10	.20	.30	.40	.50	.60	.70
No. of Items	Item Charge								
0	.00	.50	.40	.30	.20	.10			
1	.05	.55	.45	.35	.25	.15			
2	.10	.60	.50	.40	.30	.20	.10		
3	.15	.65	.55	.45	.35	.25	.15		
4	.20	.70	.60	.50	.40	.30	.20	.10	
5	.25	.75	.65	.55	.45	.35	.25	.15	
6	.30	.80	.70	.60	.50	.40	.30	.20	.10
7	.35	.85	.75	.65	.55	.45	.35	.25	.15
8	.40	.90	.80	.70	.60	.50	.40	.30	.20
9	.45	.95	.85	.75	.65	.55	.45	.35	.25
10	.50	1.00	.90	.80	.70	.60	.50	.40	.30
11	.55	1.05	.95	.85	.75	.65	.55	.45	.35
12	.60	1.10	1.00	.90	.80	.70	.60	.50	.40
13	.65	1.15	1.05	.95	.85	.75	.65	.55	.45
14	.70	1.20	1.10	1.00	.90	.80	.70	.60	.50
15	.75	1.25	1.15	1.05	.95	.85	.75	.65	.55
16	.80	1.30	1.20	1.10	1.00	.90	.80	.70	.60
17	.85	1.35	1.25	1.15	1.05	.95	.85	.75	.65
18	.90	1.40	1.30	1.20	1.10	1.00	.90	.80	.70
19	.95	1.45	1.35	1.25	1.15	1.05	.95	.85	.75
20	1.00	1.50	1.40	1.30	1.20	1.10	1.00	.90	.80
21	1.05	1.55	1.45	1.35	1.25	1.15	1.05	.95	.85
22	1.10	1.60	1.50	1.40	1.30	1.20	1.10	1.00	.90
23	1.15	1.65	1.55	1.45	1.35	1.25	1.15	1.05	.95
24	1.20	1.70	1.60	1.50	1.40	1.30	1.20	1.10	1.00
25	1.25	1.75	1.65	1.55	1.45	1.35	1.25	1.15	1.05
26	1.30	1.80	1.70	1.60	1.50	1.40	1.30	1.20	1.10
27	1.35	1.85	1.75	1.65	1.55	1.45	1.35	1.25	1.15
28	1.40	1.90	1.80	1.70	1.60	1.50	1.40	1.30	1.20
29	1.45	1.95	1.85	1.75	1.65	1.55	1.45	1.35	1.25
30	1.50	2.00	1.90	1.80	1.70	1.60	1.50	1.40	1.30

banks offer another type of checking account service that has become very popular with customers during recent years. Although this service bears many different titles, it is usually designated as special checking accounts.

Since most of these plans charge only for check activity and do not make any charge for maintenance, number of deposits, and items deposited, the fee does not reflect directly the costs of operating the accounts. Rates generally range from five to twelve and one half cents per check paid. Theoretically, the rate charged for each check paid not only pays for the handling of the check, but also compensates the bank for the costs of maintenance, deposits, transit and clearing items deposited, profit, and reserves for losses. Of course, if the balance is nominal and if the customer writes only a few checks, there is usually a loss on the account. Likewise, if the customer writes a large number of checks and the account has little or no other activity, the profit to the bank on that account could be comparatively high, depending, of course, on the rates used.

The service charges on special checking accounts are usually collected by one of two methods, either by charging the account the fee at the time each check is paid or by selling the customer a book of blank checks made up especially for this type of account.

Charges for Miscellaneous Services

The previous discussion of account analysis and service charges has been limited to regular and special checking accounts. In addition to the procedures mentioned, practically every bank has some kind of plan for miscellaneous service charges. Some plans are very brief, covering only a few transactions; others are so elaborate that management has found it advisable to furnish employees with reference guides on the subject. Ordinarily, miscellaneous service charges are imposed to place certain activities on a profitable basis. However, some charges are made with the objective of discouraging unsound practices by bank customers. For instance, when returning checks because of insufficient funds, banks frequently establish a rate considerably higher than the actual cost.

A current survey among 383 representative banks revealed considerable variation in the services for which charges were made and wide ranges in rates used and the bases for charges. For instance, 98 of the 383 participating banks charged savings customers for excess withdrawal activity. There were, however, eleven different bases for these charges, and thirty-six different rates were being applied. Among the miscellaneous services for which these 383 banks made a charge are the following:

Miscellaneous Services

Cashing out-of-town checks
Certifying checks
Imprinting and binding checks
Returning post-dated checks
Issuing traveler's checks
Replacing lost savings passbooks
Collecting coupons
Collections (in or out)
Paying out currency or coin
Closing checking accounts within specified periods
Issuing official checks, such as drafts, bank money orders, and cashier's checks
Answering credit inquiries
Handling escrows
Minimum charges on loans
Charges for night depository use
Making up payrolls
Guaranteeing signatures

Special requests for statements
Purchasing or selling stock
Transferring funds by wire
Paying checks creating overdrafts
Returning checks for not sufficient funds
Closing club accounts before completing payments
Not completing club account payments
Closing savings accounts within short periods after opening
Savings account withdrawals in excess of a specified number
Receiving currency or coin in a deposit
Originals and renewals of stop payments
Purchasing, selling, collecting or exchanging bonds

Selling Service Charges to the Bank's Customers

Customer acceptance of service charges is vital to the successful operation of any service charge plan. Selling the bank's charges to its customers is just as important and requires just as much careful planning as the development of the service charge schedules.

First, a successful service charge program should be equally fair both to the customer and to the bank. The banker who is equipped with a cost analysis of his bank's activities and with cost and earnings data for banking in general can support his service charge program with facts. Second, the service charge plan should be easy for the customer to understand. Third, the bank's directors and the entire staff should be thoroughly familiar with the service charge program and should be convinced of its fairness to the customer and to the bank. The well trained, well informed employee can often turn a disgruntled customer into a satisfied customer.

A new service charge plan may be presented to the public in a variety of ways. Some banks have launched an educational program prior to the installation of the charges by personally calling on key customers to explain the necessity for adequate service charges and to invite constructive suggestions. Other banks have written letters to all customers affected by the plan, pointing out that the charges are the result of the ever-mounting costs of doing business and the low net return to the bank from the invested assets. Booklets explaining all the costs involved in operating a bank are also often employed by banks in selling their service charge plans. Direct mail advertising confines the announcement of the plan to the customers whom the bank desires to inform, whereas a general advertising campaign reaches far beyond this group. Primarily, the selling of a schedule of service charges is a family matter between the bank and its customers.

The millions of Americans who use the services of banks wish to have strong banks. They recognize that to be strong each bank in the community must operate at a fair profit. The successful selling of a service charge plan requires that the bank's costs be explained so clearly and accurately that the customers understand and realize the need for them.

Questions Based on Chapter XVIII

1. What is the difference between the objectives of account analysis and service charges?
2. How is account analysis generally used?
3. How should the rates used in service charge plans be determined?
4. What factors should be considered in establishing programs for account analysis and service charges?
5. List the steps involved in complete analysis and in simplified analysis.
6. In the analysis of checking accounts what is the difference between the use of minimum as compared with average balances for determining the earnings credit?
7. What are the disadvantages of many flat and measured plans?
8. Why are a few of the rates for miscellaneous service charges often purposely set at figures considerably in excess of actual costs?

Questions for Investigation

1. What account analysis and service charge plans are in use in your bank?

2. How do your plans and rates compare with the plans and rates used by other banks in your area?
3. How do your bank's costs compare with bank costs in general?
4. What miscellaneous service charge program does your bank have in effect?

CHAPTER XIX

INTERNAL CONTROLS

The Purposes of This Chapter:

1. To discuss the significance of internal control through the audit function.
2. To mention the principles of audit procedures.
3. To outline the functions and scope of an audit program.
4. To describe the operations of an auditing department.

BANKS are public institutions and are, therefore, affected and influenced by public opinion. They are the arteries through which flows the economic and the financial blood of the community. They are also the custodians of other people's wealth and business affairs. Consequently, their services and their success have a lasting effect upon every individual and every community in the nation.

A sound and constructive banking system must be based upon proper procedures, practices, and operations. Such safeguards assure the safety and security of the institution and, when made known, promote the public approval. The safeguards which the Federal and various state governments have adopted through the enactment of laws and regulations to foster a strong banking system are explained in Chapter XXI, External Controls. In that chapter, also, the various government agencies which are responsible for the enforcement of these laws and regulations are described. Bank examinations by the government, however, are not all-inclusive in scope and consequently cannot give the public or the bank's stockholders complete assurance that the bank's operations are safe, sound, and efficient. Supervisory examinations cannot properly be considered as internal audits, although this misconception is not uncommon. Examinations are conducted primarily to ascertain whether bank management is complying with all regulatory requirements. A secondary purpose is that of appraising the bank's assets, policies, and internal management. These examinations also permit the regulatory authorities to verify the accuracy of the regular reports prepared and submitted by the bank.

The Principle of the Audit Procedure

The principle of audit procedure is to insure that proper internal controls and safeguards are first instituted and then constantly maintained. The prevention of carelessness and misuse of the property both of the customer and of the bank and the safeguarding of human values, as well as asset values, is the prime object of the audit program, rather than the discovery of irregularities that may have occurred. The function of an audit is to provide an independent review of the bank's condition and a continuing verification of the fact that the staff is observing the established controls and safeguards. This work is performed by an individual or by a group, consisting primarily of a bank's own employees. The internal audit must determine that accounting records, reports, and official and published statements accurately reflect the true status of the bank's condition and also that there are no undue hazards involved in any of the bank's policies, plans, operations, or procedures. In general, the function of an audit is to assure management that the general internal operations are proceeding smoothly and correctly.

The auditor or control officer of a bank is appointed by the board of directors. To derive the maximum benefit from an audit program, the bank should provide in its by-laws a brief description of the scope of the audit program and a specific statement that the auditor or control officer must report directly to the board of directors. The auditor or control officer should be responsible to the board and report directly to it, or he may be requested to attend meetings. At these meetings he, personally, should make the audit report based on the audit examination and should be available for questions and consultation on matters involving the safety and the internal controls of the bank.

The Responsibilities of the Auditor

As the representative of the bank's stockholders and directors, the auditor or control officer bears the responsibility for their protection, as well as for the protection of management. He is interested in the solvency of the institution as well as compliance with the laws. It is his duty to observe operations, to report all irregularities, weaknesses, improper practices, and to recommend necessary corrective measures. His action must be in harmony with the established policies of the board of directors. Many banks are too small to employ a full-time auditor; however, some individual is charged, as part of his duties, with the responsibility to ascertain that the auditing function is performed. To accomplish his task, he can devise a system in which the work of one individual is checked or verified by another.

THE FUNCTION AND THE SCOPE OF THE AUDIT PROGRAM

The function of an audit is to verify the fact that the program of internal safeguards is in effect a well organized and effective program. It is important that the purposes and functions of the auditor be explained to employees to avoid any misunderstanding which might arise.

In banks large enough to employ a full-time auditor, the auditor should not have authority to make or disburse loans, receive deposits, handle cash, originate entries, or sign official bank checks or drafts. It is his responsibility to set the timing of the examinations and audits without advance notice. The alert auditor, however, so schedules his activities that they do not interfere with the flow of operations. Such timing is essential to gain the cooperation of all and to prevent an increase in the operating expense. In addition, the element of surprise is essential in a successful audit program.

The Five Aspects of an Audit

The fundamental purpose of the auditing program and function is that of verification. It is the aim of the program to verify the bank's records to determine that they reflect all contractual undertakings, whether they are in an agency or in fiduciary capacity. Essentially, five aspects are involved in this program.

1. Verification of assets. The audit should verify the existence and safety of all bank assets and of all property left in the bank's custody by others. It is essential that the assets be accounted for and that they be reflected on the bank's books at their proper value.

2. Verification of liabilities. All liabilities should be verified. This procedure includes the determination that liabilities are real or contingent and are properly reflected on the bank's records.

3. Verification of income. All items of income are verified and proved to the various income accounts of the bank. It should also be determined that the bank has received all the income to which it is entitled and that such income is reflected in the accounting records.

4. Verification of expense. All expenses incurred should be verified. The auditor should make certain that they are paid and distributed to their proper designations and captions in the accounting records, that they are properly authorized and are made for legitimate purposes, and that funds are properly disbursed and are paid to the proper parties.

5. Verification of net worth. The net worth of the bank should be proved. Verify the fact that the capital accounts, including capital stock, surplus, undivided profits, and reserves are properly stated; and that proper increases, decreases, and allocations have been made. The verification may fall into three categories: statement of condition audits, spot audits, and continuous audits.

a. *Statement of condition audits* consist of verifying the assets and liabilities as of one certain day. This type of audit is used by the examining authorities and occasionally by the auditing staff.

b. *Spot audits* are the verification of certain assets and liabilities and the proving of income and expense by testing some of the transactions.

c. *Continuous audits* are, as the name indicates, a constant audit such as that used in verifying income and expense. The procedure requires the daily audit of these accounts, and if the income and expense are kept on an accrual basis, the accrual must control the cash received.

Duties of the Auditor

It is beyond the scope of this text to explain in detail the various methods and procedures for auditing and controlling each specific asset, liability, item of income and expense, and the capital structure. The student, however, should be aware that tellers' cash and reserve cash are verified by actual count. The bank's own investment securities are kept under dual control, physically counted, and compared to the investment ledger. The income is verified to ascertain that it was credited on the books. Correspondent or due from bank accounts are reconciled from statements received from banks. Notes and liability ledgers are proved to the general books and the income verified. The genuineness of the note should be determined either by direct verification, or by the auditor forwarding the payment notices to the customer. Collateral should be under dual control and verified direct to the note and periodically by direct verification with the customer. An inventory of furniture and fixtures is made periodically. Insurance coverage on these items and on the bank building should be reviewed periodically.

The verification of liabilities includes balancing the accounts with the general books by taking trial runs of the various customers' account ledgers. Commercial or checking accounts are verified by sending statements periodically to the customers and asking the customers to balance the statement with their figures in their checkbooks and advise the bank as to the correctness of the account.

Outstanding official checks and drafts are proved to the general ledgers by running outstanding items and examining the indorsements on paid checks.

Capital accounts are verified and reconciled with particular attention being given to recoveries, profits, and charge-offs, and provision being made for reserves in accordance with established formulas.

Income and expense accounts are carefully reviewed, analyzed, and proved, and certain test checks or accrual accounting can reflect the accuracy of these records.

Many other effective methods of verification can be used in the audit procedure. Such methods depend upon the wishes and abilities of the auditor and the type of item appearing in the statement of condition of a particular bank.

From this discussion it might be assumed that the auditing function is applicable only to larger banks. However, audits and controls are applied in the small bank as well as in the large metropolitan institution. The difference between an audit in a small and in a large bank is one of degree, that is, in the amount of detail involved and the extent to which certain controls can be equitably employed.

The Audit in the Small Bank

Even the small country bank can install controls which create better safeguards. Such controls might include any or all of the following:

1. Employees should be rotated whenever possible.
2. Segregation or division of duties (Employees handling cash should not post records and the reverse).
3. All employees and all officers should have an annual vacation.
4. Tellers should clear overs and shorts daily.
5. Dual control of securities, collateral, and reserve cash should be maintained.
6. Erasures on accounting ledger records should be eliminated.
7. Loan proceeds should be paid by a credit to the customer's account or by an official check.
8. All inactive and dormant accounts should be segregated and placed under dual control.

These and many other safeguards do not increase the cost of operation and provide excellent safeguards for banks.

Direct Verification

Direct verification is another method used in connection with auditing procedures. This procedure is becoming an increasingly important adjunct to an audit program. After ledger accounts are proved, the auditor prepares a notice which is sent directly to the customer. In the notice, the customer is requested to verify his checking or savings account balance. In the case of loans, the customer is requested to verify the loan balance as well as the kind of collateral, and so forth. The reason for this procedure is that, although the audit of a bank may show the records of the institution to be correct, this fact does not prove that the accounts are not being manipulated.

Auditing and proving the bank's records and then securing a confirmation from the customer is excellent proof that no one has committed an error or theft. Although direct verification alone does not afford complete internal control, it deserves an important place in every bank's audit program.

The verification notices are of two types; which type is selected usually depends on the personal preference of the auditor as well as on a consideration of the expense involved. The two types of notice are:

1. *Positive.* This type of notice contains a request for the customer's signature and the return of the notice to the bank.

2. *Negative.* This type of notice asks for a response from the bank's customer only in the event that the balance or verification shown does *not* agree with the customer's records.

Naturally, the positive type assures maximum results as it supplies tangible evidence of the correctness of the accounts, measures the staff performance, and indicates which accounts require additional audit attention.

AUDITING DIVISION

Although this chapter has referred to an auditor, a control officer, or to the auditing division, the auditing function does not pertain specifically to a large bank. While the limited auditing duties in a small bank may be performed by a single employee, in a large bank these duties are distributed among employees in a department consisting of a great number of individuals.

In the small bank the auditing function can be performed by an officer having other duties; or such a nonofficer employee as the general bookkeeper or officer's secretary (whose other duties would not include the handling of cash, the signing of drafts, or the originating of entries) may report to the board of directors concerning his auditing duties. In the small bank there may be an occasional violation of auditing practices. If so, the board as well as management should realize the bank's exposure.

The large bank audit division is under the supervision of the auditor who conducts the audit. The work is divided among employees who handle and specialize in specific asset or liability audits. Certain employees handle reconcilements, accountant confirmations, securities, statements, accrual supervision, and so forth. These employees report and are responsible to the auditor who in turn reports to the board of directors.

Activities in both areas are closely supervised and kept secret to prevent the various departments and employees from becoming aware of the major activities of the audit department; thus the essential element of surprise is maintained.

DIRECTORS' EXAMINATIONS

In addition to the internal auditing procedures performed by the auditor (or in a small bank by the person responsible for the auditing) and the examinations performed by supervisory authorities (state bank examiners, national bank examiners, Federal Reserve bank examiners, and Federal Deposit Insurance Corporation examiners), there is another type of examination known as the directors' examination. In some states the directors' examination is required by law. Although the National Bank Act, under which national banks operate, does not specifically require such examinations, nevertheless, the Comptroller of the Currency, as a matter of policy, usually will not approve the by-laws of a national bank unless they make provision for directors' examinations.

In some banks, especially small banks in which the auditing is necessarily a part-time duty of one individual, the board of directors conducts its own examination through a committee of the board appointed for the purpose. In most banks, however, the board of directors has examinations made for it by outside agencies such as certified public accountants. In some cities, the clearing house association has a staff of examiners whose duties are to examine the member banks for the directors. If errors or unsound practices are uncovered by the examination and the directors fail to correct such conditions, the directors may be held personally liable.

It is a requirement that each director review the report of the various examinations made. A bank's directorate should be informed as to its moral and legal responsibility with respect to fraud.

Questions Based on Chapter XIX

1. What is the principle of audit procedure?
2. Who appoints the auditor or control officer?
3. To whom is the auditor or control officer responsible?
4. What is the fundamental purpose of the audit program?

5. What is a statement of condition audit?
6. What is a spot audit?
7. What is a continuous audit?
8. What is meant by direct verification?
9. What controls are recommended to create better safeguards?
10. What is the positive type of direct verification?

Questions for Investigation

1. Who performs the auditing duties in your bank?
2. What agency of the supervisory authorities examines your bank and how often?
3. Does the board of directors conduct examinations of your bank?

CHAPTER XX

HOW BANKING GREW

The Purposes of This Chapter:

1. To outline our commercial banking structure.
2. To discuss the many influences responsible for the development of the banking system.
3. To present a brief history of banking in the United States.

How DID our banking system grow? What influences shared in its development? In this chapter we discuss the development of our commercial banking system, with emphasis on banking as a system. Obviously, banks do not operate apart from other banks; instead they work together as part of a larger whole, in other words, they work together as parts of a system. Our commercial banking system grew slowly; more than a century was consumed in its evolution.

The Elements of the Banking System

A visitor from abroad observing our banking system might remark, "State banks, national banks, banks that are members of the Federal Reserve System, nonmember banks, banks that insure their deposits, banks that do not! I cannot understand your system; it is so very complicated."

Compared with the simple banking structure in other countries, the American system is complex. Consider the commercial banking system of Great Britain. In Britain there are five large banks, that is, five independent banking organizations. They are privately owned and have numerous branches serving the commercial and industrial interests of Great Britain. In addition to the five large commercial banks, there is one central bank, the Bank of England, which now is owned by the government, although its ownership was in private hands until 1946.

Authority and control are centralized to a high degree in the British banking system. The bankers of Great Britain may hold a luncheon meeting at which five top executives discuss their common problems and interests. Add a sixth member to the luncheon party, perhaps the Chancellor of the Exchequer, and the meeting may discuss money and credit problems involving the interest of the government. Such problems as whether to refund maturing government securities or whether to ease or restrict bank credit might be decided at the meeting.

Contrast the British system with the American system. Instead of authority and ownership control centralized in five giant branch banks, there are in the United States not ten, nor 100, large banks with many branches but more than 14,000 separately owned independent banks. Among the 14,000 banks, moreover, there are several forms of organization and management, thus adding not only to the complexity but also to the flexibility of our commercial banking system and to the adaptability of banks in catering to local needs and in serving local communities.

1. Some banks have but one office or place of business and have no formal or corporate connections with other banking businesses. Their only connections with other institutions consist of the usual voluntary interbank relationships. Such a bank establishes its own policies and has its own stockholders; it is known as a *unit bank*.

2. A *branch bank* maintains a head office and one or more branch offices controlled by the head office. The branches may be located in the same city as the main office or may operate in a trade territory or throughout a state, depending on state laws and regulations. The general policies and activities of a branch are always determined by the head office or central authority.

3. The term *chain banking* refers to an arrangement by which the control of a number of banks is exercised through stock ownership by a group of individuals, who take an active part in formulating the policies of the banks in the group.

4. The term *group banking* refers to an arrangement by which a substantial proportion of the stock of each bank in the group is held in a holding company engaged in the business of banking. The identity of the local bank remains intact, with policies and operations determined by its own board of directors.

The benefits to the bank itself, the possibilities of increased service to customers, the prospective benefits to stockholders and depositors, and the effects of local competition are all factors determining the selection of one form of organization in preference to another where state law permits a choice. The form does not, of course, insure the stability of the bank, for the principles of sound banking apply in any case.

There is a further classification. Approximately one-half of the banks are members of the Federal Reserve System (member banks). However, most of the nonmember banks are small and their combined resources are a small fraction of the total banking resources of the country. More than ninety percent of total bank resources are held by member banks.

The Dual Banking System

Presently bank charters may be obtained from the Federal Government, each of the forty-eight states, the Territories of Hawaii and Alaska, the Commonwealth of Puerto Rico, the Government of the Virgin Islands, and certain of the possessions of the United States. With more than fifty government bodies issuing bank charters and exercising external controls over banking operations, the question well may be asked, "Wherein is the dual feature of the banking system?" Despite the multiplicity of chartering and supervising bodies, the term dual system is used for the reason that the organizers of a bank have but one choice of two charters. They may choose only between a Federal charter and a charter of the state in which the bank is to be located. There are no other alternatives. If the decision is take out a Federal charter, the bank becomes a national bank and is classified as a member of the national system. The two classifications of banks, national system and state system, make up the dual banking system.

Close to 5,000 of all the banks have their charters from the Federal Government and therefore constitute the national system. The remaining banks are state banks, inasmuch as their charters are issued by the states or comparable bodies. State banks are the more numerous, but the combined resources of the national banks are much larger in total.

Supervision of Banks

The legal structure of our banking system is further complicated by the multiplicity of government bodies with supervisory powers over banks. State banks that are neither members of the Federal

Reserve System nor insured by the Federal Deposit Insurance Corporation are subject only to the supervision of authorities of the state which chartered them. A nonmember state bank that has its deposits insured by the Federal Deposit Insurance Corporation is supervised both by the state government and by the Federal Deposit Insurance Corporation. State member banks must have their deposits insured; therefore, they are subject to the supervisory powers of the state government, the Federal Deposit Insurance Corporation, and the Federal Reserve System. A national bank is supervised by the Federal Government, the Federal Deposit Insurance Corporation, and the Federal Reserve System.

Hence it is evident that banking in the United States is a much supervised industry. Voluntary arrangements among the supervisory authorities reduce the number of periodic examinations to which banks are subject. In the American system there is an overall complexity that is in sharp contrast with the British system where the supervisory controls are few and are primarily internal controls rather than the external controls of government.

The foreign visitor, however, would be greatly mistaken if he were to go away with the impression that this complexity of structure results in confusion and disorder in our system. Quite the contrary is the fact. In its functioning, the American system has a degree of unity rivaling that of the British system. In addition, it has a measure of flexibility and responsiveness to new credit needs that is not always present when banking control is concentrated in a few hands.

The American banking system was not transplanted from the Old World nor did it grow in a vacuum. It grew as part of the developing American scene. The same factors that are responsible for the growth of the United States (from a few straggling communities on the eastern seaboard into a great and populous nation with productive powers attained by no other people) are also responsible for the growth of the American banking system. The American system characterized by structural complexity and functional unity is peculiarly an American product.

The Shaping of the American Banking System

The commercial banking system of the United States was molded by many influences. Some of these influences were psychological, some were political, and some were economic and geographic. Some of these influences caused diversity and decentralization of control; others caused unity and integration. Some influences fostered a driving initiative that stimulated the development of new forms of credit and enabled banking to keep pace with the needs of an expanding and ever changing economy. Other influences contributed to the stability and security of the system.

1. The traditions of free enterprise and independent action were strong. The new Americans were a restless, impatient, ambitious, and optimistic people with little regard for the restraints of Old World traditions. In their minds, the right to engage in any occupation, which promised success, was considered the heritage of free men. The early Americans did not distinguish between establishing a bank and starting any other kind of enterprise. Furthermore, early banking practices seemed often to be an exercise of license rather than of responsible liberty.

2. There was a strong and deeply felt hostility to monopoly of all kinds, particularly to a money monopoly. It was this tradition which led Congress during the first decades of the Republic to reject the establishment of a permanent central bank.

3. There was the political system of the United States. The United States is a republic composed of a central government and forty-eight sovereign states. The central government has only such powers as are expressly delegated to it, all other powers being reserved to the states. Under these arrangements both the Federal Government and the state governments are empowered to issue bank charters, thus bringing a dual banking system into existence.

4. There were the disastrous experiences of those periods of free banking when little or no control was exercised over the banks. In response to the demand for easy credit and easy money, particularly on the part of the frontier communities, many banks issued more bank notes than they could redeem and made loans that were based on little more than hopeful anticipations.

5. There was the expansive territory of the United States with its variety of resources and of industries, each presenting a different credit need calling for specialized knowledge and experience on the part of the banker. This geographic fact encouraged the decentralization of banks and supported the belief that a unit bank, in close touch with the community and identified with its well

being, would serve the American people better than would a few giant branch or chain systems, controlled by distant central offices.

6. There was the fact that the economic life of the people of the United States was becoming more unified. The expansion of railroads and the invention of the telegraph and the telephone gradually changed the economic organization of the United States from a collection of local communities into a national economy. This unifying trend was reflected in banking as well as in industry; it was expressed in the National Bank Act of 1863 and even more in the Federal Reserve Act of 1913.

7. There was a growing understanding of their industry on the part of bankers. They came to realize that although banking is a private business seeking profits, it is a private business with social responsibilities greater than those of any other business enterprise. As custodians of the people's money and as suppliers of credit, the bankers know that the well-being of every individual depends on how well they do their job.

Considering the many influences which shaped the banking system of the United States, we should not be surprised that the formative period lasted over a century. The result is that the banking system so molded has a high degree of unity and central control. Yet the system retains a large measure of free and independent action. Although it remains responsive to local interests and needs, it paces the credit needs of a dynamic economy and assures a high degree of safety for the funds of its depositors.

Let us now turn briefly to the history of American banking and the story of how it grew.

Early Efforts To Establish a Sound Banking System

Colonial banks were hardly worthy of the name. They were few in number and often were managed in disregard of sound banking principles. To satisfy the hunger of the colonists for money, the banks obligingly issued bank notes in ever increasing abundance. And the usual consequences followed: Money declined in value, prices increased, speculative excesses mounted, and economic collapse followed. Some banks were soundly managed, and some efforts were made to establish banking on a sounder foundation. In general, however, colonial banking was synonymous with a plethora of bank notes and bank failures.

Partly as a consequence of the unhappy colonial experience, but
mainly through the influence of Alexander Hamilton, the new
Federal Government attempted to reform the banking system. In
1791, Congress chartered the Bank of the United States, commonly referred to as the first Bank of the United States. The Bank
acted as the fiscal agent of the government. It made loans to the
Government and to industrial and commercial enterprises. The
Bank's power to issue notes was restricted, and it maintained an
adequate specie reserve to redeem its notes in hard cash. Since
its affairs were managed along conservative, prudent lines, the
Bank prospered financially and its stock was sought not only at
home but also abroad.

However, the Bank did not prosper politically. Some policies
were unpopular, especially its collection policy. When in the course
of business the Bank received the notes of local banks, it presented
those notes for redemption in specie (gold or silver coin) as quickly as messengers on horseback could carry them. To pay in hard
cash was an unpleasant experience for the local banks, particularly since there was so little hard cash in the country. This aggressive collection policy made the first Bank extremely unpopular,
not only among the bankers who could not redeem their notes,
but also among the people in the local communities who were
often left without specie and without banks. Investments and
business undertakings suffered severely from the resulting collapse
in values.

The frontier communities also opposed the first Bank because
they feared it would develop a banking monopoly serving primarily the needs of the large cities, such as Philadelphia, Boston,
and New York.

In 1811 the Bank's charter expired, and Congress considered extending the life of the Bank. Congress rejected by a close vote the
application of the Bank for an extension of its charter. The Bank
closed, redeeming its outstanding stock at a premium and selling
its assets to the Girard Bank of Philadelphia.

During the next five years, several factors combined to encourage the issue of bank notes.

1. There was little effective pressure for specie redemption.

2. States liberalized their banking laws, some of them exempting
banks from all requirements of specie redemption.

3. The Federal Government financed the war of 1812 by borrowing from the state banks, that is, in effect through the issue of bank notes by the state banks.

The historical pattern repeated itself. Bank notes became increasingly plentiful. Their value became increasingly less. Prices became increasingly higher. Speculation and money disorders flourished. The situation led to a demand for the establishment of a Federal bank. The second Bank of the United States was chartered in 1816.

The basic factors which led to the political demise of the first Bank persisted. The supply of capital was less than the demand for it. Easy money and liberal credit seemed a quick solution, especially in the debt ridden rural communities. Issues of state bank notes multiplied, and the efforts of the second bank to secure the redemption of bank notes were rewarded with a mounting hostility. In 1836 the renewal of the Bank's charter was rejected, this time by the Presidential veto of Andrew Jackson.

The Period of Free and Easy Banking

Banks were freed from the restrictions imposed on them by the aggressive collection policies of the second Bank of the United States; only the state legislatures and the good sense of bankers were left to restrain the expansion of credit and money. But prudence and caution were not in harmony with the temper of the times. This period was one of change, growth, and unlimited optimism; this optimism was not without foundation.

The first railroad was opened for traffic in 1830; in that year forty miles of trackage were built. By the end of the 1830's some 2,200 miles had been added to railroad trackage. In the 1840's more than 6,000 miles were added; the rate of construction was nearly three times that of the preceding decade. In the decade before the Civil War new railroad trackage mounted to 22,000 miles, nearly four times the mileage added in the forties. By 1860, the railroads had grown from the little industry of 1830 to a billion dollar industry.

Growth and expansion were not limited to railroads. Older industries expanded, and new industries came into being. The factory method of production had come into general use in such major food processing industries as flour milling and meat packing as well as the tobacco industry. In addition to satisfying a growing domestic demand, these industries were exporting their products in ever increasing amounts to Europe and South America.

Population increased. New areas were opened for settlement. Villages became towns, and towns grew to city size.

This was a period of dynamic growth, not only in banking but in many other fields, particularly industry, transportation, and agriculture. The opportunities for making money seemed limitless, if only one could get enough credit. Merchants, manufacturers, and farmers needed money; they obtained it from the banks that issued bank notes with accommodating abundance.

A period of such turbulent growth was bound to have its casualties; one of its casualties was sound banking. Bank failures occurred frequently, and when an economic crisis impended, banks failed in waves. When times improved, a new generation of banks arose as fruitful of credit and as optimistic of the future as before. A succinct picture of this period is given in the Institute text, Money and Banking.

There were a few examples of sound banking during this period, but on the whole the era of state banking was a sorry episode in American banking history. Banks were able to start business under lenient state laws (which might not even be enforced), with inadequate capital, and with little or no intention of providing a currency as good as specie. The principal object was to issue and lend notes in order to collect interest on the loans. If the volume of notes was restricted by redemption, the profitableness of the banks was reduced. Hence all kinds of difficulties were thrown in the way of people who might want gold or silver for their notes. The notes might be redeemable only at the head office of a bank. This office would then be so successfully hidden on a back road that no one could find it. The terms "banking among the wildcats" and "wildcat banking" became common. Each of the hundreds of state banks had its own notes designed and printed; hence there was no uniformity of design, thus making counterfeiting easy.[1]

Financial confusion and chaos ultimately disrupt business and trade. Massachusetts, New York, and Louisiana each moved to reform its banking system. The more important development, however, was the re-entry of the Federal Government into the field of banking.

---

[1] Money and Banking, p. 119. American Institute of Banking, New York, 1950

UNIFICATION AND STABILIZATION OF THE BANKING SYSTEM

Congress passed the National Currency Act (now known as the National Bank Act) primarily because the Secretary of the Treasury, Salmon P. Chase, wished to facilitate the sale of government bonds. The Act provided the basis for a much stronger commercial banking system. The Act included provisions for:

1. *A national and uniform currency,* known as national bank notes, secured by United States Government bonds and by funds deposited with the Secretary of the Treasury.

In 1865, Congress passed a law imposing a heavy tax (10%) on the note issues of all state banks, thus making the issue of notes a very unprofitable undertaking for those banks. As a consequence, national bank notes became the only notes circulating in the United States. In view of their sound backing and restricted issue, these notes maintained their value and were accepted at par throughout the country.

From 1865 to 1913, the national bank notes formed the greater part of the currency system. After 1913, they were gradually supplanted by the Federal Reserve notes, and in 1935 the issuance of national bank notes came to an end. Since that date, when national bank notes are received by a bank, they are forwarded immediately to the Secretary of the Treasury for redemption. However, we may well observe that long before the national bank notes were supplanted in our monetary system, the use of checks had superseded the bank note as the chief instrument used in money payments.

2. *A system of national banks* located in all parts of the country and subject to uniform laws and regulations.

Regulations governing the chartering of national banks were designed to assure that, as far as possible, institutions chartered by the national banking authorities would be constructive additions to the banking system. Before a charter was granted, the organizers of the proposed bank had to demonstrate to the Comptroller of the Currency that the institution, if organized, not only would meet the requirements of the National Bank Act but also would be in the public interest. Some of the considerations that are likely to influence the Comptroller to act favorably upon an application for a bank charter are:

a. That proposed national bank will have capital adequate to serve the financial needs of its community,

b. That there is need for a new bank in the community,

c. That those connected with the organization (that is, the proposed stockholders, directors, and officers) are individuals of good character and financial responsibility, and

d. That the proposed bank has a prospect of operating profitably and therefore of future growth.

These requirements of the National Bank Act are still operative today, and they aid in the avoidance of unsound banking. Once chartered, a national bank was and still is subject to systematic regulation and supervision as long as it exists.

3. *The establishment of the Office of the Comptroller of the Currency.* The Comptroller was the first official to exercise Federal authority over banks. He held both regulatory and supervisory powers.

The National Bank Act provided "That there shall be in the Department of the Treasury a bureau charged with the execution of all laws passed by Congress relating to the issue and regulation of a national currency secured by the United States bonds . . . the chief officer of which bureau shall be called the Comptroller of the Currency and shall perform his duties under the general directions of the Secretary of the Treasury." The Comptroller retains all the powers given him under the National Bank Act.

Although the first and major duty of the Comptroller of the Currency was regulating the issuance of national bank notes, his regulatory powers are far broader in scope. Supervision of national banks is accomplished by various means, the most important of which are bank examinations and statements calls.

The Basic Weaknesses of Our System of Commercial Banking

The national banking system made many important contributions to our financial stability. It set standards for sound banking. It established a national bank currency. It expanded credit facilities to support an expanding economy. It added elements of safety to the banking structure. But it also had serious weaknesses which became increasingly apparent and economically dangerous, particularly in view of the successive industrial and commercial crises.

The collection of checks on out-of-town banks was a slow and costly process. Checks drawn on other banks within the town or city limits were quickly collected through local clearing arrangements. Checks drawn on out-of-town banks, particularly those on distant banks, often traveled a long and circuitous course. A check deposited in Texas drawn on a bank in a small town in Maine might well tour a large part of the country, moving from one bank to another, accumulating indorsements along the way, and taking weeks or months to reach the home bank. Since deposit credit was gradually supplanting the bank note as a means of payment, this situation was a most undesirable one.

Although national bank notes were a uniform and standard currency, the quantity of notes in circulation tended to fluctuate not with but counter to trade requirements for currency. When the number of transactions increased and an increase in the supply of currency was required, banks sometimes found it more profitable to retire their notes, and conversely, they found it more profitable to expand their note issues when there was less need for currency. Thus national bank notes were commonly referred to as constituting an inelastic currency.

There were other weaknesses in the system. The reserves (namely, the cash funds that banks are required to set aside to support their deposits) tended to concentrate bank funds in the large financial centers, mainly in New York. As a consequence, bank credit was often scarce and costly in agricultural areas.

The more serious weakness, however, was the fact that the operations of the commercial banking system under the regime of the National Bank Act tended seriously to accentuate industrial and commercial crises. Periods of severe financial stringency heralded the oncoming of a depression. A money panic was often the first phase of a descending business cycle. The result was that the instability of the economy as a whole was greater, and the depressions were more severe than otherwise they might have been.

These deficiencies finally led to action by Congress. As a result, the Federal Reserve Act was passed and became effective with the signature of President Wilson on December 23, 1913.

Summary

The American system is very complex in its structure. In

functioning, however, it is highly unified. The American banking system was not transplanted from any other country; it is peculiarly and uniquely American in its development and organization. Many influences, among them the ideals of free and private enterprise, the size and diversity of the American continent, the traditional American hostility toward monopoly, and the gradual growth of national unity, are reflected in the development of the American banking system. The brief history of American banking indicates that in its growth banking has passed through many phases. This chapter traces the development of banking as far as the passage of the Federal Reserve Act. In a later chapter, the tracing of the growth of our banking system is completed with a discussion of the Federal Reserve System and its functions and the establishment of the Federal Deposit Insurance Corporation.

Questions Based on Chapter XX

1. Discuss the elements that constitute the American banking system.
2. What government bodies have authority to supervise banks?
3. Name seven influences that shaped the American banking system.
4. Trace the history of banking from colonial times to the Civil War period.
5. Why did Congress refuse to renew the charter of the first Bank of the United States? Why did the President veto the bill extending the charter of the second Bank of the United States?
6. What deficiencies in the American banking system were corrected by the National Bank Act?
7. What factors does the Comptroller of the Currency consider in chartering a national bank?
8. What were the basic weaknesses of our commercial banking system after the passage of the National Bank Act?

Question for Investigation

Find out which supervisory agencies examine your bank. How often is your bank examined?

CHAPTER XXI

EXTERNAL CONTROLS

The Purposes of This Chapter:
1. To explain the external controls by which American banks are regulated and supervised.
2. To indicate why banks are subject to external controls.
3. To discuss the granting of charters as a method of external controls.
4. To point out the importance of bank examinations in our system of external controls.

All of us in one way or another are subject to external controls by government authority. To drive a car without fear of arrest, an individual must have a driver's license issued by the government of the state of which he is a citizen. To qualify for such a license many states require proof of competence to drive, knowledge of traffic regulations, and adequate vision. Driving itself is subject to control by traffic authorities, and it is regulated and supervised by local and state police.

Business enterprises also are subject to external controls by government. In some cases, the controls are very few, and the intervention of government affects but slightly the day-by-day operations of business. In other cases (for example, public utilities, transportation, and airlines) the regulations are numerous and comprehensive. There is no business or industry, however, in which regulation and supervision by government is as comprehensive and as far reaching as in banking.

The Reason for External Controls over Banks

It is a cardinal principle of government that the sovereign authority shall control and regulate the nation's money. Because banks participate with government in the money function, they are subject to government supervision and regulation.

In ancient days when the money supply of nations consisted only of metallic currency, the sovereign easily regulated the quality and quantity of the money through exercise of control over the mint at which the coins were struck. When governments began to supplement the metallic currency with national paper currency, the controls had to be increased. The gold or silver bullion on which the paper currency was based had to be kept separately, the plates from which the money was printed had to be controlled, and a register of notes issued and redeemed had to be maintained in order to prevent the paper money outstanding from exceeding the amount authorized.

In later periods when governments had to enlarge their money systems, they sought a currency which could be expanded and contracted in accordance with the changing needs of industry, trade, and commerce. Bank note currency proved advantageous for many forms of debt settlement. Hence this third form of money was adopted by most modern nations. Bank note currency consists of promises on the part of the issuing banks to pay the sums stated on the paper note in metallic currency (legal tender) at the time and place specified. The adoption of bank note currency as a kind of money resulted in a further enlargement of governments' money control systems. In addition to regulating the quality and the quantity of the metallic and national paper currencies, it became necessary to make periodic appraisals of the assets pledged by the banks to secure their note issues.

Within the past century the banking industry has perfected a new form of currency, which has completely superseded bank note currency in this country. This new currency is the most efficient form of money yet devised for the general settlement of debts which do not require the use of legal tender money. It is estimated that ninety-five per cent of the business transactions in the country are settled with this new money, termed bank deposit currency.

Bank deposit currency is created whenever the proceeds of loans made by banks are credited directly to deposit accounts. Conversely, bank deposit currency is retired whenever bank loans are paid through debits to deposit accounts. Bank deposits in effect are currency and are a part of the national supply of money because the owners of such deposits may convert them at will into legal tender money through the drawing and encashment of checks drawn against their balances.

The ability of banks to pay the checks drawn by their depositors depends on the money "goodness" of loans, investments, and other assets that the banks own. If loans and similar assets are uncollectable and the capital accounts of the holding banks are insufficient to absorb the losses, then insolvency exists and the deposit currency is impaired. Therefore with the advent of bank deposit currency, the government, in the performance of its responsibility to regulate the nations' money, was again called upon to enlarge its bank supervisory programs. Governments now must supervise all activities in which banks engage since these activities usually bear upon the deposit function.

Thus it is obvious that the public interest requires sound banking. Consider these facts.

1. No other business creates money. In earlier chapters it is pointed out that all but a small part of the money supply comes from banks.

2. No other business enterprise is charged with the responsibility of holding and protecting the people's money.

3. No other business assumes the obligation of paying on demand the debts it owes. The greater part of a commercial bank's debts are payable on demand, and the remainder are payable upon brief notice.

4. In no other business is the ratio of capital to debt so low as it is in the banking business. In the case of banks, the capital ratio may be as low as ten per cent or less.

5. The economic well being of the country is closely, directly, and continuously dependent upon day-to-day operations of banks far more than on the activities of other businesses or industries. The transportation industry, particularly the railroads, may be as subject to detailed regulations as are the banks.

In the light of these facts, it is understandable that the external controls exercised over banks are so many and so detailed and that government authorities conduct regular examinations of the financial condition of the banks.

THE SCOPE OF EXTERNAL CONTROLS

External controls are very wide in scope. They affect all the daily activities of the banker. It may properly be said that external controls by the government begin with the organization of the bank, continue throughout the life of the bank, and preside over its liquidation, if by misfortune, the bank should suffer so unhappy a fate.

To start a bank, the organizers must satisfy a banking authority that (1) the bank is needed in the community, (2) the bank has a reasonable prospect of success, (3) the capital resources of the bank are adequate for the task ahead, and (4) those who are undertaking the management of the bank are men who have successfully demonstrated their business responsibility. The uses to be made of the capital resources of the bank may also be prescribed. The supervisory authority, for instance, may set the maximum percentage of capital that may be invested in the bank building.

The controls extend to the area of operation, including such matters as the kind of loans and investments the bank may make and the quality of the loans and investments they have made. There are frequent examinations by trained and skilled examiners who check the records of the bank in fullest detail to determine whether the operations of the bank are consistent with the spirit and letter of the regulations.

The complex system of external controls reflects the governmental structure of the United States. In the United States, the sovereign powers of the government are distributed between the central government and the state governments. Each of these bodies is sovereign, and as an incident of its sovereign power can charter banks, examine banks, and supervise bank operations.

THE BANK SUPERVISORY ESTABLISHMENT

The system of external controls to which our banks are subject is unique among modern nations. It is natural that our supervisory establishment should be large because our banks are numbered in the thousands. It is natural also that our supervisory system should be of complex character by reason of the decentralized form of our government and because of the strong public advocacy of free enterprise in all forms of business activity.

In the discussion of our dual banking system in Chapter XX, it is pointed out that this term indicates the existence of the alternative sources of bank charters and that bank supervision is not lodged solely with one government body.

The chartering of banks in the United States has been decentralized to prevent the formation of banking monopolies. Abhorrence of monopoly is characteristic of the American public, and nowhere is it more apparent than in our banking history. During the early years of our national life, Congress was impelled on two occasions, when financial peril threatened, to create a bank affiliated with the Federal treasury.[1] In both instances the banks served the country well, and on the basis of each record, a renewal of the charter was warranted. In each case, however, the public so greatly feared the possibility of a bank monopoly that each bank was dissolved at the expiration of the term of its charter.

Today our bank supervisory establishment is made up of some fifty-three separate banking departments. The Comptroller of the Currency in Washington, D. C. exercises supervisory authority over all national banks. The Comptroller also supervises the district banks of the District of Columbia. Each of the forty-eight states has an established banking department for the supervision of its respective state banks. Similar departments have been established by Hawaii, Alaska, Puerto Rico, and the Virgin Islands. Two agencies, which are described elsewhere in this text, are the Federal Reserve System and the Federal Deposit Insurance Corporation.[2] Although they are not supervisory bodies in the technical sense, they do exercise important supervisory powers in the performance of their function. For this reason they are generally regarded as important elements of the nation's bank supervisory establishment. The supervisory controls over the nation's banks are graphically illustrated in Chart 12.

Controls over the Establishment of a Bank

A group seeking to organize a bank first must decide on the character of the charter to be sought. If a national bank is desired,

---

[1] The first Bank of the United States was established in 1791. The second Bank of the United States was chartered in 1816.

[2] The Federal Deposit Insurance Corporation may conduct examinations of any insured bank. However, in practice it examines only state nonmember insured banks. The Federal Reserve System may examine any member bank but in practice it examines only its state member institutions. The Office of the Comptroller of the Currency makes available to the two agencies copies of the examination reports of national banks. Also, the Federal Reserve System makes available to the Federal Deposit Insurance Corporation copies of its examination reports of state member banks. Thus ordinarily no national or state bank is examined by more than one Federal examining agency.

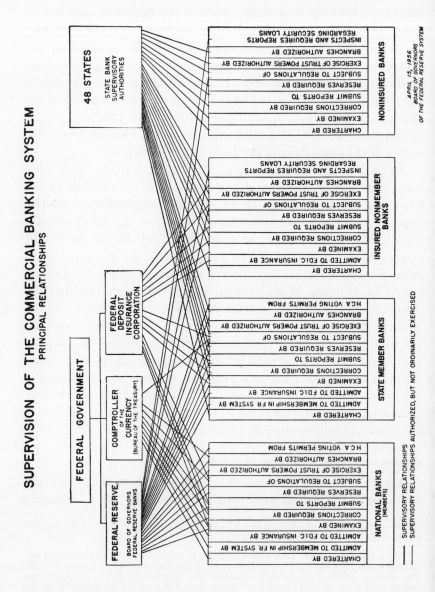

CHART 12. GRAPHIC PRESENTATION OF SUPERVISORY CONTROLS OVER BANKS

a formal application must be submitted to the Comptroller of the Currency in Washington, D. C. In the application, the organizers propose a name for the institution, state the amount of the contemplated capitalization (allocated as to common stock and paid in surplus), and furnish information as to the financial worth, occupation, business affiliations, and prior connections with other financial institutions of any of the proponents, prospective directors, and officers.

Following receipt of the application, the Comptroller of the Currency directs the appropriate district chief national bank examiner to make an investigation and report with his recommendation for action on the proposal. The Comptroller also gives notice of the proposal to and requests advisory recommendations from the Board of Governors of the Federal Reserve System and from the Federal Deposit Insurance Corporation. These two instrumentalities are not chartering bodies but, inasmuch as member bank and insured bank status are mandatory for national banks, it is the policy of the Comptroller of the Currency to invite their consideration and recommendations.

The investigation of a proposal for a new bank is not limited in scope. It ranges over all the aspects that are pertinent to each application. The examiners for the three agencies usually conduct a portion of their investigation concurrently, but they prepare separate reports for submission through agency channels. These reports have one feature in common. Each report gives detailed consideration to five factors, (1) adequacy of the capital structure, (2) future earnings prospects, (3) the general character of management, (4) conveniences and needs of the community to be served, and (5) consistency of corporate powers.

State bank chartering procedure is generally similar to the procedure employed in chartering a national bank, although the technique varies from one state to another. The formal application for charter is filed with the state banking department of the state of domicile. Unlike national banks, however, the issuance of a state bank charter does not carry with it membership in the Federal Reserve System or insured status in the Federal Deposit Insurance Corporation. A separate application must be filed to obtain either or both of these benefits.

Should a newly organizing state bank desire both insured and member bank status, it must file a separate application with the Board of Governors of the Federal Reserve System. However, if insured bank status exclusive of Federal Reserve System membership is desired, the bank files an application with the Federal Deposit Insurance Corporation. In either event the five factors previously mentioned are considered before the application is approved. State chartering officials need not consider these specific factors but it may be said that they have established policy standards and guides which are generally equivalent in scope and objective.

Controls over Existing Banks

Bank examinations are essential for effective bank supervision. Each of the state and national bank supervisory bodies maintains or is authorized to engage a staff of examiners to carry out this function. Each of the Federal Reserve banks, and also the Federal Deposit Insurance Corporation, has established a staff of bank examiners. Thus an impression is created that there is much costly duplication in the bank examination process. However, those who have studied the subject are in general agreement that significant savings would not be realized and that efficiency would not be promoted were there but one body of bank examiners for all the banks in the country.

National banks are examined by the examining staff of the Comptroller of the Currency; state banks are examined by the staffs of the respective state supervisory authorities. Inasmuch as national banks are also member banks and insured banks, they may be examined by their Federal Reserve bank and by the Federal Deposit Insurance Corporation. In practice, however, neither of these two agencies examines national banks. Copies of the reports of examinations of national banks are made available to the two agencies by the Comptroller of the Currency. Since the standards, policies, and the forms of the report of examination are closely proximate, there is little likelihood for national banks in satisfactory condition to be examined by any agency other than the office of the Comptroller of the Currency.

State banks which have applied for and have been admitted to the benefits of membership in the Federal Reserve System or the Federal Deposit Insurance Corporation are subject to examination by

Federal authority as well as by their state authority. Technically a state member bank may be examined by the Federal Reserve bank examiners and the Federal Deposit Insurance Corporation examiners. However, for the reasons given in the previous paragraph, examinations of state member banks are conducted by the district Federal Reserve bank and a copy of the examination report is made available to the Federal Deposit Insurance Corporation. State banks which are insured banks but not member banks are examined by the Federal Deposit Insurance Corporation examiners. Possible duplication of examining effort is further reduced in practice because the two Federal agencies conduct their examinations concurrently with the state authority, if the latter so desires, and they interchange information which is of common interest.

THE BANK EXAMINATION FUNCTION

Notwithstanding the fact that each banking department is a separate authority operating independently of the others, the responsibility of each is common to all. The function of each is (1) to enforce the banking laws to which their chartered banks are subject and (2) to determine whether the banks under their supervision are operated in a safe and sound manner. The performance of this function requires that visitations be made to the banks at periodic intervals for a determination of the facts. These visitations are made by bank examiners who make written reports of their findings at the conclusion of each visitation. The reports of examination thus provide the head of the banking department or equivalent supervisory authority with the information and factual data on which practically all supervisory actions may be based.

The Frequency of Examinations

Examinations are scheduled at irregular intervals and without prior notice to the banks. Some jurisdictions conduct two regular examinations annually but the trend appears to be in the direction of one regular annual examination. Special examinations are made of banks whose condition is less than satisfactory, or on the occurrence of events which may adversely affect their condition. There is no limit to the number of special examinations which may be made, but the managements of banks on the special list usually make extra efforts to correct the faulty conditions in order to be freed from the extra close supervision. The matter of expense is also a powerful influence on management to conform to approved standards for the cost of examinations are borne by the banks. The only exceptions are that the expense of examinations conducted by the Federal Reserve bank and the Federal Deposit Insurance Corporation is paid from their general funds. However, these two instrumentalities are supported by their members and hence the taxpayers' money is not used to defray the costs of bank supervision and examination in either case.

The Purpose of the Examination

Banks are examined in order to determine as of a given date (1) their true financial condition, (2) the fact of conformance or nonconformance with applicable banking laws and regulations, (3) whether the loan and investment policies are prudent, (4) the profitability of operations, (5) the adequacy of the accounting and control methods, and (6) the effectiveness of the directors' supervision. The scope of a bank examination may be better appreciated by noting the index of an examination report as reproduced in Form 40.

Examination Procedures

The procedures generally followed in conducting examinations include, (1) proving the asset and liabilities accounts of record to the general ledger control, (2) physical inspection or verification of the assets, (3) evaluation of the assets to determine their intrinsic value in relation to their book values, and (4) studies of bank operations, accounting procedures and records to enable the formulation of accurate judgments in relation to the objectives previously mentioned. The techniques and mechanics of examinations vary according to the character and size of individual banks.

Examinations usually are started shortly before banks open for business or immediately after they close in the afternoon. On entering the bank, the examiners take possession or custody of all assets, control ledgers, deposit ledgers, the general ledger, and other key records. Since there are not a sufficient number of examiners to deal simultaneously with all aspects of the exami-

Examined Close of Business_____   Number_____

SCHEDULE OF EXHIBITS
I ANALYSIS OF ASSETS

II ANALYSIS OF LIABILITIES

III NONBOOK ASSETS AND LIABILITIES

IV GENERAL INFORMATION

FORM 40. SCHEDULE OF EXHIBITS

nation, official seals are used to control vaults, safes, chests, or other containers of assets and records until their contents may be processed in an orderly manner. As soon as the proof, verification, and evaluation are completed, the records and assets are returned to the bank's personnel to facilitate normal conduct of business.

Classification of Bank Assets

The standard in use for the classification of bank assets is common to most of the bank supervisory and examining authorities. Assets which contain no more than normal risks are not classified in examination reports. Assets which appear to be possessed of greater than normal risks are listed in the report and are classified according to the degree of risk. In addition to the listing, the examiner includes appropriate comments in support of the classifications that he has applied. Three classifications are generally used—substandard, doubtful, and loss.

Capital Ratios

This chapter would be incomplete were capital ratios unmentioned. The three ratios most commonly referred to are (1) capital to assets, (2) capital to deposits, and (3) capital to risk assets. The ratios are usually expressed as a percentage and are computed by dividing (1) adjusted assets into adjusted capital, (2) total deposits into adjusted capital, and (3) adjusted assets minus (a) cash, (b) due from banks, and (c) investments in United States securities into adjusted capital.

The capital to assets ratio indicates the percentage by which a bank's assets may shrink in value before a state of insolvency comes into existence and depositors' funds become impaired. The capital to deposit ratio indicates the percentage relationship between the stockholders' investment and the depositors' fund. The capital to risk ratio seeks to measure capital in terms of those assets which present business risks. It depends for its validity on the theory that cash and United States Government securities are devoid of credit risk. It is recognized that Government securities are subject to market, but the proponents of the ratio hold that only in exceptional and isolated instances would involuntary sales of such assets under depressed markets be required to meet the needs of general deposit withdrawals.

Capital ratios are indicators merely of quantity and not of quality. To illustrate the necessity for caution in the use of capital ratios, Institute Bank with a capital to assets ratio of 10% and a risk ratio of 11% may not be as sound as Instruction Bank with a capital to assets ratio of 6.8% and a risk ratio of 16%. For these and other equally pertinent reasons bank supervisory officials predicate their conclusions and decisions on their qualitative analyses rather than on capital ratios alone.

Report of Examination

The results of the examination are incorporated in the official report by means of schedules and exhibits. Additional schedules and exhibits include a comparative analysis of earnings, expenses, and profit and losses over a three to five year period; a listing of items which do not conform to applicable laws and regulations, if such there be; a listing of borrowings, if any, by directors, officers, employees, or their interests; an analysis of deposit trend over a period of years; and a review of the adequacy of accounting and control procedures and of the effectiveness of the supervision exercised by the board of directors. The completed report is forwarded to the supervisory authority with the examiner's statement or letter of conclusions concerning the condition of the bank and with his recommendations for such supervisory action as he deems to be appropriate.

Review of the Examination Report

The report of the examination receives careful study by the supervisory official. The various schedules, exhibits, and details of the report are given close attention; comparisons with prior reports are made to determine what trends may be in progress and to evaluate their significance.

On completion of the review of the report a copy of it is transmitted to the bank's board of directors with a letter setting forth the supervisory official's observations, critical comments, and requirements. In due course the bank's board of directors is required to respond in writing to advise that adjustments have been made, that actions have been initiated to correct any unsatisfactory conditions which may exist, and that compliance has been accorded to the directives of the supervisory authority. Under more extreme conditions conferences may be held in the supervisor's office, but ordinarily satisfactory adjustments are achieved through correspondence.

Summary

Bank supervision and bank examinations are complex processes and are more extensively organized in the United States than elsewhere in the world. Had the public so willed, our banking system could have been formed in the pattern of the Old World with a very few banks located in the financial centers from whence banking facilities spread outward over the nation and downward in diminishing scale to the community levels. Under such circumstances, bank supervision is a relatively simple process. But the American public willed that our banking system should be founded in free enterprise. In consequence our banks originate at the grass roots level and, more often than not, in response to demands for credit facilities rather than for deposit facilities. With our banks numbered in the thousands, instead of in tens as with other nations, it is inevitable that our supervisory and examining bodies should be large and complex.

Questions Based on Chapter XXI

1. What does the term insured nonmember bank signify?
2. Why should examiners take custody of all bank assets at the start of an examination?
3. Examinations usually are started prior to the bank's opening for business in the morning or just after closing at the end of the business day. Why should examinations not be started at any time during the business day?
4. Although banks, merchants, and manufacturers are engaged in private enterprise, only banks are subject to close supervision by government. Why should they be supervised?

Questions for Investigation

1. Which government agency conducts the examination of your bank?
2. How often has your bank been examined during the last three years?

CHAPTER XXII

THE FEDERAL RESERVE SYSTEM
AND THE
FEDERAL DEPOSIT INSURANCE CORPORATION

The Purposes of This Chapter:

1. To discuss some of the services provided by the Federal Reserve banks for member banks and for the Government.
2. To point out the influence which Federal Reserve exerts over general credit policy.
3. To describe the organization of the Federal Reserve System.
4. To mention briefly the Federal Deposit Insurance Corporation and to note some of its activities.

THE DEVELOPMENT and operation of the Federal Reserve System and of the Federal Deposit Insurance Corporation are described in detail in the Institute's textbook, "Money and Banking." The brief discussion of these institutions in this chapter is focused on those activities that bear directly on the practical bank operations of every bank.

THE FEDERAL RESERVE SYSTEM

The Federal Reserve System renders many services to member banks. Federal Reserve also exerts a dominant influence in the formulation and in the execution of the monetary and credit policies of the Federal Government and renders essential services to the Government.

Services to Banks

Many of the preceding chapters contain references to the activities of the Federal Reserve System. The Federal Reserve banks perform for their member banks many of the services that the latter perform for their customers. Therefore, they are sometimes called "bankers' banks." Among these services are those relating to:

1. Cash
2. Cash collection
3. Noncash collection
4. Wire transfer
5. Rediscounting.

Each service meets a specific need of the member banks and is performed expeditiously for them by the Federal Reserve banks.

1. *Cash*. When a customer has more cash than he wishes to keep, he deposits the excess in his bank; when he needs more cash, he withdraws it from his bank. The bank, of course, decides how much cash it wishes to keep as a working fund and as vault cash. When a member bank acquires more cash than it wishes, it sends the excess to its Federal Reserve bank to increase its reserve balance or to a correspondent bank, which sends its excess to the Federal Reserve bank. If a member bank runs short of the desired amount of cash, it will draw on its reserve balance. Nonmember banks generally get their cash from a member bank.

The Federal Reserve banks keep a large stock of all kinds of paper money and coin to meet the demand of member banks for cash. Some of this cash, principally silver certificates, United States notes, and coin, is issued by the Treasury. The Reserve banks pay for such Treasury currency by crediting the Treasury's account on their books. The largest amount, however, consists of Federal Reserve notes which the Federal Reserve banks are authorized to issue. Thus the Treasury, the twelve Federal Reserve banks, and the thousands of local banks throughout the country distribute cash promptly as needed and retire it when the need has passed.

2. *Cash collection*. Payments are made by check many times more frequently than they are made with paper money and coins. A rapid collection system has assisted in making checks an acceptable means of payment. The way commercial banks facilitate the use of checks is discussed in Chapter IV and Chapter XIII.

The Federal Reserve banks clear and collect checks and provide commercial banks with a means of settling for the checks that they clear and collect. Included in this system are checks collected by city correspondent banks and local checks collected by banks through clearing houses or by direct presentment to one another. The settlement or payment for such checks on member banks is made directly or indirectly through member bank reserve balances with the Federal Reserve banks.

Checks collected and cleared through the Federal Reserve banks must be paid in full by the banks on which they are drawn; in other words, they must be payable at par without deduction of a fee or a charge. Federal Reserve banks will not collect checks drawn on nonpar banks.

An example of the way the Federal Reserve banks directly facilitate the clearing and collecting of checks follows. Suppose a manufacturer in Albany, New York sells $5,000 worth of equipment to a dealer in Portland, Oregon, and receives in payment a check on the dealer's bank in Portland. The manufacturer deposits the check in his bank in Albany. He does not wish cash in exchange for the check; he wishes to have credit in his deposit account. The Albany bank does not want currency in exchange for the check, but wants credit in its reserve account with the Federal Reserve Bank of New York. The Albany bank might begin the collection process by sending the check to the Federal Reserve Bank of New York, which would send it to the Federal Reserve Branch in Portland, which in turn would present it to the clearing house of the bank upon which it is drawn. The Portland bank charges the check to the account of the depositor who wrote it, and the Federal Reserve Branch in Portland charges the Portland bank's reserve account according to its availability schedule and credits the Federal Reserve Bank of New York. The Federal Reserve Bank of New York then credits the Albany bank's reserve account and the Albany bank credits the depositor's account at the time of deposit. The net effect is a reduction of the reserves and deposits of the purchaser's bank in Portland, and an increase in the reserves and deposits of the seller's bank in Albany. The Federal Reserve banks shift reserves from one account to the other. In order to facilitate the collection process, Federal Reserve banks extend to member banks which handle a substantial volume of checks payable in other Federal Reserve districts the privilege of sending their checks directly to other Federal Reserve banks. This eliminates the first step. The Albany bank, therefore, might have sent the $5,000 check directly to the Federal Reserve Branch in Portland at the same time informing the Federal Reserve Bank in New York of its action. The

Federal Reserve Bank of New York would credit the Albany bank's reserve account on the basis of this information.

3. *Noncash collection.* Checks are not the only items that banks convert into usable funds. Notes, acceptances, certificates of deposit, drafts, bills of exchange, bonds, and bond coupons are other items. The handling of these items by the collection department of commercial banks is described in Chapter XIII.

The Federal Reserve System has a noncash collection service much like that of a large commercial bank.

4. *Wire transfer.* The Federal Reserve banks operate a leased wire system that connects every Federal Reserve bank and branch with every other Federal Reserve bank and branch. A member bank may use this service to establish balances or immediately to pay funds in other parts of the country. Such transfers of funds are debited and credited to the reserve accounts of the member banks involved.

5. *Rediscounting.* One of the advantages of membership in the Federal Reserve System is the privilege of borrowing from a Federal Reserve bank. A member bank may rediscount one or more of its customers' notes with a Reserve bank. Also, a member bank may secure an advance from its Federal Reserve bank by giving its own note secured by loans or bonds from its holdings. In either case, the Reserve bank gives the member bank credit in its reserve account. This credit increases the reserve deposit of a member bank at the Reserve bank. For this service a Reserve bank charges interest at a rate known as the *discount rate*.

A Reserve bank is not obliged to grant credit automatically when requested by a member bank; its decision rests on judgment as to the applicant's need and the use to be made of the funds. A discount or advance from a Reserve bank is considered available to member banks to meet temporary requirements or unusual banking situations.

Services for the Government

The Federal Reserve banks are used by the Government as fiscal agents, custodians, and depositories. They carry the principal checking accounts of the United States Treasury, are responsible for a large part of the work in issuing and redeeming Government obligations, and perform other fiscal duties for the Government.

1. *Treasury deposits.* The Government receives and spends funds in all parts of the country. Receipts come mainly from taxpayers and purchasers of Government securities. Most receipts are deposited initially to the Treasury's account in the commercial banks and are then transferred to the Reserve banks when they are needed by the Treasury. The Government spends by check, and checks are charged to Treasury accounts at the Reserve banks.

2. *Government debt.* Reserve banks take applications for the purchase of Government securities, make allotments as instructed by the Treasury, deliver the securities to the purchaser, receive payment, and credit the amounts of the payments to the Treasury account. Reserve banks redeem Government securities as they mature, make exchanges, and pay interest coupons. They also issue and redeem Savings Bonds.

In size, these services run into astronomical figures. For example, in 1953 the Federal Reserve banks handled more than three billion checks worth more than a trillion dollars!

Monetary Policy

It should be observed that some Federal Reserve operations affect the reserve balance of the member bank. Monetary policy is important because individual banks are sensitive to their own reserve position and because the Federal Reserve System exercises its credit controls primarily through influencing the supply, availability, and cost of reserves.

The member bank is sensitive to its reserve position because it is required by law to keep a percentage of its deposits in the form of reserves. It must keep this reserve on deposit with its Federal Reserve bank. Nonmember banks are subject to reserve requirements that vary from state to state. A bank cannot permit its reserve account to fall below its requirements without suffering penalties. On the other hand, a bank ordinarily does not wish to keep its reserve account above its requirements because it receives no income from such excess reserves. As banks acquire excess reserves they tend to lend and invest more readily, and credit becomes easier. As they lose excess reserves they tend to become more selective in their loans and investments, and credit grows tighter.

The Federal Reserve System, in turn, can ease or tighten credit by influencing the volume of reserves. It has three general instruments for this purpose:

1. Changes in reserve requirements
2. Open market operations
3. Discounting.

These instruments provide the Federal Reserve banks with a considerable amount of flexibility in dealing with credit conditions.

1. *Changes in reserve requirements.* The Board of Governors of the Federal Reserve System is authorized to change, within limits, the minimum percentage of deposits that member banks must keep as reserves. By reducing reserve requirements, the Board of Governors increases excess reserves of member banks. This increase in excess reserves induces member banks to lend and invest more readily. On the other hand, when reserve requirements are increased, member banks (unless they have excess reserves) must acquire additional reserves to meet the higher requirements, and credit grows tighter.

2. *Open market operations.* The Federal Reserve System can put reserves into the banking system directly by buying Government securities; Federal Reserve can take the reserves out of the banking system by selling Government securities in the open market. The System pays for securities with a check drawn on itself. Typically, the seller of the securities deposits the check in his bank. Then the bank in turn deposits the check to its reserve account at the Federal Reserve bank. Since no bank has lost reserves, the operation increases the excess reserves not only of the original receiving bank but also of the banking system as a whole. When the Federal Reserve buys securities in the market, credit tends to become easier. Conversely, a sale of securities by the System will be paid for by checks, which will reduce both deposits and the reserve balances of the member banks on which the checks are drawn. This action tends to cause both credit and money to become tighter.

3. *Discounting.* A member bank that is short of reserves may restore its position by borrowing from its Federal Reserve bank and depositing the proceeds of the loan to its reserve account. The Reserve banks can influence the volume of reserves created in this way by changing the rate of discount on such borrowing, discouraging borrowers by a higher and encouraging by a lower rate

STRUCTURE OF THE FEDERAL RESERVE SYSTEM

The organization of the Federal Reserve System is illustrated in Chart 13. Instead of establishing a single central bank, the statute divided the country into twelve districts and a city was selected in each district for the location of a Federal Reserve bank.

Member Banks

National banks within the continental United States are required to be members of the Federal Reserve System. Most of the large state-chartered banks have elected to join the System. Thus, although less than half of all banks belong to the System, member banks hold about three-fourths of the total bank deposits.

Members are eligible to use all of the System's facilities and must abide by certain regulations for the protection of the public interest. In addition to the services provided by the System, which are described earlier in this chapter, member banks share in the informational facilities of the System. They participate in the election of six of the nine directors of the Federal Reserve bank of their district, and they receive a cumulative statutory dividend of six per cent on paid-in capital stock of the Reserve banks which the members own.

Federal Reserve Banks

Every member bank must subscribe to a prescribed amount of the capital stock of the Federal Reserve bank in its district. Each member bank subscribes to the extent of six per cent of its capital and surplus, of which three per cent is paid in and an additional three per cent may be called if required. Each Federal Reserve bank has nine directors. Three of them are known as Class A directors; three as Class B directors; and three as Class C directors. Class A and B directors are elected by member banks. One of each class (two directors) is elected by small banks; one of each class by banks of medium size; and one of each class by large banks. The three Class A directors may be bankers. The Three Class B directors must be actively engaged in the district in business, agriculture, or some other commercial pursuit. The Class B directors must not be officers, directors, or employees of any bank whatsoever.

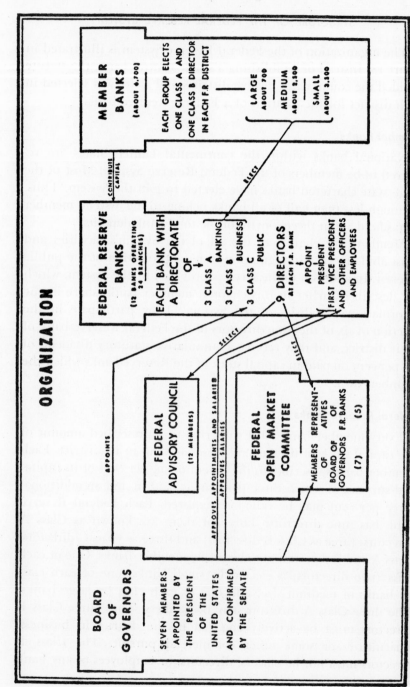

CHART 13. THE FEDERAL RESERVE SYSTEM

The three Class C directors are selected by the Board of Governors of the Federal Reserve System. They must not be officers, directors, employees, or stockholders of any bank.

The directors are responsible for the conduct of the Reserve bank in the public interest, subject to supervision by the Board of Governors. Directors of the Reserve banks set the discount rate for their respective districts, subject to review and determination by the Board of Governors. The officers of each Federal Reserve bank are appointed by its board of directors, but the law requires that the president and first vice president be approved by the Board of Governors.

The Board of Governors of the Federal Reserve System

The Board of Governors of the Federal Reserve System has seven members appointed by the President and confirmed by the Senate. Board members give their full time to the business of the Board of Governors. Appointments are for fourteen years, so arranged that the term of office of one member expires every two years. The Board supervises the operations of the Federal Reserve System. The Board exercises authority in formulating credit policy of the Federal Reserve System. The importance of the Board's influence is obvious from the following list of its activities.

1. It establishes the reserve requirements of member banks.
2. It reviews and determines the discount rates established by directors of the Reserve banks.
3. Board members constitute a majority of the members of the Federal Open Market Committee.
4. The Board sets maximum rates of interest that member banks may pay on savings and other time desposits.
5. It is responsible for setting margin requirements for stock market credit.

Federal Open Market Committee

Seven members of the Board of Governors and five representatives elected by the Reserve banks constitute the Open Market Committee. This Committee decides on changes to be made in the System's portfolio of Government securities; in other words, when, how much, and under what conditions to buy or sell in the market. Reserve banks are required by law to carry out these decisions.

Committee decisions are influenced by national and regional considerations. Purchases and sales of securities for the System open market account are divided among the twelve Reserve banks in accordance with the relative asset size of each.

Federal Advisory Council

This twelve member body confers with the Board of Governors on business conditions and makes recommendations regarding the affairs of the System. One member of the Committee is selected annually by the board of directors of each Reserve bank.

FEDERAL DEPOSIT INSURANCE CORPORATION

The Federal Deposit Insurance Corporation protects small depositors of insured banks against loss. The most important ways that it affords this protection are as follows:
1. Insured banks must conform to F.D.I.C. standards.
2. It regularly examines insured banks to make certain that these standards are maintained.
3. When despite precautions an insured bank is in trouble, the F.D.I.C. provides the cash to protect depositors.

All member banks of the Federal Reserve System are required to participate in the F.D.I.C. plan. Nonmember state banks and mutual savings banks may obtain this insurance if they meet F.D.I.C. standards. In 1952, about 93% of all banks, holding 96% of the deposits, were insured by F.D.I.C. Deposit insurance does not cover all deposits in insured banks. Only the first $10,000 of each deposit account is insured; thus in 1952 about 54% of the dollar total of deposits in insured banks was covered.

Insured banks pay to the F.D.I.C. an assessment of one-twelfth of 1% of their yearly deposit liabilities. In years when F.D.I.C. income exceeds expenses, a percentage of this excess is refunded to the insured banks and the remainder is added to the F.D.I.C. surplus. F.D.I.C. invests the surplus, and the interest on the investment provides part of the funds for F.D.I.C. operations. If additional funds are needed, the United States Treasury is directed to lend the Corporation as much as three billion dollars.

The Federal Deposit Insurance Corporation does not have to close an insured bank before taking action. F.D.I.C. may make a loan to a distressed bank, purchase assets from it, or deposit with it to keep it from failing. F.D.I.C. may also make loans or purchase assets to bring about a merger or consolidation of the distressed bank with a stronger insured bank in the same area. Generally, such an action is taken if the F.D.I.C. determines that it will benefit the community or it will reduce F.D.I.C. losses. It should be noted that when the F.D.I.C. chooses to act to prevent a bank failure it is, in effect, protecting all deposits. When the F.D.I.C. allows an insured bank to close, it customarily pays each depositor's claim up to $10,000. It may make deposit accounts on another bank available to those who held insured deposits in the closed bank.

Each demand and time or savings deposit is insured up to $10,000 by the F.D.I.C., but a depositor cannot increase the insurance by placing his deposits in two or more accounts in the same bank. In other words, all deposits maintained in the same ownership are insured to $10,000. Accounts maintained in different ownerships, however, are each insured to $10,000.

The Federal Deposit Insurance Corporation is managed by a three-man board of directors. They appoint all officers and employees of the Corporation and determine policy. One of the directors is the Comptroller of the Currency; the other two are appointed by the President, with the advice and consent of the Senate. The appointed members hold office for six years, and one is Chairman of the Board. The three members may not all be of the same political party. None of the three may hold any office or be employed by an insured bank while serving on the Board of the Federal Deposit Insurance Corporation.

Questions Based on Chapter XXII

1. Why are the Federal Reserve banks frequently called bankers' banks?
2. In what ways does the Government use the Federal Reserve banks?
3. Explain how the Federal Reserve System influences commercial bank credit policies by changes in reserve requirements, purchases and sales of Government securities in the open market, and the discount rate.
4. Do all large banks have to be members of the Federal Reserve System?

5. In what ways are the Federal Reserve banks different from commercial banks?
6. Is the Board of Governors composed of three bankers, three businessmen, and three representatives of the general public?
7. How does the Federal Deposit Insurance Corporation protect smaller depositors of insured banks?
8. Is the Comptroller of the Currency affiliated with the Federal Deposit Insurance Corporation?

Questions for Investigation

1. Which Federal Reserve services does your bank use?
2. How do Federal Reserve policies influence the operations of your bank?

CHAPTER XXIII

BANKING AND PUBLIC SERVICE

The Purposes of This Chapter:

1. To indicate the ways in which banks cooperate with each other.
2. To mention bankers associations that promote cooperative action.
3. To discuss the educational programs supported by bankers associations.
4. To point out the many community activities in which bankers participate.

AN INDIVIDUAL bank does not exist unto itself alone, any more than does an individual employee in a bank. This point has already been made clear in the chapter on the operations of banks. The clearing of checks, for example, makes it necessary for banks to maintain continuous cooperative relations with each other. Clearing arrangements, correspondent bank relations, and exchanges of credit information are among the ways in which banks cooperate with each other.

In no other industry are the agencies of cooperation as highly developed as in banking. Bankers join in associations, conferences, institutes, and discussion groups to consider their common problems and to exchange ideas. There is continuous study and research into all phases of banking from the smallest detail of bank operations to the larger aspects of banking. The educational activities sponsored and supported by bank organizations are unique in their scope and comprehensiveness.

In this chapter we shall discuss areas of cooperation among bankers. They are (1) bankers associations, (2) the educational activities sponsored and supported by bank organizations, and (3) the community activities of bankers.

BANKERS ASSOCIATIONS

The complexity of our banking system is symbolized by the many and varied associations of bankers in the United States. Banks operate under a variety of circumstances, and they have many interests in common. Associations of bankers are organized along geographical lines, such as national, state, city, county, district, and regional associations; they are organized also on the basis of the kind of charter, such as national bank, state bank, trust company, or savings bank. Banks also have organized clearing houses that, in addition to the clearing function, carry on other activities such as public relations and educational programs. Some associations of bankers are organized on a functional basis, such as credits, investments, mortgages, and public relations.

Thus an individual bank may be a member of many associations. It may be a member of a county bankers association concerned chiefly with the problems and projects arising in the local area. The interests of the bank, however, extend beyond the limits of the county in which it is located to a larger area, and thus it may participate with other banks in a regional grouping. In some respects the interests of banks are statewide, and thus the banks join a state bankers association. All banks, moreover, are affected by national developments; therefore, they find it advantageous to participate in and to support associations whose activities are national in scope. Approximately 98% of all banks are members of the American Bankers Association.

THE ACTIVITIES OF BANKERS ASSOCIATIONS

A complete compilation of the activities of all the associations through which bankers order their cooperative activities would be massive. It would be much too large to treat in this chapter; therefore, some of the major types of activity characteristic of bank associations are summarized briefly in this chapter.

Maintaining Contacts with Legislators

Banking laws are constantly expanded, revised, amended, and extended. New interests, changing practices, and the recognition of new needs and new hazards motivate proposals for new legislation. Some of the proposals for new laws are wise; others are poorly conceived without any understanding of their effect on banking. Some are beneficial to banking, others are harmful; some strengthen the economy, others weaken it. Therefore, banks watch pending legislation that affects banking in order to present the bankers' viewpoint on legislative measures under consideration. In fact, legislators often wish to hear the bankers' opinions concerning proposed laws. The bills introduced in the state and federal legislature are usually quite complicated. They must be analyzed carefully and in some instances the analysis may require extensive research. Furthermore, legislators often request time for informal discussions, and bankers are also requested to attend committee hearings, which may extend over a considerable period of time.

An individual banker cannot possibly devote adequate time and energy to these activities. Only through organized effort can individual bankers be represented effectively. Thus it is one of the duties of a bankers association to represent bankers' interests at state legislatures. The American Bankers Association, as a national organization, sometimes presents the bankers' viewpoint to Congressional committees.

Cooperation with Government Agencies

Banks have an interest not only in the lawmaking process but also in the policies and practices of the executive agencies of government. There are several federal agencies which directly exercise control over bank operations in such sensitive areas as the cost and availability of credit, the management of the federal debt, and the loan policies and practices of the banks. Other federal agencies influence bank operations through the loaning function. For instance, loans to farmers for the storage of their crops, loans to consumers for the purchase of automobiles, loans to investors for the purchase of securities, and loans to prospective homeowners for the purchase of their homes are but a few of the kinds of bank loans which are influenced by one or another government agency.

That it is necessary for banks to maintain continuous close contact with government agencies is obvious. It is as important for the government agencies to understand the problems of bankers as it is for banks to understand the purposes and objectives of the government agencies and the reasons for the rules and regulations of the agencies.

In this area of banker-government relationships, the bankers associations perform valuable services. They serve as a liaison between the government agencies and the banks. When necessary, they present the banking viewpoint to the agencies and seek to adjust any difficulties and problems which may arise. They provide information and offer recommendations and suggestions to banks and to the government agencies.

Study and Research in All Phases of Banking

In no industry is study and research more continuous, more comprehensive, and more thorough than it is in banking. No detail of bank operations is too small to be the subject of investigation and study. Through the research activities of bankers associations, the experience and knowledge of bankers are assembled in a common pool. Through the information services of the associations, accumulated knowledge and experience is made available to all bankers.

Some idea of the scope of the study and research activities of the national association, the American Bankers Association, is indicated in the following partial list of subjects which at one time have been studied or are under continuous study. The subjects studied include such matters of operating detail as the size and design of checks and drafts, currency straps, coin wrappers, packaging, account analysis, and service charges. In the field of personnel relations, we find such topics as job analysis and employee merit rating, on-the-job training, and job relations training for supervisors. Included also are topics of broader scope, such as the relationship between farm income and farm expense, the agricultural lending procedures of banks in comparison with the procedures of competing agencies, current economic and monetary trends, international financial developments, and social and economic legislation.

The study and research activities of bank employees have great value for banking both in the present and in the future. The results of the studies and the recommendations based upon them are communicated to bankers through conferences, association meetings, in the publication of books, in pamphlets, in articles published in Banking[1] and in other magazines for bankers. Thus the best thought that banking is able to bring to bear on its many problems is made available to all bankers. New and improved

---

[1] Published monthly by the American Bankers Association

systems and methods do not remain the trade secrets of the banks who originate them, but they quickly become the common knowledge of all.

Conferences and Other Meetings

Bankers regularly assemble in conferences sponsored by their associations to hear and participate in discussions of their common problems. The list of speakers usually includes bankers, representatives of other industries, economists, and public officials. At an agricultural credit conference, for example, a representative of one of the farm organizations may present the financial problems and credit needs of agriculture. At an instalment credit conference, there may be a speaker from the automobile industry to discuss trends and new developments in his industry. An economist may be asked to discuss general monetary and economic trends and their effect on banking. A banker may discuss some new method or system which his bank found helpful in cutting its operating costs and increasing its profits. These meetings also provide time for personal contacts between bankers and an opportunity to make new friendships. The conferences and meetings also provide opportunities for the interchange of ideas among bankers.

There are many more activities which characterize organized banking, but these are probably sufficient to suggest to the student the larger world of which his job and his bank are a part.

THE EDUCATIONAL ACTIVITIES OF ORGANIZED BANKING

The educational activities of organized banking are a unique phenomena not only in banking but in American education. There is no other industry in the United States which provides an educational program as comprehensive and as well organized.

The American Institute of Banking

First and foremost among the educational institutions sponsored by organized banking is the American Institute of Banking. It is the educational section of the American Bankers Association. It was organized in 1900 in response to a petition from bank employees in various cities urging the Association to establish an institute similar to the one in successful operation in England.

The Institute carries on its educational program through local chapters, through study groups in localities where the number of bank employees is not sufficient to maintain a chapter, and through individual correspondence courses. Enrolment in Institute classes is open to the personnel of all banks that are members of the American Bankers Association and to the personnel of the bank supervisory agencies. Student enrolments in Institute classes total close to seventy thousand a year; this number exceeds the number of students in even the largest universities.

The objective of the Institute is fourfold: (1) to aid the student in developing his intellectual capabilities, (2) to aid the student in acquiring knowledge and understanding of the basic processes of banking, (3) to give the student an opportunity for advanced study in the various fields of specialized study such as mortgage lending, investments, instalment credit, bank management, and (4) to give the student an understanding of the larger aspects of banking, of our monetary system, and of our credit economy.

The course of studies has three divisions: Pre-Standard, Standard, and Graduate. The study programs which lead to the Pre-Standard and Standard certificates are designed to give the students a grasp of the rudiments of banking and a working knowledge of the basic tools. This course of study includes such subjects as Principles of Bank Operations, Effective Bank Letters, Negotiable Instruments, Accounting I, Accounting II, Money and Banking, and Economics. The Graduate program permits the student to specialize in the field of his special interest.

The educational standards are uniformly high and compare favorably with those of many colleges and schools of commerce. The approximately 2500 faculty members are drawn from the ranks of bank executives, from college faculties, and from the law and accounting professions. To write its textbooks, the Institute selects skilled writers from colleges and universities, outstanding bankers who have distinguished themselves in the various specialized areas of banking, and professional men who are noted for their work in a particular field.

The Stonier Graduate School of Banking

The Stonier Graduate School of Banking is conducted by the American Bankers Association in cooperation with Rutgers University. This school offers a comprehensive study of the problems of banks to bank executives. About a thousand bank officers enroll each year. Each student who attends three resident sessions of two weeks each, completes written extension work in the intervals between these sessions, submits an acceptable thesis, and passes the final oral examinations receives a diploma issued jointly by Rutgers University and by The Stonier Graduate School of Banking. All students are required to attend lectures on economics and monetary policy.

Foundation for Education in Economics

In celebration of its fiftieth anniversary, the American Bankers Association created an endowment fund of $500,000 to be administered by the American Bankers Association Foundation for Education in Economics. From the income of the fund, the Foundation provides loan scholarships for the study of banking and economics in institutions of higher learning and in The Stonier Graduate School of Banking, Rutgers University.

Other Bank-Sponsored Schools for Advanced Study

In recent years several state bankers associations have established schools for advanced study in banking subjects in conjunction with state universities. Some of these schools are Pacific Coast Banking School—University of Washington, School of Banking of the South-Louisiana State University, and School of Banking at the University of Wisconsin. They are conducted along lines similar to that of The Stonier Graduate School of Banking. The course of studies places special emphasis on those fields of banking activity which predominate in the local areas.

THE BANKS AND COMMUNITY RELATIONS

Banks perform many services which contribute to the economic life of their communities. In turn, a bank depends for its success largely on its reputation in the community. The public regard toward banking is important to banking as a whole. Banks should make themselves respected and liked in their communities and should cooperate actively in community life.

We find, therefore, that alert and progressive bankers have an active community program. The community activities of banks center around three areas, (1) banking education in schools, (2) civic and social activities, (3) business associations.

Banking Education in Schools

In promoting banking education, banks do not try to sell the services of a particular bank. Instead, they try to serve both teachers and students by relating the banking story to appropriate subjects in the curriculum. Their purpose is primarily educational; it is to convey to the students a clear conception of what banks do and why they do it. An effective medium is the use of films and other visual techniques. A local banker may be asked to lead a discussion in the classroom and to answer any questions that may be raised concerning banking.

Civic and Social Activities

There are many ways in which banks contribute to the civic and social activities of their community. In addition to their monetary donations to charities, bankers may contribute their experience, knowledge, and facilities to charitable drives; some of the large banks assign groups of their employees to give their full time to such financing programs. Smaller banks may assign one or several employees to aid the charitable organizations in preparing for and in conducting drives.

Community fund drives are only one of the activities which enlist the help of bankers. Bankers serve on school boards, on local education committees, and in local chambers of commerce. They may sponsor junior achievement companies, and work with such organizations as 4-H Clubs, Future Farmers of America, or the Boy Scouts. Banks provide speakers for civic clubs, sponsor women's financial forums, and open their quarters for civic meetings. Bankers may serve on church boards and work with slum clearance projects.

If the bank is in a rural area, it may work with local county agents to promote reforestation, contour plowing, or it may erect demonstration stations to educate farmers in new ideas and new agricultural techniques. Bankers may work on committees sponsoring country fairs.

Business Associations

Some business men, in spite of their continuous use of banking facilities, remain uninformed about many services bankers are able to render. What is equally important, many business men have only a limited understanding of how the banking system works, of the extent to which the lending policies of a bank are influenced by such external factors as a change in monetary policy by the Board of Governors of the Federal Reserve System. Thus there is a need for banks to present the banking story to business clubs, associations, and conferences.

The Bank and the Community

A bank does not exist unto itself alone. It is part of a larger association of banks. It also is part of a community with its many civic and social activities. Banks cooperate with each other through the activities of many organizations, local, state, and national. Bankers have many interests in common, including contacts with lawmaking bodies and with the many government agencies. They are interested in the study of the common problems. They hold frequent meetings and conferences for the interchange of ideas and the discussion of banking practices. An outstanding activity of bank associations is the development of educational programs. The many local activities indicate the extent to which banks assume their responsibilities as citizens of the communities in which they live and work.

THE ROLE OF BANKS AND BANKERS

The primary emphasis of this text is on the various functions that banks perform and the many financial services they render. Beginning with the receiving of deposits, chapter by chapter the book unfolds the story of bank operations. It makes clear how each of the several processes is related to the others and to the operations of the bank as a whole. But banks do not exist merely as separate entities; their very operations require that they cooperate with each other and that their activities be coordinated into a larger system. This coordination of the activities of the many unit banks is achieved through correspondent bank relationships as well as through a system of external controls by government authorities. These smooth operating arrangements were not achieved overnight but over a period of more than a century of trial and error.

In addition to the coordination of bank activities prescribed by law, banks cooperate with each other on a voluntary basis through associations. The activities of these associations express the many interests that bankers have in common.

The Requisites of a Career in Banking

To anyone who intends to follow banking as a career an understanding of banking as a series of interrelated processes is indispensable. An individual who limits his interest to his particular assignment may develop competence in a particular task, but his comprehension, his perspective, and his imagination remain limited by the routine requirements of his position. If, on the other hand, he has a larger understanding of the working of the bank as a whole, his own particular task becomes alive with an appreciation of its importance and purpose. He knows the relationship of his work to that of the people around him. He knows why his work is essential to the bank and why it is performed in that particular way. He becomes more versatile and more capable, and he is better prepared to advance to a position of greater responsibility.

Principles of Bank Operations is the first and basic text in a series of studies that, together, give the student a comprehensive picture of banking's many phases and of its specialized services. The student who is ambitious to advance in the field of banking will find it to his advantage to continue his studies in such basic subjects as accounting, negotiable instruments, and effective letter writing. To enlarge his understanding of banking and its role in our economic life, he will turn to such subjects as money and banking, business administration, and economics. Later as he advances in his career, he will seek to obtain further training in the specialized fields that constitute his primary occupation or that come within the area of his executive responsibilities.

The functions and the operations of the commercial bank are all designed to provide the people of the community with essential banking and monetary services. These services are discussed briefly in this text. You are now ready to think about your relationship with your bank and with banking. You can now decide which bank function you wish to study in detail. For your future, it does not matter in which function of banking you choose to specialize if you plan to become a technician in one field. However, any path may lead you to the summit if you wish a broad career in banking.

Among the presidents of the great banks of the nation are men who began in credits, in instalment loans, in trusts, in auditing, in bank examinations, in operations, in commercial loans, and as bookkeepers or tellers, but none started at the top. Furthermore, some of the presidents of the largest banks began their careers in small banks, and some of the men who are heading smaller banks started out in large banks.

As you know, banking is one of the few fields of endeavor in which there are no political or geographical boundaries. A banker who is a good banker in New York is a good banker in Illinois or Texas. Not so a lawyer; a lawyer must stay in his own state. Not so a doctor or an accountant; each must practice his profession in a particular state. A banker may change his connection at will. Neither government nor geography prevents him from moving to any locality that offers a desirable opportunity.

The opportunities are there; they are limited only by your imagination. But a career in banking is not for everyone. Banking is a service business. It serves people in their most sensitive area—their purses. Therefore, it demands quality traits of those who work within its portals. Only those who have outstanding traits of character can qualify for leading roles; that is, those who have courage, integrity, accuracy, and trustworthiness. Combining these qualities with imagination and a deep desire to serve your fellow man, you have much to offer banking, and banking has need of you.

What does banking offer? Opportunity, unbounded opportunity to grow in stature and in strength. Opportunity to serve the present and shape the future for coming generations. Never did banking offer more rewarding opportunities for growth, for change, and for moulding the future.

In banking, automation is moving rapidly ahead. As highly specialized machines take over the clerical tasks, people are released from mechanical work for thought work. Therefore, you must be prepared to think harder and faster, for with automation the banks will need more and better technicians and more and better administrators.

You can see that banks must build executive talent from within. They cannot buy executive talent as can other business.

In any other business or profession, to get ahead you must single-heartedly serve *only* that business or profession. But to serve banking well, you must also cater to the needs, the hopes, the ambitions, and the welfare of every business, every trade, every service, and every profession in the community. You have the prospect of a life spent in constantly pursuing the frontiers of knowledge, in spreading the benefits of industry, and in encouraging the growth and stability of the business in your area of activity. Always the banks and the bankers must serve all phases of the nation's growth. Always they must demonstrate with hard cash their belief in the nation's future and their faith in their fellow citizens.

Questions Based on Chapter XXIII

1. Give some concrete illustrations of the way that banks cooperate with each other.
2. Into what kinds of associations are banks organized?
3. Why do banks have a common interest in maintaining contact with lawmaking bodies?
4. Do banks have an interest in the rules and regulations of government executive and administrative agencies? Why?
5. Name some of the topics in which banks support research and studies.
6. What are the educational programs of the American Bankers Association and other bank organizations?
7. Why are banks interested in their community relationships?
8. What are some of the activities of banks which come under the heading of community relations?

Questions for Investigation

1. To what organizations does your bank belong?
2. What are the community activities in which your bank participates?
3. In what community activities do you participate?

APPENDIX

A.B.A. Numerical System

Approximately forty years ago the American Bankers Association developed a plan for the numbering of all banks in the country so that each bank would have a specific identifying number. The plan, as developed, provided for a hyphenated number (for example, 1-45 or 90-567). The digit (or digits) preceding the hyphen, called the prefix number, designates the city or state in which the bank is located; the number after the hyphen, termed the suffix number, refers specifically to one bank in that given area. Under this plan, prefix numbers from 1 to 49 are assigned to cities which are normally large centers of economic activity (1 for New York, 2 for Chicago, 3 for Philadelphia, etc.); numbers from 50 through 99 are assigned to states (50 for New York, 90 for California, etc.). At this time the number 89 is not assigned, and the number 59 is used for the territories of Hawaii, Alaska, and Puerto Rico. The remainder of the numbers cover the 48 states. The numbers of all banks are listed in the Key to the Numerical System and in various bank directories under authority of the American Bankers Association, and the listing is revised periodically to reflect current changes.

Check Routing Symbol

To facilitate the handling and routing of transit items through banks throughout the United States, a check routing symbol plan was developed by the American Bankers Association and the Federal Reserve System during the 1940's. The check routing symbol is the denominator of a fraction, the numerator of which is the A.B.A. transit number assigned to the drawee bank. The entire fraction is located in the upper right corner of the check above the figure amount line. The check routing symbol, for example

$$\frac{1\text{-}45}{210} \text{ or } \frac{97\text{-}18}{1243},$$

is composed of three elements.

1. The first digit of a three-digit number (or the first two digits of a four-digit number) designates the Federal Reserve district. Thus the 2 in 210 indicates the Second Federal Reserve District and the 12 in 1243 indicates the Twelfth Federal Reserve District.

2. The next to the last digit designates the Federal Reserve bank or branch serving the territory in which the drawee bank is located. The head office is indicated by figure 1. Branches, if any, arranged alphabetically are indicated by figures 2 to 5. Figures 6 to 9 are used (or reserved) to designate special collection arrangements. For example: The 1 in 210 indicates that the bank is served by the head office; the 4 in 1243 indicates that the bank is served by the Salt Lake City Branch. In the Twelfth Federal Reserve District, figure 1 stands for the head office in San Francisco; the Los Angeles branch is 2, the Portland branch is 3, the Salt Lake City branch is 4, and the Seattle branch is 5.

3. The final digit serves two purposes: first, it facilitates the separation of items which are receivable for immediate credit from those which are receivable for deferred credit (without respect to the number of days of deferred availability), and second, it facilitates the sorting of items by states in any case when that is convenient.

If the number is 0, it indicates that an immediate credit will be given upon receipt of the check by the Federal Reserve bank or branch in time for that day's clearings; any other digit means a deferred credit without indicating whether it is deferred one or two days. This information is most helpful in separating city and country items. The final digit also indicates, in alphabetical progression, the state in which the drawee bank is located. Thus, in the number 1243, the 3 stands for Utah, 1 being used for Idaho banks served by the Salt Lake City Branch of the Federal Reserve Bank of San Francisco, and 2 for Nevada.

GLOSSARY OF BANKING TERMS

Acceptance. A time draft (bill of exchange) on the face of which the drawee has written the word "accepted," the date it is payable, usually the place where it is payable, and his signature. Thus an acceptance is an obligation which the drawee has agreed to pay at maturity. After accepting the draft, the drawee is known as the *acceptor. See also* bank acceptance *and* trade acceptance.

Accommodation indorser. One who indorses a negotiable instrument for the accommodation of another party, having no right of ownership but simply guaranteeing fulfilment of the contract to subsequent holders of the instrument. *See also* indorsement *and* indorser.

Accommodation paper. A note or similar obligation the payment of which is guaranteed by some party other than the one who receives the benefit. Thus, before advancing funds, a bank may require the indorsement of a director of known means upon the note of a corporation of doubtful strength.

Account analysis. The process of analyzing a checking account to determine the profit or loss incurred by the bank for servicing the account over a given period, usually one month. If the analysis shows that the customer is not maintaining sufficient balance to pay for the services rendered, a service charge is usually applied to offset the difference. The objective of account analysis and service charges is to obtain fair and reasonable compensation for services rendered to customers. *See* service charge.

Accounts receivable. The accounts receivable of a business enterprise represent money owed by customers for merchandise sold to them on open account—that is, without the giving of a note or other evidence of debt.

Accrual system. The system of recording expenses and earnings as they actually occur without regard to the date of payment or collection.

Accrued interest. Interest earned but not yet due. On a bank statement, Accrued Interest Payable represents interest earned by depositors on interest-bearing accounts, but not as yet paid by the bank. Accrued Interest Receivable represents interest earned by the bank on loans, but not as yet collected from the borrowers.

Administrator. A person or an institution appointed by a court to settle an estate when the decedent has left no will, when no executor has been named in the will if the decedent has left one, or when the named executor has died or is unwilling to serve.

361

Agent. A person who is authorized to represent or act for another person, called the principal, in dealing with third parties.

Alternate account. An account in the names of two or more persons, any of whom may draw against the account without further authority from the others. *See also* joint account *and* survivorship account.

American Bankers Association (A.B.A.). The national organization of banking organized in 1875 to "promote the general welfare and usefulness of banks and financial institutions." The Association consists of about eighty working groups, including four divisions, seven commissions, and a number of councils and committees. The A.B.A. (as it is generally known) has over sixteen thousand members, representing over ninety-eight per cent of all the banks in the United States and over ninety-nine per cent of the banking resources.

A.B.A. numerical system. The system of bank numbers whereby each bank in the United States and Territories is provided with a definite number of its own which constitutes a numerical name used only by that bank.

American Institute of Banking (A.I.B.). The educational section of the American Bankers Association, organized in 1900. Through the medium of about four hundred chapters and study groups and the correspondence method of study, the Institute devotes itself to the education of bank personnel in the theory and practice of banking and in those principles of law, economics, and accounting that pertain to the banking business. Membership is restricted to employees, officers, and directors of banks and other financial institutions that are members of the American Bankers Association.

Amortization. The gradual reduction of a debt by means of equal periodic payments sufficient to meet current interest and extinguish the debt at maturity. When the debt involves real property, often the periodic payments include a sum sufficient to pay taxes and insurance on the property.

Antedated check. A check which is dated prior to the date on which it is issued—that is, delivered or mailed to the payee. If a check dated July 15, for example, is not issued until July 20, it is an antedated check.

Asset. Anything owned by a business or by an individual which has commercial or exchange value. Assets may consist of specific property or of claims against others, in contrast to obligations due to others (liabilities).

Availability date. The date on which a check drawn on an out-of-town bank will be considered as having been converted into cash.

Average daily balance. The average amount of money that a customer keeps on deposit, determined by adding the daily balances of his account for a given length of time and dividing the total by the number of days covered.

Balance sheet. A detailed listing of assets, liabilities, and capital accounts (net worth) showing the financial condition of a company on a given date. The balance sheet of a bank is generally referred to as a statement of condition.

Bank acceptance. A draft drawn on a bank and accepted by the bank.

Bank call. The demand made upon a bank by a supervisory authority for a sworn statement of the bank's condition as of a certain date.

Bank directors. Persons selected by the stockholders of a bank from among their own number. The directors are responsible to the stockholders for profitable management and to government supervisory authority for operation of the bank according to law and sound banking principles.

Bank draft. A check drawn by a bank against funds deposited to its account in another bank.

Bank examination. An examination made by representatives of a federal or state bank supervisory authority, to make certain that a bank is solvent and is operating in conformity with banking laws and sound banking principles.

Bank examiner. A person who as the representative of a federal or state bank supervisory authority examines the banks under its jurisdiction with respect to their financial condition, management, and policies.

Bank note. A noninterest-bearing promissory note of a bank issued for general circulation as money and payable to the bearer on demand. In the United States only the Federal Reserve banks now issue bank notes.

Bank statement. A statement of a customer's account which the bank gives him periodically, usually monthly, for his information. It shows all the deposits made and all the checks paid during the period as well as the balance; the statement is accompanied by the customer's canceled checks.

Bank statement of condition. *See* statement of condition.

Batch. A group of deposits, or a group of other items, which are proved in one operation. Also termed *block*.

Bearer. Holder or person in possession of money, or of a check, bill, note, or other instrument. "The person in possession of a bill or note which is payable to bearer" (Negotiable Instruments Law).

Beneficiary. 1. The person in whose favor a letter of credit is issued. 2. The person designated to receive the income or principal of a trust estate. 3. The person who is to receive the proceeds of or benefits accruing under an insurance policy or annuity.

Bid and asked price. The price at which an owner offers to sell (asked) and the price at which someone has agreed to buy (bid). Said of unlisted stocks and bonds but may apply to any property in which there is an active trade.

Bill of exchange. *See* draft.

Bill of lading. A document issued by a railroad or other carrier. It acknowledges the receipt of specified goods for transportation to a certain place, it sets forth the contract between the shipper and the carrier, and it provides for proper delivery of the goods.

Block. Same as batch.

Board of Governors of the Federal Reserve System. A board of seven members (located at Washington) which supervises, coordinates, and controls the operations of the twelve Federal Reserve banks and branches, and the Board has regulatory powers with respect to member banks.

Bond. An interest-bearing debt certificate under seal which promises that the issuer (a government or a corporation) will pay a certain sum of money to the holder of the bond at a specified date. In effect, it is a long term loan by the bondholder (lender) to the issuer (borrower).

Bondholder. One who owns bonds and therefore is a creditor of the issuer.

Bond of indemnity. A written instrument under seal by which the signer, usually together with his surety or bondsman, guarantees to protect another against loss. It is generally required to protect the drawee bank when the drawer issues a stop-payment order against a certified check. Such an agreement without sureties and not under seal is called an *indemnity agreement.*

Bond power. A signed instrument in the form of a power of attorney by which the owner of registered bonds authorizes another party to sell and transfer the bonds.

Book value. The amount at which an asset is carried on the books of the owner. This may be less or greater than the price that could be obtained at a given moment.

Branch bank. A bank that has a head office and one or more branch offices.

Broker. A middleman who brings together buyers and sellers of the same security or commodity and executes their orders, charging a commission for the service.

Cable transfer. The transfer of funds in a foreign country through instructions sent by cable.

Call. *See* bank call.

Call Loan. A loan made on a day-to-day basis, callable on twenty-four hours' notice. Typically, loans made to members of the New York Stock Exchange to facilitate the exchange of securities.

Capital. In an accounting sense, the excess of assets over liabilities. In a corporation, it is the sum of the various capital stock accounts, surplus, and undivided profits; hence capital is synonymous with net worth.

Capital loan. A loan which cannot be repaid without disposing of capital assets, in contrast to a loan, for example, to purchase merchandise, the sale of which will provide funds to repay the loan.

Cashier's check. A check drawn by a bank on itself and signed by the cashier or other authorized officer. Also called *officer's check.*

Cash items. Items (commonly checks and coupons) which a bank accepts for immediate credit to depositors' accounts.

Cash surrender value. The amount which an insurance company will pay the insured on the cancelation of a policy.

Central proof. A system for effecting economy of operation by proving a large number of independent operations in a single group called a batch or block.

Certificate of deposit. A formal receipt for funds left with a bank as a special deposit, generally interest-bearing. Such deposits may bear interest and be payable at a definite date in the future, or they may be non-interest bearing demand deposits. These deposits are payable only upon surrender of the formal receipt properly indorsed, and they are carried on the general ledger of the bank under heading "Certificate of Deposit" rather than on the individual ledgers under the name of the person to whom the certificate was originally issued.

Certified check. A depositor's check across the face of which an officer of the bank or some other authorized person has stamped the word "certified" and the bank's name and then signed his own name. By its certification the bank guarantees that sufficient funds have been set aside from the depositor's account to pay the check when payment is demanded.

Chain banking. A term used to refer to an arrangement by which control of a number of banks is exercised through entire or majority ownership of stock by a group of individuals, who take an active part in formulating the policies of the banks in the group. *See also* group banking.

Charge ticket. Same as debit ticket.

Charter. A document issued by a bank supervisory authority (national or state) giving a bank the right to do business, enumerating its powers, and prescribing the conditions under which it may operate.

Chattel mortgage. A mortgage with title to some form of personal property given as security.

Check (sometimes spelled cheque). **A draft drawn on a bank and payable on demand.**

Checking account. A bank account against which checks may be drawn.

Check routing symbol. A device to facilitate the handling and routing of transit items through banks that remit at par throughout the United States. The check routing symbol is the denominator of a fraction, the numerator of which is the A.B.A. transit number assigned to the drawee bank. The entire fraction is located in the upper right corner of the check above the figure amount line. The check routing symbol (denominator of the fraction) is composed of three or four digits. The first digit in a three-figure number or the first two digits in a four-figure number identify the Federal Reserve district in which the drawee bank is located. The next to the last digit designates the Federal Reserve bank head office or branch through which the item should be cleared and also any special clearing arrangement. (The head office is indicated by the figure "1." Branches, if any, arranged alphabetically are indicated by figures "2" to "5." Figures "6" to "9" are used to designate special collection arrangements.) The last digit serves two purposes: First, it shows whether the item is acceptable for immediate or deferred credit. (Figure "0" designates items which are receivable for immediate credit. All other numbers, "1" to "9" inclusive, designate items which are acceptable for deferred credit but the numbers do not indicate the number of days of deferred availability.) Second, the last number also designates the state in alphabetical progression in which the drawee bank is located.

Checks on us. Checks drawn on a bank and presented to it for deposit or payment.

Clearing. *Domestic* clearing (clearing within a country) is the offsetting of bank counterclaims and the settlement of balances; it may be either local or nationwide. *International* clearing is the settlement of balances between countries through the medium of foreign exchange.

Clearing house. A place where representatives of the banks in the same locality meet each day at an agreed time to exchange checks, drafts, and similar items drawn on each other and to settle the resulting balances.

Clearing house association. A voluntary association of banks in the same locality for the purpose of maintaining a clearing house arrangement and possibly taking concerted action on matters of common interest.

Coin. In banking terminology, refers to metallic money only.

Collateral. Specific property which a borrower pledges as security for the repayment of a loan, agreeing that the lender shall have the right to sell the collateral for the purpose of liquidating the debt if the borrower fails to repay the loan at maturity.

Collateral loan. A loan which is secured by the pledge of specific property, the borrower depositing with the lender either the property itself or a document bearing evidence of title to the property.

Collateral note. A promissory note which is secured by the pledge of specific property.

Collection items. Items (drafts, notes, acceptances, etc.) which are received by a bank subject to collection before payment will be credited to depositors' accounts. Also termed *collections*.

Co-maker. A person who signs the note of another as an additional maker for the purpose of strengthening the credit of the principal maker.

Commercial bank. A banking corporation which accepts demand deposits subject to check and makes short term loans to business enterprises, regardless of the scope of its other services.

Commercial letter of credit. An instrument by which a bank lends its credit to a customer to enable him to finance the purchase of goods. Addressed to the seller, it authorizes him to draw drafts on the bank under the terms stated in the letter.

Commercial loan. A short term loan made by a bank to a business enterprise for use in the production, manufacture, or distribution of goods or in the financing of related services.

Commercial paper. Short term negotiable notes, drafts, bills of exchange, and acceptances which arise from transactions involving the production, manufacture, or distribution of goods.

Common stock. The class of capital stock which represents the last claim on the dividends and assets of a corporation—in other words, the ownership not allocated to other classes of stock. Dividends cannot be paid on common stock until interest on all bonds and other debt and dividends on preferred stock issues have been paid. On the other hand, common stock generally carries superior voting rights as compared with other classes of stock.

Compound interest. Interest upon principal plus accrued interest.

Comptroller of the Currency. An appointed official who is responsible for the chartering, supervision, and liquidation of national banks. His office is located in the Treasury Department.

Consular invoice. A copy of an invoice for merchandise shipped from one country to another, prepared by the shipper and certified at the shipping point by a consul of the country of destination. The consul's certification applies to the value of the merchandise, the port of shipment, the destination, and in certain cases the place of origin of the merchandise.

Consumer credit. Credit granted to an individual for personal use.

Contingent liability. A secondary liability which arises out of a business relationship or accommodation and which at some future date may become an absolute liability upon the fulfilment or lack of fulfilment of certain conditions.

Contra. Placed on a debit or a credit ticket, this word indicates the account to which the offsetting credit or debit entry is made.

Control. A system under which all transactions or balances of a given type are included in a single total, so that the accuracy of their recording may be proved.

Correspondent bank. One which carries a deposit balance for a bank located in another city or engages in an exchange of services with that bank.

Counter check. A form of check provided by a bank for the convenience of the depositor. A counter check can be cashed only by the drawer personally.

Counter-error. In accounting, an error (over or short) which is offset by an error of equal amount, thus creating a balance which is correct without disclosing that two or more of the transactions apparently proved are actually in error.

Counterfeit money. Money illegally manufactured in imitation of genuine money (currency or coins).

Counter item. In item received over the counter.

Countersign. To sign what has already been signed in order to verify the authenticity of an instrument.

Country collections. Collection items on out-of-town points which a bank sends to its correspondents for collection and credit or for remittance after payment.

Coupon. One of a series of promissory notes of consecutive maturities attached to a bond or other debt certificate and intended to be detached and presented on their respective due dates for payment of interest.

Credit. An advance of cash, merchandise, or other commodity in the present in exchange for a promise to pay a definite sum at a future date, with interest if so agreed. *Long term* credit is credit granted for a long period of time. It is generally obtained by the sale of bonds or mortgages. *Short term* credit, as the term is ordinarily used, is credit granted to a business enterprise for a short period of time (usually a few months to one or two years) for the purpose of supplying the temporary commercial needs of the business. Short term credit granted to an individual for personal use is called *consumer* credit.

Credit ticket. A bank bookkeeping memorandum or posting medium on which the transaction leading to a credit entry in a ledger account is described in detail.

Currency. Technically, any form of money which serves as a circulating medium and includes both paper money and metallic money (coins). In banking terminology, however, the term generally refers to paper money only.

Debenture. One of a series of unsecured long term promissory notes issued by a corporation (and sometimes by a governmental body), usually in a distinctive printed form similar to a bond.

Debit ticket. A bank bookkeeping memorandum or posting medium on which the transaction leading to a debit entry in a ledger account is described in detail.

Decedent. A person who has died. A term used in connection with inheritance, estates, wills, etc. A decedent who had made no will is called an intestate decedent; one who had made a will is called a testator.

Deed. A written document which transfers the title to real property from the seller to the buyer.

Demand draft. A draft that is payable on demand. Also called *sight draft.*

Demand loan. A loan that is payable on demand.

Deposit. In a banking sense, a deposit consists of funds (cash, checks, drafts, etc.) left with a bank to be used according to banking practice. A deposit balance in a bank is merely a credit; it represents the depositor's right to receive an equivalent sum of money from the bank.

Deposit function. The business of receiving money on deposit for safekeeping and convenience. This function includes the receiving of demand deposits subject to check and the receiving of savings (time) deposits at interest.

Depositor. Any person, firm, corporation, or association which has placed funds in a bank.

Depository. A bank in which funds or securities are deposited by others, usually under the terms of a specific depository agreement. Also, a bank in which government funds are deposited or in which other banks are permitted by law to maintain required reserves. The term "depository" and "depositary" have come to be used interchangeably in banking.

Deposit slip. An itemized memorandum of the cash and other funds which a customer (depositor) presents to the receiving teller for credit to his account.

Discount. 1. The amount of interest withheld when a note or draft is purchased. 2. A note on which the interest is paid in advance. 3. The process of making a loan by requiring a note larger by the agreed interest charge than the amount paid to the borrower or credited to his account. A discount is distinguished from a loan by the fact that interest on a loan is collected at the time the note is paid or at regular intervals during the term of the loan, as in case of a demand loan.

Dishonor. 1. The refusal of the drawee to accept or to pay a check, draft, or bill of exchange when it is presented to him for acceptance or for payment, as the case may be. 2. The refusal of the maker to pay a note when it is presented to him for payment.

Dividends. The proportion of the net earnings of a corporation paid to the stockholders as their share of the profits. Dividends become payable only when declared by the board of directors. They are commonly distributed at regular intervals (quarterly, semiannually, or annually).

Domestic bill of exchange. Same as inland bill of exchange.

Dormant account. An account which has shown no activity, either by increase through deposits or decrease through withdrawals, over a long period of time.

Draft (bill of exchange). A signed written order addressed by one person (the drawer) to another person (the drawee) directing the latter to pay a specified sum of money to the order of a third person (the payee).

Drawee. The party who is directed to pay the sum specified in a check, draft, or bill of exchange.

Drawer. The person who makes and signs an order (check, draft, or bill of exchange) for the payment of money. *See also* maker.

Equity. The value of collateral over and above the amount of the obligation it covers.

Escrow. A written agreement between two or more parties by which an instrument (bond, deed, or other paper) and certain funds, securities, or other property are deposited with a third party known as an *escrow agent* for safekeeping, the instrument and the property to be delivered by the escrow agent only upon the fulfilment of the condition or conditions set forth in the agreement and only in accordance with its terms.

Exchange. 1. An amount charged for the collection of a check or other financial instrument. 2. The volume of funds available for use in another city or country. 3. An organization for trading in securities or commodities.

Exchange charge. The term "exchange charge" has a variety of meanings. 1. Sometimes it refers to a remittance charge which is a charge that some banks deduct in paying checks drawn upon themselves when they are presented through the mails from out-of-town points for the service of remitting the proceeds to these distant points. 2. Sometimes it refers to a charge for drafts on other cities. 3. Sometimes it refers to a charge which banks make for collecting out-of-town items. Generally called collection charges.

Exchanges. Items on banks in the local area presented for collection through the clearing house.

Executor. A person or an institution named by an individual in his will to settle his estate in accordance with the terms of his will.

Export credit. A commercial letter of credit issued for the purpose of financing a shipment of goods to a foreign country.

Face value. Same as par value.

Federal Deposit Insurance Corporation. A corporation established by federal authority to provide insurance of demand and time deposits in participating banks up to a maximum of $10,000 for each depositor.

Federal Reserve banks (twelve in number plus branches). Federal banking corporations that deal principally with their member banks and with the government. They deal with the general public only to a limited extent.

Federal Reserve note. A noninterest-bearing promissory note of a Federal Reserve bank issued for general circulation as money and payable to the bearer on demand.

Federal Reserve System. The central banking system of the United States, created by an act of Congress (Federal Reserve Act) in 1913. It consists of regional bankers' banks (twelve Federal Reserve banks and their branches), which are controlled and supervised by the Board of Governors in Washington, and national and state member banks.

Fiduciary service. A service performed by an individual or a corporation acting in a trust capacity. A banking institution authorized to do a trust business may perform fiduciary services, for example, by acting as executor or administrator of estates, guardian of minors, and trustee under wills.

Financial statement. A summary of figure facts showing the financial condition of a business. It is an itemized listing of assets (what the business owns), liabilities (what the business owes), and net worth or capital account (the owners' equity in the business). A balance sheet of a bank is called a *statement of condition*.

Float. The portion of a bank's total deposits or of a depositor's account which represents items (checks, coupons, etc.) in the process of collection. The same thing as uncollected funds.

Foreign bill of exchange. A bill drawn in one state or country and payable in another state or country.

Foreign exchange. 1. The system by which the balances arising out of transactions between countries are settled. 2. The currency used in making the settlement.

Foreign exchange rate. The price relationship between the currencies of two countries.

Forged check. One on which the drawer's signature has been forged.

Frozen asset. An asset which is believed to have value but which cannot be converted into cash readily; also cash which, because of some regulation or order, the owner cannot withdraw from his deposit in a bank.

Future exchange contract. A contract for the purchase or sale of foreign exchange to be delivered at a future date and at a rate determined in the present.

General banking law. The banking law of an individual state under which the banks organized in that state are authorized to do business.

General ledger. A bank's general book of accounts, the functions of which are: (1) to provide, in summary form, a record of changes in the bank's financial status; (2) to provide control accounts for the detailed records maintained by the various operating units of the bank (Bookkeeping, Loans and Discounts, etc.); (3) to provide a basis for statements of condition and operation for the bank's management, supervisory authorities, stockholders, and the public.

Good delivery. A term used to describe the conditions that must exist to effect the transfer of the ownership of property by means of an instrument or document bearing evidence of title. These conditions are: (1) that the instrument or document is genuine, (2) that the person making the transfer has title to the property, and (3) that the instrument or document is in negotiable form.

Group banking. A term used to refer to an arrangement by which a substantial proportion of the stock of each bank in the group is held by a holding company engaged in the business of banking. The identity of the local bank remains intact, and its policies and operations are determined by its own board of directors.

Guaranty. A written promise by one person (the guarantor) to be liable for the debt of another person (the principal debtor) in the event that the principal debtor fails to perform his obligation and provided the guarantor is notified of that fact by the creditor. A guaranty must be in writing to be enforceable at law.

Guardian. 1. An individual appointed by a court to manage the affairs or person (or both) of a minor or a mentally incompetent individual. 2. A corporation appointed by a court to manage the affairs of a minor or a mentally incompetent person.

Hypothecate. To give to a creditor the right to cause personal property of his debtor to be sold in satisfaction of a debt. If the property offered as security is delivered to the creditor (lender), the hypothecation is generally called a *pledge*. In a true *hypothecation*, the debtor (borrower) usually retains possession of the property until such time as he defaults in meeting his obligation.

Import credit. A commercial letter of credit issued for the purpose of financing the importation of goods.

Income statement. A record of income and expense relating to the operations of a business; a summary of transactions resulting from the sale of goods or services. *Operating statement* and *profit and loss statement* are other terms that are sometimes applied to this accounting record.

ndemnity agreement. *See* bond of indemnity.

ndependent bank. *See* unit bank.

ndirect liability. A secondary, or contingent, liability assumed by he indorsement or guaranty of an obligation for which another party s primarily liable. It becomes an absolute liability only upon the failure of the primary party to live up to his agreement.

ndividual account. An account in the name of one individual, as ontrasted with an account of a corporation, a partnership, or an account in two or more names.

ndorsee. The holder of a negotiable instrument to whom it has)een transferred by indorsement.

ndorsement. The signature plus any other writing on the back of n instrument by which the indorser transfers his rights in the instrunent to someone else.

ndorser. A person who signs his name on the back of a negotiable nstrument, such as a check, draft, or promissory note, for the purpose •f transferring his title to the instrument or of guaranteeing payment.

nsufficient funds (sometimes abbreviated N.S.F., not sufficient funds). A term used by a bank to indicate that the drawer's deposit balance is maller than the amount of a check presented for payment.

nsured bank. A bank that subscribes to the deposit insurance plan •f the Federal Deposit Insurance Corportion. A state banking institution which does not subscribe to this plan is referred to as a *non-nsured* bank.

ntangible asset. Something to which a business enterprise attaches n arbitrary dollar value, not because it has real value in itself but •ecause it helps to produce real values in a going business. Patents, rademarks, franchises, and goodwill are examples of intangible assets.

nterest. The sum paid for the use of money or credit.

nvestment banking. The business of underwriting and distributing orporate and government securities.

nvestment banking house. One which engages in the merchandising •f corporate and government securities by purchasing them in large)locks and selling them to investors. It helps to finance the capital, or ong term, credit requirements of business organizations, whereas the ommercial bank finances their short term credit requirements.

tems (as used in bank collections). A flexible term broad enough to nclude instruments payable in money generally. The term is often ised in combinations such as cash items, non-cash items, collection tems, city items, and out-of-town items.

•oint account. An account in the names of two or more persons, a ombination of signatures being required for the withdrawal of funds. *ee also* alternate account *and* survivorship account.

Journal sheet. A record on which transactions are entered in chrono logical sequence. *See* ledger.

Ledger. 1. The accounting record of final entry, on which tran actions are entered according to the accounts they affect. The ledge is posted from a journal, which is the book of original entry. 2. I connection with depositors' accounts, a grouping of accounts for ea in locating errors in trial balances. *See* general ledger.

Ledger sheet (or Ledger card). A sheet or card used for the recordin of transactions on a given account. It shows all credits, such as deposi and all debits, such as checks paid and withdrawals, the dates on whic these transactions occurred, and the balance in the account.

Legal reserve. A bank's legal reserve is the portion of its deposi (demand and time) which it is required by law to maintain in th form of cash or readily available balances to meet the demands depositors. Members of the Federal Reserve System must keep the legal reserves on deposit with the Federal Reserve banks of the respective districts.

Legal tender. Any kind of money (coin or currency) which the la prescribes as acceptable in payment of debts, unless there is a contra which calls for payment in a particular kind of money.

Letter of credit. An instrument issued by a bank to an individu or corportion by which the bank substitutes its own credit for that the individual or corporation. *See also* commercial letter of credit *an* traveler's letter of credit.

Line of credit. A term applied to the maximum amount of cred which a bank will extend to a particular borrower (usually a busines concern) over a stated period, subject to certain conditions whic must be met by the borrower, such as maintaining a specified balanc in his checking account.

Loan. *See* call loan, collateral, demand, discount, *and* time loan.

Loan function. The employment of a bank's deposits and capit funds in the making of loans.

Maker. The person who makes and signs a negotiable instrumen *See also* drawer.

Margin. The excess value of collateral over the amount of a loan fo which it is pledged as security. This is the lender's *margin of safety.*

Market value. The price of a security or commodity as determine by current market transactions.

Maturity. The due date of a note, draft, acceptance, bond, or othe instrument.

Member bank. The term applied to any bank, either national o state, that is a member of the Federal Reserve System. A state bank tha is not a member of the system is termed a *nonmember* bank.

Money. In bank operations, money refers to *cash* and includes both currency (paper money) and coin (metallic money).

Money order (bank). A draft sold by a bank to a customer for a fee, which usually varies according to the amount of the order.

Mortgage. An instrument by which the borrower (mortgagor) gives the lender (mortgagee) a lien on real estate as security for a loan. The borrower continues to use the property, and when the loan is repaid, the lien is removed.

Mortgage loan. A loan secured by a mortgage on real estate. Also called a real estate loan.

Multiple banking. A term sometimes used to refer to branch banking and group banking together, as distinguished from unit banking.

Mutual savings bank. A bank that is owned by the depositors and managed for them by a self-perpetuating board of trustees. It has no capital stock and therefore no stockholders.

National bank. A corporation organized under a federal banking law (National Bank Act) and authorized to do a general or commercial banking business—that is, receive deposits subject to check and make loans. It usually performs a variety of other functions as well. A national bank must have the word "national" in its corporate title.

National numerical system. The plan under which every bank in the United States has a distinctive number, which is usually printed below or beside the bank name on all forms in external use, including checks. It is used in listing checks on deposit slips and transit letters and in many other ways. *See also* transit number.

Negotiable instrument. An unconditional written order or promise to pay money which can be transferred by one person to another free from defenses between the original parties. The law sets forth certain standards with which an instrument must conform in order to be negotiable.

Nonpar items. Items for which the drawee bank will not remit to a collecting bank without deducting an exchange charge.

No protest. A waiver of notice of nonpayment of an item. It is evidenced by a stamped impression made on the face of the item by the indorser.

Notary public. A quasi-public official appointed by a state governor or other appointing authority to perform designated duties, such as attesting signatures on documents and administering oaths.

N.S.F. *See* insufficient funds.

Numerical transit system. Same as national numerical system.

Officer's check. Same as cashier's check.

"On us checks." *See* checks on us.

Overdraft. The amount by which checks paid against an account exceed the balance on deposit in the account.

Par items. Items for which the drawee bank will remit to another bank without charge.

Par list. A list (issued by the Federal Reserve System) of banks which will remit in full for items payable by them.

Par value. The principal or nominal value appearing on a bond, note, coupon, or other instrument calling for the payment of money.

Passbook. In general, a book supplied by a bank to a depositor for record purposes. A *savings* passbook contains a complete record of the customer's account, showing deposits and withdrawals as well as the interest credited at regular periods; it must be presented to the bank for proper entry of these transactions. A *checking account* passbook is the customer's deposit receipt book, in which the teller receipts for deposits as they are made.

Pay. 1. To pay a check in cash, as when a check is paid by the paying teller. 2. To charge a check against a customer's account, as in the case of a check coming through the clearings.

Payee. The person named in an instrument calling for the payment of money as the one to whom, or to whose order, payment is to be made.

Paying teller. A representative of the bank who is responsible for the proper paying or cashing of checks presented at the window. *See also* unit teller system.

Personal loan. A loan (usually small in amount) made to an individual for his personal needs.

Postdated check. A check dated ahead. It is not an effective order on the bank until the future date is reached. Thus, if a check dated July 15 is issued on July 1, it cannot be collected from the bank until July 15.

Power of attorney. A document, usually acknowledged before a public officer or witnessed, authorizing a named person to perform certain acts in place of the signer. It is void on the death of the signer.

Preferred stock. Stock which usually has a right to receive a specified share of the profits of a corporation before any distribution can be made on the common. In liquidation, it is usually entitled to share in the assets ahead of the common stock.

Principal. 1. The sum of money stated in a contract, account, or financial instrument as distinguished from the sum actually to be paid. 2. A person who appoints another person to act for him as agent.

Private bank. An unincorporated institution which is owned and operated by an individual or a partnership. It may or may not be subject to supervision by the banking authorities, depending on the laws of the particular state in which it is located.

Profit and loss statement. Same as income statement.

Promissory note. A written promise made by one person (the maker) to pay a sum certain in money to another person (the payee), or to his order, on demand or at a determinable future date.

Proof. 1. An operation for testing the accuracy of a previous operation, as relisting the checks and adding their amounts to determine the accuracy of the total shown on a deposit slip. 2. Applied to the *proof sheet,* the record on which the test is made. 3. Also used to describe the method by which a type of transaction is proved, as *transit proof.* Proof is generally effected when a total agrees with another total of the same items arrived at in a different manner; it is then said to be *in balance.*

Protest. A written statement by a notary public, or other authorized person, under seal for the purpose of giving formal notice to parties secondarily liable that an instrument has been dishonored, either by refusal to accept or by refusal to make payment.

Raised check. One on which the amount has been fraudulently increased.

Recap. Short for recapitulation, the gathering together of numerous totals, which have been proved individually, for a general proof and thus provide the summary total for application to a general ledger balance.

Receiving teller. A representative of the bank who receives and verifies deposits and issues receipts for them. *See also* unit teller system.

Reconcilement of account. A comparison of a statement of account rendered by another bank with the bank's own record for the period, to determine whether the two records are in agreement and to adjust any differences that are found to exist.

Rediscount. 1. The process by which a Federal Reserve or other bank discounts for a member of customer bank the notes, drafts, or acceptances which the member or customer bank has already discounted for its customers. 2. The rediscounted paper itself.

Registered check. A check purchased from a bank.

Registrar. A bank or a trust company which has been appointed by a corporation to keep an accurate record of its shares of stock and to see that the number of shares issued does not exceed the total amount authorized.

Rehypothecate. To transfer to another a note which is secured by the hypothecation of property. *See also* hypothecate.

Reserve. A portion of the bank's funds which has been set aside for the purpose of assuring its ability to meet its liabilities to depositors in cash. Minimum reserves to be maintained against demand and time deposits are usually specified by banking law. *See also* legal reserve.

Routing symbol. The latest step in the direction of faster sorting and greater efficiency in collecting items. The routing symbol appears on checks as the denominator of a fraction, the numerator of which is the transit number. The routing symbol may have three or four digits. The first digit of a three digit symbol or the first two digits of a four digit symbol designate the Federal Reserve district in which the bank is located. The next to the last digit indicates whether the territory in which the bank is located is served by the main office or a particular branch of the Federal Reserve bank, and the last digit has reference to the availability of credit under the Federal Reserve bank time schedules. For further description, *see* Appendix.

Return item. An item returned unpaid by a payor bank.

Safekeeping (deposit for). The receipt by a bank of custody of specific property to be returned as contrasted with an ordinary deposit to be repaid in money and with a safe deposit where the property is placed in a safe deposit box, rented to a customer, to which the renter rather than the bank has access.

Savings bank. A corporation chartered by the state to receive savings deposits primarily from people of moderate means. It invests those deposits for the most part in securities (bonds) and real estate mortgages.

Savings deposit (savings account). A fund which a person gradually accumulates from earnings and on which the bank usually pays interest. *See also* time deposit—open account.

Seal. In law: any impression, device, sign, or mark which is recognized by judicial decision or by statute law as making the instrument on which it is placed enforceable at law.

Service charge. A charge made by a bank for the cost of handling a depositor's account.

Sight draft. A draft which is payable on presentation to the drawee—in other words, on "sight" or demand.

Special interest account. A term used by some commercial banks to apply to a deposit of savings (time deposit) when the state law restricts the use of the term savings account to exclusively savings institutions.

Stale check. One that has been held an unreasonably long time after issue before being presented for payment to the bank on which it is drawn.

State bank. A corporation organized under the general banking law of a state and authorized to do a commercial banking business—that is, receive deposits subject to check and make loans. It usually performs a variety of other functions as well. In a broader sense, a state bank is any bank chartered by the state.

Statement of condition. A detailed listing of a bank's resources, liabilities, and capital accounts showing its condition on a given date.

On requests (calls) by supervisory authorities several times a year, banks are required to submit sworn statements of condition. In general accounting, this type of financial report is known as a balance sheet.

Statute of limitations. The periods fixed by statute within which suits must be brought if legal redress is to be obtained. At the expiration of these periods, suits are forever barred. Periods vary in the several states and within a state according to the rights to be enforced.

Stock. A claim which gives the owner (stockholder) a right to share in the profits of the issuing corporation and in its property upon liquidation. A stockholder is thus a part owner of the corporation. *See also* common stock *and* preferred stock.

Stock certificate. A document which certifies that the person whose name it bears owns a stated number of shares of stock in the issuing corporation.

Stock exchange. 1. An association of brokers and dealers engaged in the business of buying and selling securities. 2. The place where such brokers and dealers meet to do their trading.

Stock power. A signed instrument in the form of a power of attorney by which the owner of stock authorizes another party to sell and/or transfer the stock.

Stop-payment order. An order issued by a depositor to his bank instructing it to refuse payment of the check specified in the order.

Surplus. The accumulated profits of past periods left invested in a business. In a bank it represents the amount paid in by the stockholders in addition to their capital stock subscriptions when the bank is organized and amounts (not available for dividends) added to capital from earnings.

Survivorship account. An account in the names of two or more persons, each signature alone being sufficient authority for the withdrawal of funds, the balance in the account belonging to the survivor or survivors on the death of the other or others. *See also* alternate account *and* joint account.

Tax waiver. Permission by inheritance or estate tax authorities for the payment of an account or the transfer of property despite the provisions of statutes or regulations.

Teller. A bank representative who, in one capacity or another, transacts over-the-counter business with customers.

Tickler. 1. A maturity index. 2. A memorandum record carrying the details of certain transactions, as a list of the checks on other banks cashed by the paying teller for the convenience of customers. Also called a *scratcher.* Such a record generally has no further usefulness after the transactions noted have passed through other departments and been entered in the permanent records.

Time deposit—open account. A deposit with respect to which there is in force a written contract with the depositor that neither the whole nor any part of the deposit may be withdrawn within thirty days after the date of the deposit or prior to the expiration of the period of notice given by the depositor in writing not less than thirty days in advance of withdrawal.

Time draft. A draft that is payable at a fixed or determinable future time.

Time loan. A loan that is payable at some specified future date.

Title. The right to ownership of property.

Trade acceptance. A draft drawn by the seller of goods on the buyer and accepted by the buyer. On its face there often appears a statement indicating that the acceptor's obligation arises out of the purchase of goods from the drawer of the draft. *See also* acceptance.

Trade (assumed) name. A name assumed by persons, not incorporated, for trade or business purposes. In some states, trade names must be filed in a public office.

Transfer agent. A bank, a trust company, or an individual appointed by a corporation to see that all the requirements are met in connection with the transfer of its stock.

Transit items. Cash items which are payable outside the town or city of the bank receiving them for credit to customers' accounts.

Transit letter. A letter or form of deposit slip on which a bank lists and describes transit items.

Transit number. A key to the name and location of a drawee bank under the national numerical system. The transit number has two parts; the prefix or first part designates the city or state in which the bank is located, and the second part indicates the name of the bank. The transit number appears on checks today as the numerator of a fraction, the denominator of which is the routing symbol (*see* Appendix, check routing symbol).

Traveler's checks. Special checks supplied by banks and other companies at small cost for the use of travelers.

Traveler's letter of credit. A letter addressed by a bank to its correspondent banks either in the same country or in foreign countries, authorizing the person named in the letter to draw drafts on the correspondent banks to the extent of the credit specified. The person in whose favor the letter of credit is issued deposits with the issuing bank a sum of money equal to the total amount of the credit plus the bank's charges for this service.

Treasurer's check. *See* cashier's check.

Trust. An arrangement by which an individual or a corporation as trustee holds the title to property for the benefit of one or more persons, usually under the terms of a will or a written agreement.

Trust business. The business of settling estates, administering trusts, administering guardianships, and performing agencies.

Trust company. A corporation chartered by the state to engage in the trust business for both individuals and business organizations. It may or may not perform banking functions as well, depending on the powers granted in its charter.

Trustee. *See* trust.

Trust institution. Applied to both a trust company and a banking corporation (either national or state) which has the power to perform trust services, regardless of the scope of its other services.

Trust receipt. A trust agreement (in receipt form) between the bank and the borrower which is temporarily substituted for other collateral securing a loan. By means of this receipt the bank releases documents, merchandise, or other property without releasing its title to the property, and the borrower agrees to keep the property, as well as any funds received from its sale, separate and distinct from his own property and subject to repossession by the bank in the event that he fails to comply with the conditions specified in the agreement.

Two-name paper. Notes on which two persons are liable for payment.

Uncollected funds. *See* float.

Undivided profits. Undistributed earnings available for dividends and for the writing off of bad debts or special losses.

Unearned discount. Interest collected but not yet earned.

Unit bank. A single independent bank which conducts all its operations at one office.

Unit banking. A term used to refer to the type of banking in which an individual bank is separate and distinct from every other bank in operation, management, and control.

Unit teller system. An arrangement for the convenience of customers who wish to make deposits and withdrawals at the same time. When this system is in use, the bank representative at each window handles both receiving and paying operations.

Unlisted market. The market made by person-to-person transactions, usually between brokers, for securities which are not listed on an organized stock exchange.

"Us" *or* **"on us" checks.** *See* checks on us.

Warehouse receipt. A receipt for goods stored in a warehouse and an agreement between the warehouseman and the person storing the goods. By its terms the warehouseman promises to keep the goods safely and to redeliver them upon the surrender of the receipt, properly indorsed, and payment of the storage charges. The receipt is also evidence that the owner or holder has title to the stored goods.

Will. A formal written instrument by which a person gives explicit instructions regarding the disposition to be made of his property after his death.

Wire transfer. An order to pay or to credit money transmitted by telegraph or cable.

Index

Estates
  settling, 212
Examinations, 324, 328
  bank, 299, 363
    cost of, 330
  directors', 306
  frequency of, 329-330
  function of, 329-334
  procedures, 330
  purpose of, 330
  reports of, 329, 333
    review of, 333-334
  supervisory, 299
Examiner
  national bank, 327
Exchange, 370
  charges, 54, 264, 370
  foreign. See Foreign exchange.
  stock, 379
Executive responsibilities
  training for, 356
Executor
  account of, 112
  as safe deposit customer, 241
  bank as, 13
    duties of, 212
  definition of, 370
  of joint depositor, 104
  signature of
    authorized, 75
Expense (s)
  accounting for, 254, 264
  reserves for, 275
  verification of, 302
Export credit, 371
Exporter, 232, 238
  services to, 228

Face value, 371
Farmers
  financing of, 2-3
Federal Advisory Council, 344
Federal Deposit Insurance Corpo-
    ration, 344-345
  controls exercised by, 325-328
  definition of, 371
  regulations of, 116, 117, 118
  supervision of
    state banks by, 311

Federal Government
  debt of, 9, 339, 349
Federal open market committee,
    343-344
Federal Reserve
  Act, 313, 319
  collection service
    cash, 336-338
  collection service
    noncash, 338
  notes, 10, 336, 371
Federal Reserve Bank of New
    York, 51
Federal Reserve banks
  availability schedule, 58-61
  balances with, 269
  cash service, 336
  definition of, 371
  directors, 341-343
  discount rates of, 343
  discounting by, 340
  operating letter, 208
  par collection system, 58, 61
  rediscount with, 145
  rediscounting by, 338
  reserve account with, 47
  routing checks through, 64
  organization, 341-343
  services, 335-338
  settlement by, 58-61
  stock, 271
  transfer of funds through, 65
  transit functions of, 53
Federal Reserve System, 335-344,
    371
  as element of banking system,
    308, 310
  Board of Governors of the, 343
  description of, 364, 371
  Interdistrict Settlement Fund,
    61
  loan limitations by, 139. See
    also Regulations F, G.
  recommendations of, 325, 327,
    328
  trust authority granted by,
    219, 220
  credit
    controls, 339
    instruments, 339-340

Federal Reserve System (*continued*)
  Interdistrict Settlement Fund, 61
  monetary policy of, 355
  noncash collection service, 203, 208-210, 338
  open market operations, 340
  regulations of, 117, 118
  reserve requirements, 340
  structure of, 341-344
  supervisory powers, 311, 325
  transfer of funds through, 81
  transit collection through, 58, 61
Fictitious name. *See* Trade name.
Fiduciary (ies), 216, 218
  accounts, 111-112
  as safe deposit customer, 241
  definition of, 111
  records, 301
  service, 371. *See* Trust services.
Financial condition of bank, 255
Financial statement, 164-165, 371
Float, 284, 286, 287, 288, 292
  calculation of, 64
  charge for, 57
  definition of, 27, 371
Foreign
  banking, 237
  bill of exchange, 371
  exchange, 228
    conversion of, 122
    rate, 371
  financial services, 226-238
  department
    services of, 226-228
    operations, 228-229, 236-238
Forgery, 74, 129
  report of
    by customer, 101
  Foundation for Education in Economics, 353
Fraud
  liability of bank for, 102
Funds
  availability of, 115-119
  insufficient, 295, 373
  uncollected, 57, 90, 381
Furniture and fixtures, 272-273
  inventory, 303
Future exchange contracts, 372

General bank accounting, 254-278
General banking laws, 372
General bookkeeper. *See* Bookkeeper, general.
General books, 63, 83, 116, 269, 303
  as journal, 262-265
  recording cash letters in, 65
General ledger, 90, 260, 262
  balancing with, 86
  bookkeeping and, 83
  proving, 86
General window system, 23
Good delivery, 372
Government
  agencies, 219
    cooperation with, 349
  bonds, 271
  debt, 9, 339, 349
  loans to, 8-9
  local
    as borrower, 9
  securities, 343
    sale of, 339
Group banking, 309, 372
Guaranty, 372
Guardian (s)
  account of, 112
  bank as, 13, 212, 213, 214-215
  definition of, 372
  signature of
    authorized, 75
Guardianships, 212, 214-216

Head teller, 81, 82
History of banking, 2, 3, 308-320
Hold, 74, 78-79, 90
Holder, 69
  in due course, 127
  Holds, 91, 92
Hypothecate, 372

Identification, 102, 235
  of customer, 79
    safe deposit, 240, 248
Import credit, 372
Importer, 232, 238
  services to, 226-228

Inactive accounts, 93, 99
In-clearings procedure, 48-49
Income
accounting for, 254, 263-265
statement, 255, 372
verification of, 302
Incompetent as safe deposit customer, 252
Indemnity agreement, 373
Individual (s)
accounts, 102-104
identification of, 102
loans to, 173-179
Indorsed loan, 146
Indorsee, 373
Indorsement (s), 79-80, 86, 94
clearing house stamp as, 38
conditional, 127, 128-129
definition of, 127, 373
guarantee of prior, 38
kinds of, 127
of sending bank, 66
guarantee of prior, 129
in blank, 127
qualified, 127, 128
restrictive, 127, 128
special, 127, 128
validity of, 22
Indorser, 22, 126, 127, 132
definition of, 373
financial responsibility of, 80
general
liability of, 129-130, 131
notice of dishonor to, 131
signature, 146
warranties of, 129
Indorsing bank
return items to, 66
Inheritance taxes. See Taxes, Inheritance.
Instalment collections, 204
Instalment contracts
as collateral, 152, 156-157
Insufficient funds, 295, 373
Insurance, 213-214
coverage, 303
policy, 229, 231
Insured bank (s), 327, 328
definition of, 373
examination of, 344-345

Interdistrict Settlement Fund, 61
Interest
accrued, 361
calculation of, 185
compound, 367
definition of, 373
on loans, 264
accrual of, 265
on time deposits, 264
rate of, 141, 343
reserve for, 275
Intermediate term credit, 8
Internal controls, 299-306
Interview, 164, 180-182
Investigative division, 182-183
Investment (s)
bank, 271
correspondent bank's, 63
function, 4
securities, 302-303
trust, 221
types of, 144-159
Items, 373
return, 378
transit, 380
See also Cash items, Collection items.

Joint account, 104-107. See also Accounts
Journal, 260
general books', 262
sheet, 374

Large bank
credit work in, 170-173
Ledger (s), 374
Boston, 84
card, 79
customers, 256
entries, 293
general, 303, 372. See also General ledger.
individual, 84, 90
investment, 303
liability, 185, 186
photographing, 91
posting to, 95, 96, 97